DARK HORSE
NEW
RECRUITS

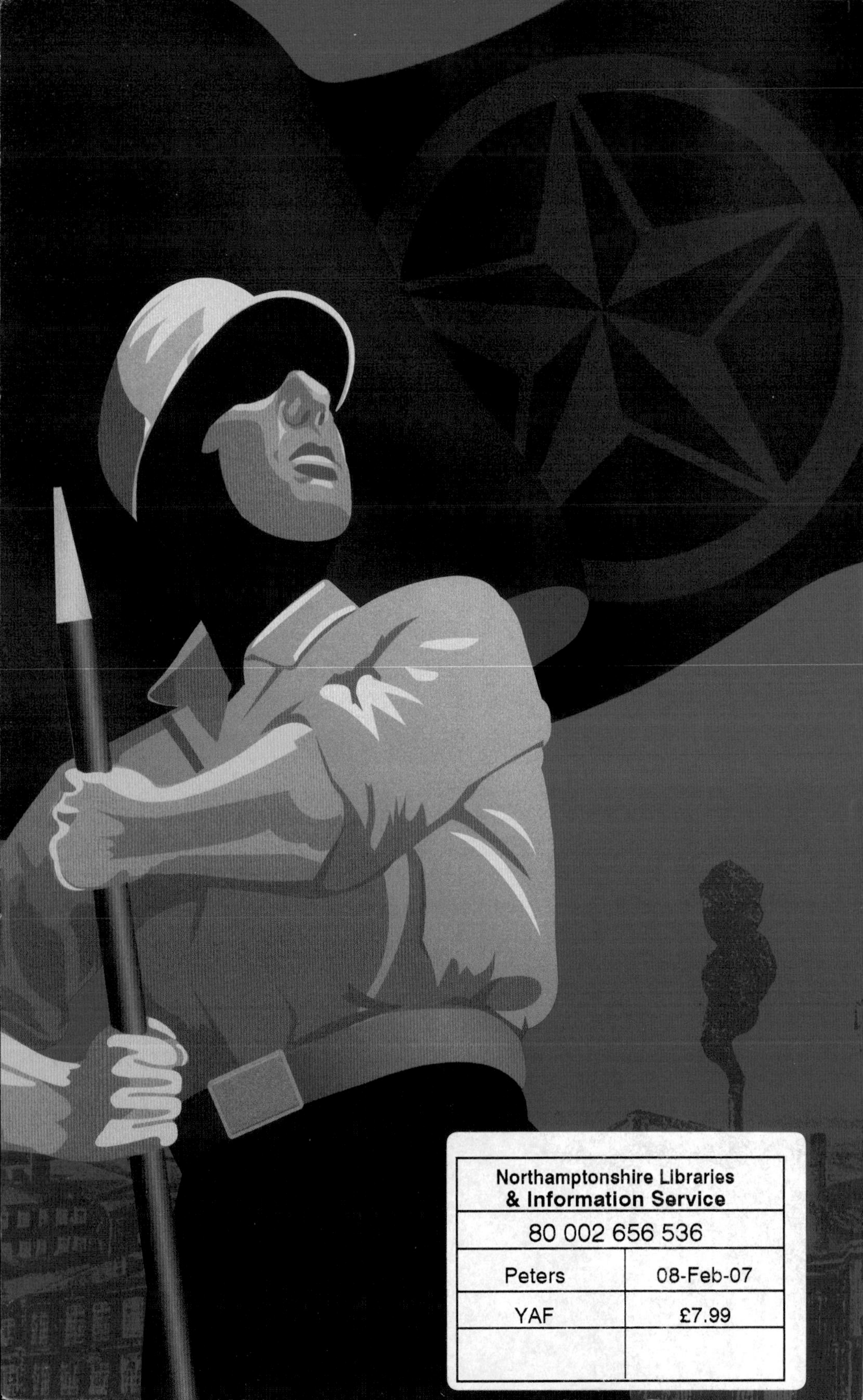

DARK HORSE
NEW
RECRUITS

ADAM ADAMOWICZ

JACOB CHABOT

IAN CULBARD

ANDREW KRAHNKE

NICK PLUMBER

RHS

cover art by
IAN CULBARD

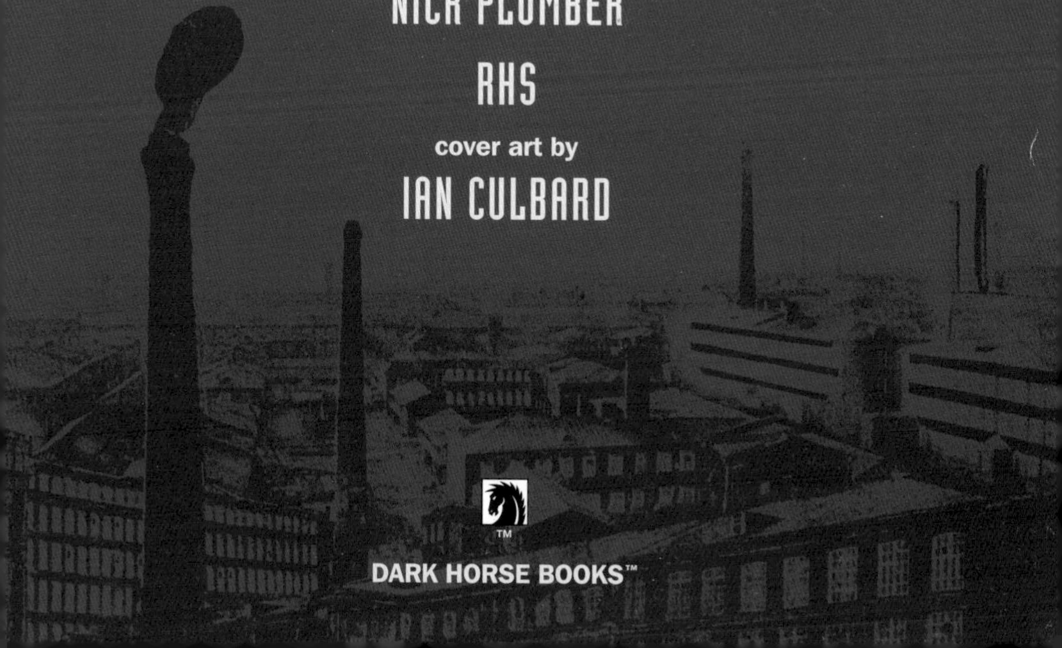

™

DARK HORSE BOOKS™

publisher
MIKE RICHARDSON

editor
MICHAEL CARRIGLITTO

designer
DARIN FABRICK

art director
LIA RIBACCHI

thanks to all of you who sent us your submissions for the New Recruits program

special thanks to **Davey Estrada** and **Scott Allie**

DARK HORSE NEW RECRUITS™

Wild Talents™ and The Way of All Flesh™ are trademarks of Ian Culbard. The Mighty Skullboy Army™ is a trademark of Jacob Chabot. The Pied Piper™ is a trademark of Nick Smith, and is © 2005 by Nick Smith and Adam Adamowicz. Discreet Despair™ is a trademark of Rafael Higino da Silveria. Zombiekiller™ is a trademark of Andrew Krahnke. All prominently featured characters are trademarks of their respective creators. New Recruits™ is a trademark of Dark Horse Comics, Inc. Text and Illustrations of the stories in New Recruits are © 2005 by their respective creators. All other material, unless otherwise specified, is © 2005 Dark Horse Comics, Inc. No portion of this publication may be reproduced by any means without written permission from Dark Horse Comics, Inc. No similarity between any of the names, characters, persons, and/or institutions in this publication an those of any preexisting person or institution is intended, and any similarity that may exist is purely coincidental. Dark Horse Books™ is a trademark of Dark Horse Comics, Inc. Dark Horse Comics® is a trademark of Dark Horse Comics, Inc., registered in various categories and countries. All rights reserved.

Published by
Dark Horse Books
A division of Dark Horse Comics, Inc.

Dark Horse Comics, Inc.
10956 SE Main Street
Milwaukie, OR 97222

darkhorse.com

To find a comics shop in your area, call the Comic Shop Locator Service toll-free at 1-888-266-4226

First edition: December 2005
ISBN: 1-59307-383-6

1 3 5 7 9 10 8 6 4 2

Printed in China

CONTENTS

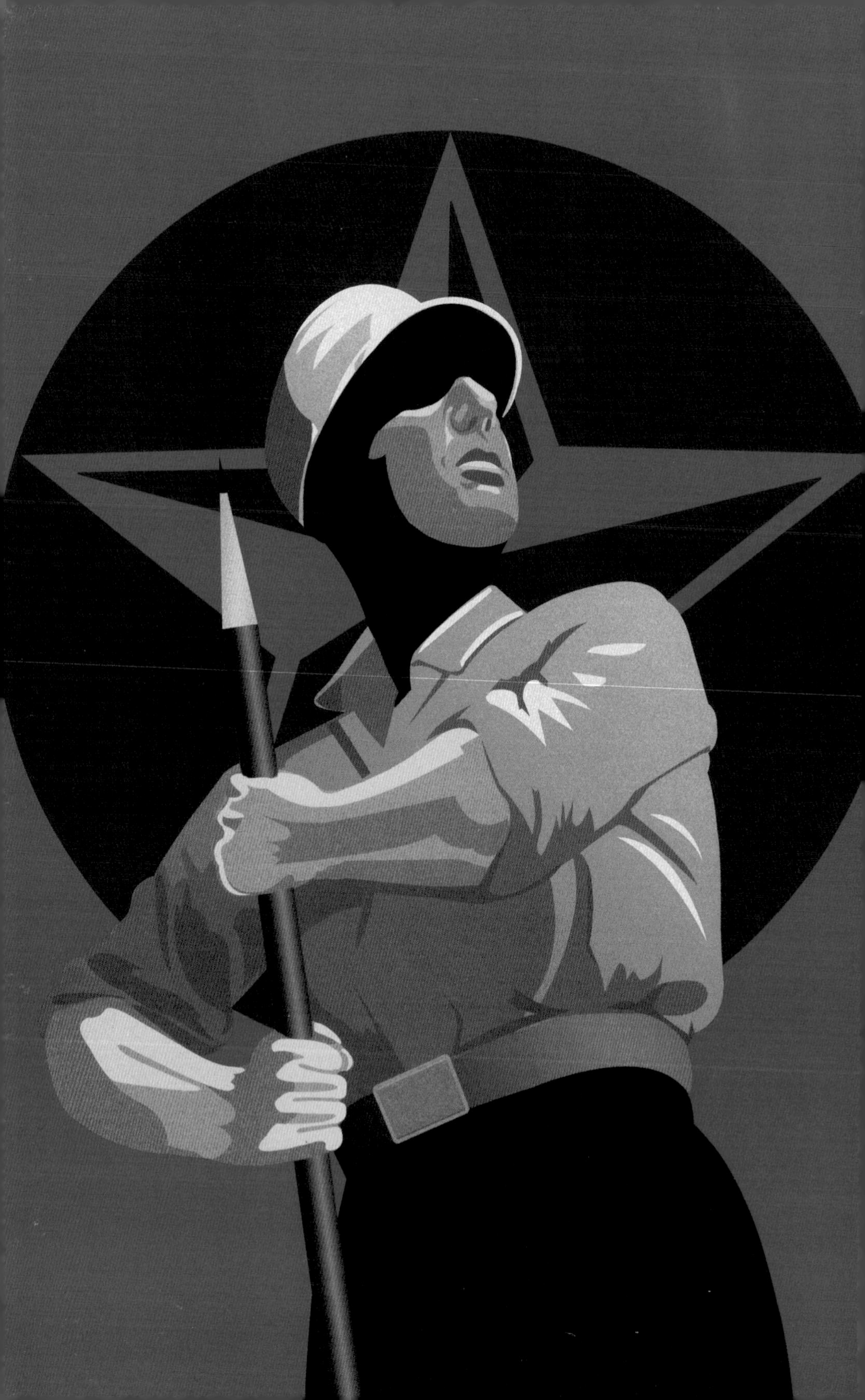

Twenty years ago, I called Randy Stradley and told him this crazy idea I had about starting a different kind of comic book company. This new company would be built around the premise that comics creators would do their best work if given the opportunity to pursue their own unique visions. Of course, I wasn't the first to feel this way. Creators such as Will Eisner had always followed their own path. A short time later, Randy and I began our own talent search, leading to a string of hits by a group of relative newcomers, including Paul Chadwick's *Concrete*, Chris Warner's *Black Cross,* and Mark Verheiden's *The American*. The success of these titles, and others like them, laid the foundation for our fledgling company's success.

As the years have passed, Dark Horse Comics has published work by many of the industry's greatest names. Creators such as Will Eisner, Frank Miller, Mike Mignola, and Stan Sakai have continually proven the truth of that initial, founding premise. It is interesting to note the similarities between Eric Powell and Paul Chadwick, who both won Eisner awards on the same night earlier this year. Eric's character, the Goon, has built a devoted fan base in recent years and his reputation as a premier creator continues to grow. Concrete continues to draw fans and win awards two decades after Paul first introduced him. Both of these artist/writers have devoted themselves to telling stories they want to tell, with characters they

own and control. This is exactly what we intended in the beginning.

In the wake of big-name creators and best-selling licensed titles, it is sometimes easy to neglect the young comics writers and artists looking to get their foot in the door. With our company's origin in mind, the New Recruits program was created to address just that problem.

Once the word was out, it didn't take long before we were flooded with submissions. We reviewed hundreds of projects, searching for stories that echoed those early Dark Horse characters and creators, if not in content, then in spirit. The book you hold in your hands is the result of that search: individual creators with unique voices and the talent to express themselves through graphic storytelling — in other words, storytellers making good comics.

This is the first of what we hope to be a series of books resulting from our New Recruits program. If you are a reader, enjoy what might be your first look at a future comics superstar. If you have the ambition and talent to be a comics professional, then hopefully you'll find the inspiration within these pages to enter our next search.

In the end, we hope that you will enjoy discovering these works as much as we did. A group of talented creators pursuing their own unique visions. Sounds great, doesn't it?

— Mike Richardson

I. N. J. Culbard is an animation director who hopes to one day just write and draw comic books (his preferred weapon of choice) all day, every day.

He was raised on a diet of history and myth and as a child did nothing but draw comics and pretend he was a dog. His first foray into comics was a self-published title which enjoyed a print run of ten and was well received by five of its devoted readers. He lives in Nottingham, England, with his wife and newborn son.

Wild Talents is just the tip of a large and dangerous iceberg.

WILD TALENTS:
THE GOD MACHINE

WRITTEN & ILLUSTRATED BY I. N. J. CULBARD

LONDON, 1888

CONSIDER THE FACTS, MISTER CHIMES.

A SERIES OF MURDERS, EACH COMMITTED WITH EXTRAORDINARY RAPIDITY AND UNDER COVER OF DARKNESS.

THE VICTIMS WERE ALL PROSTITUTES; EACH SUBJECTED TO MUTILATION.

POLICE DISCOVERED A MESSAGE SCRAWLED ON A WALL IN GOULSTON STREET; SUPPOSEDLY FROM THE KILLER.

"THE JUWES ARE THE MEN WHO WILL NOT BE BLAMED FOR NOTHING."

BELIEVING IT MIGHT FUEL ANTI-SEMITIC VIOLENCE, POLICE COMMISSIONER SIR CHARLES WARREN ORDERED THE WRITING BE SCRUBBED OFF.

HE HAD GOOD REASON TO BE CONCERNED ABOUT CIVIL UNREST.

A YEAR AGO, HE STAMPED OUT POLITICAL MEETINGS IN TRAFALGAR SQUARE; AN ACTION WHICH RESULTED IN MANY CASUALTIES AND THE RATHER UNFORTUNATE DEATH OF ONE MAN.

THOUGH THE PRESS CONDEMNED HIM, WARREN WAS ONLY OBEYING ORDERS FROM THE SECRETARY OF STATE.

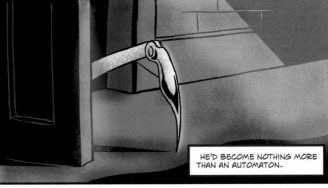

HE'D BECOME NOTHING MORE THAN AN AUTOMATON.

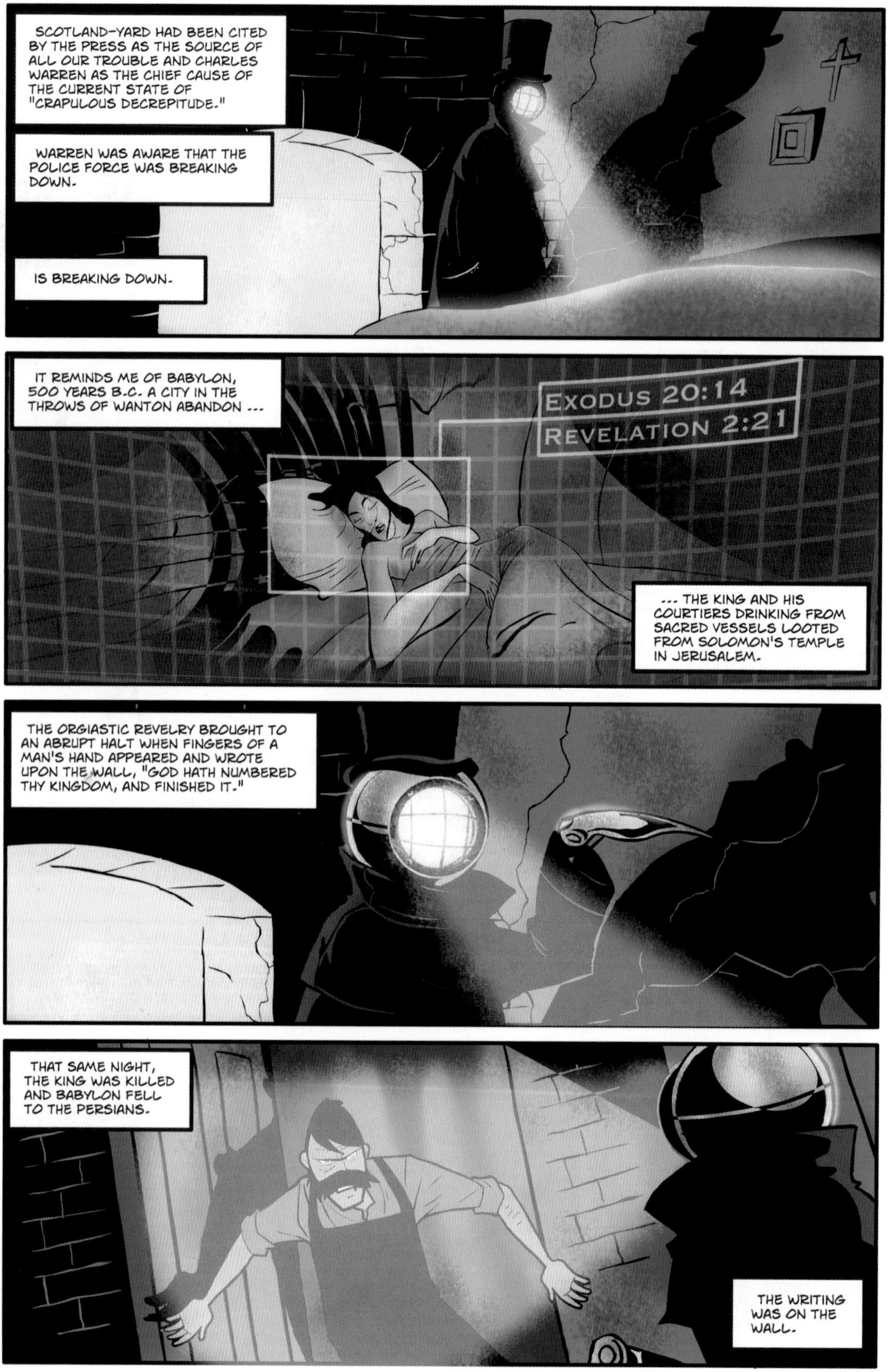
SCOTLAND-YARD HAD BEEN CITED BY THE PRESS AS THE SOURCE OF ALL OUR TROUBLE AND CHARLES WARREN AS THE CHIEF CAUSE OF THE CURRENT STATE OF "CRAPULOUS DECREPITUDE."
WARREN WAS AWARE THAT THE POLICE FORCE WAS BREAKING DOWN.
IS BREAKING DOWN.
IT REMINDS ME OF BABYLON, 500 YEARS B.C. A CITY IN THE THROWS OF WANTON ABANDON ...
EXODUS 20:14
REVELATION 2:21
... THE KING AND HIS COURTIERS DRINKING FROM SACRED VESSELS LOOTED FROM SOLOMON'S TEMPLE IN JERUSALEM.
THE ORGIASTIC REVELRY BROUGHT TO AN ABRUPT HALT WHEN FINGERS OF A MAN'S HAND APPEARED AND WROTE UPON THE WALL, "GOD HATH NUMBERED THY KINGDOM, AND FINISHED IT."
THAT SAME NIGHT, THE KING WAS KILLED AND BABYLON FELL TO THE PERSIANS.
THE WRITING WAS ON THE WALL.

LUDGATE CIRCUS

WHAT DOES THE WRITING ON THE WALL MEAN TO YOU, MISTER CHIMES?

WELL, THAT THE JEWS ARE THE ONES WHO DONE IT AND ARE GOING TO GET AWAY WITH IT, OF COURSE.

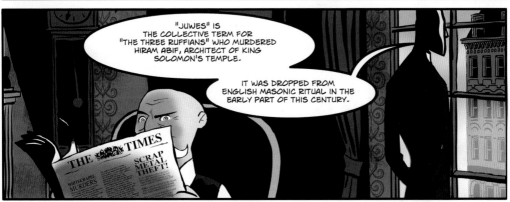

"JUWES" IS THE COLLECTIVE TERM FOR "THE THREE RUFFIANS" WHO MURDERED HIRAM ABIF, ARCHITECT OF KING SOLOMON'S TEMPLE.

IT WAS DROPPED FROM ENGLISH MASONIC RITUAL IN THE EARLY PART OF THIS CENTURY.

THE TIMES

SCRAP METAL THEFT!

WHITECHAPEL MURDERS

THEN THE FREEMASONS ARE THE ONES WHO DONE IT?

MY DEAR CHIMES, THE "JUWES" WERE THE ENEMY OF THE FREEMASONS.

THEN IT WAS THE ENEMY OF THE FREEMASONS WHO DONE IT?

THE WRITING IS ON THE WALL, CHIMES, A DECLARATION OF WAR ...

"THE JUWES ARE THE MEN WHO WILL NOT BE BLAMED FOR NOTHING."

A DOUBLE NEGATIVE WITH A SIGNIFICANT DOUBLE MEANING ... ONE, I WOULD WAGER, WARREN WAS WELL AWARE OF.

HIS RESIGNATION WAS A WHITE FLAG TO THE ENEMY.

HANG ON. ARE YOU SUGGESTING THAT WARREN IS A FREEMASON, MUNDI?

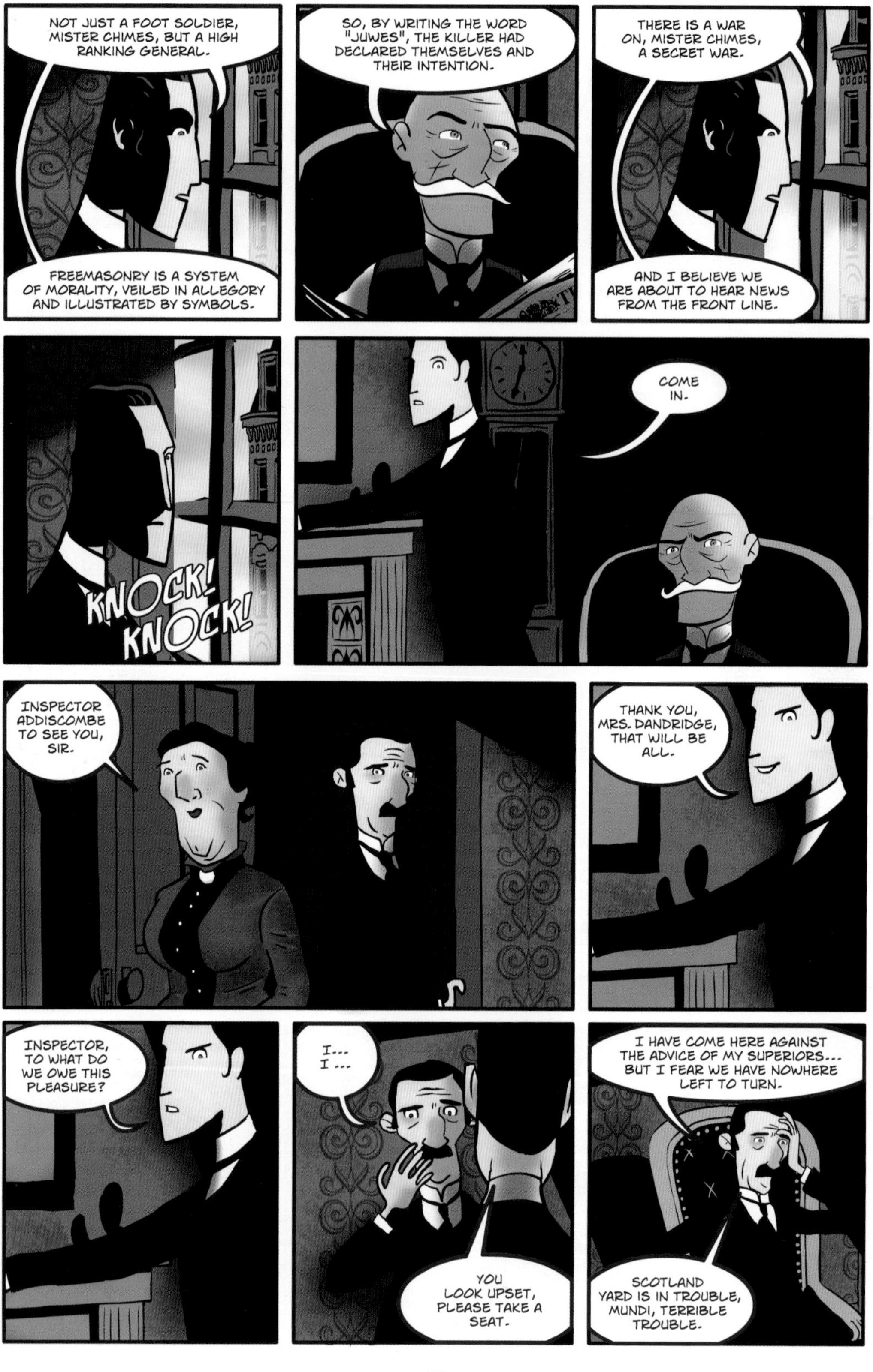
NOT JUST A FOOT SOLDIER, MISTER CHIMES, BUT A HIGH RANKING GENERAL.
FREEMASONRY IS A SYSTEM OF MORALITY, VEILED IN ALLEGORY AND ILLUSTRATED BY SYMBOLS.
SO, BY WRITING THE WORD "JUWES", THE KILLER HAD DECLARED THEMSELVES AND THEIR INTENTION.
THERE IS A WAR ON, MISTER CHIMES, A SECRET WAR.
AND I BELIEVE WE ARE ABOUT TO HEAR NEWS FROM THE FRONT LINE.
KNOCK! KNOCK!
COME IN.
INSPECTOR ADDISCOMBE TO SEE YOU, SIR.
THANK YOU, MRS. DANDRIDGE, THAT WILL BE ALL.
INSPECTOR, TO WHAT DO WE OWE THIS PLEASURE?
I... I ...
YOU LOOK UPSET, PLEASE TAKE A SEAT.
I HAVE COME HERE AGAINST THE ADVICE OF MY SUPERIORS... BUT I FEAR WE HAVE NOWHERE LEFT TO TURN.
SCOTLAND YARD IS IN TROUBLE, MUNDI, TERRIBLE TROUBLE.

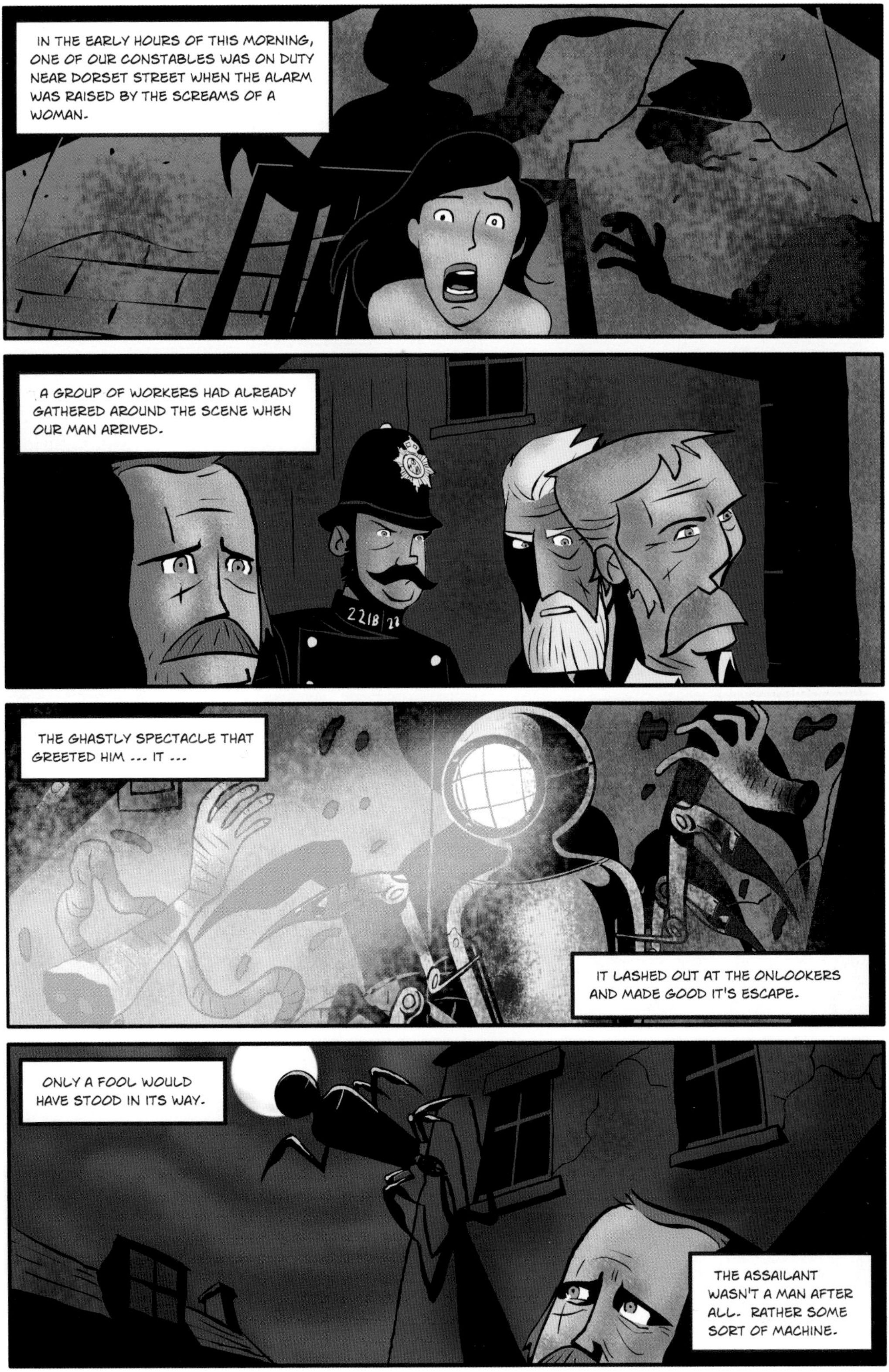
IN THE EARLY HOURS OF THIS MORNING, ONE OF OUR CONSTABLES WAS ON DUTY NEAR DORSET STREET WHEN THE ALARM WAS RAISED BY THE SCREAMS OF A WOMAN.
A GROUP OF WORKERS HAD ALREADY GATHERED AROUND THE SCENE WHEN OUR MAN ARRIVED.
221B 28
THE GHASTLY SPECTACLE THAT GREETED HIM --- IT ---
IT LASHED OUT AT THE ONLOOKERS AND MADE GOOD IT'S ESCAPE.
ONLY A FOOL WOULD HAVE STOOD IN ITS WAY.
THE ASSAILANT WASN'T A MAN AFTER ALL. RATHER SOME SORT OF MACHINE.

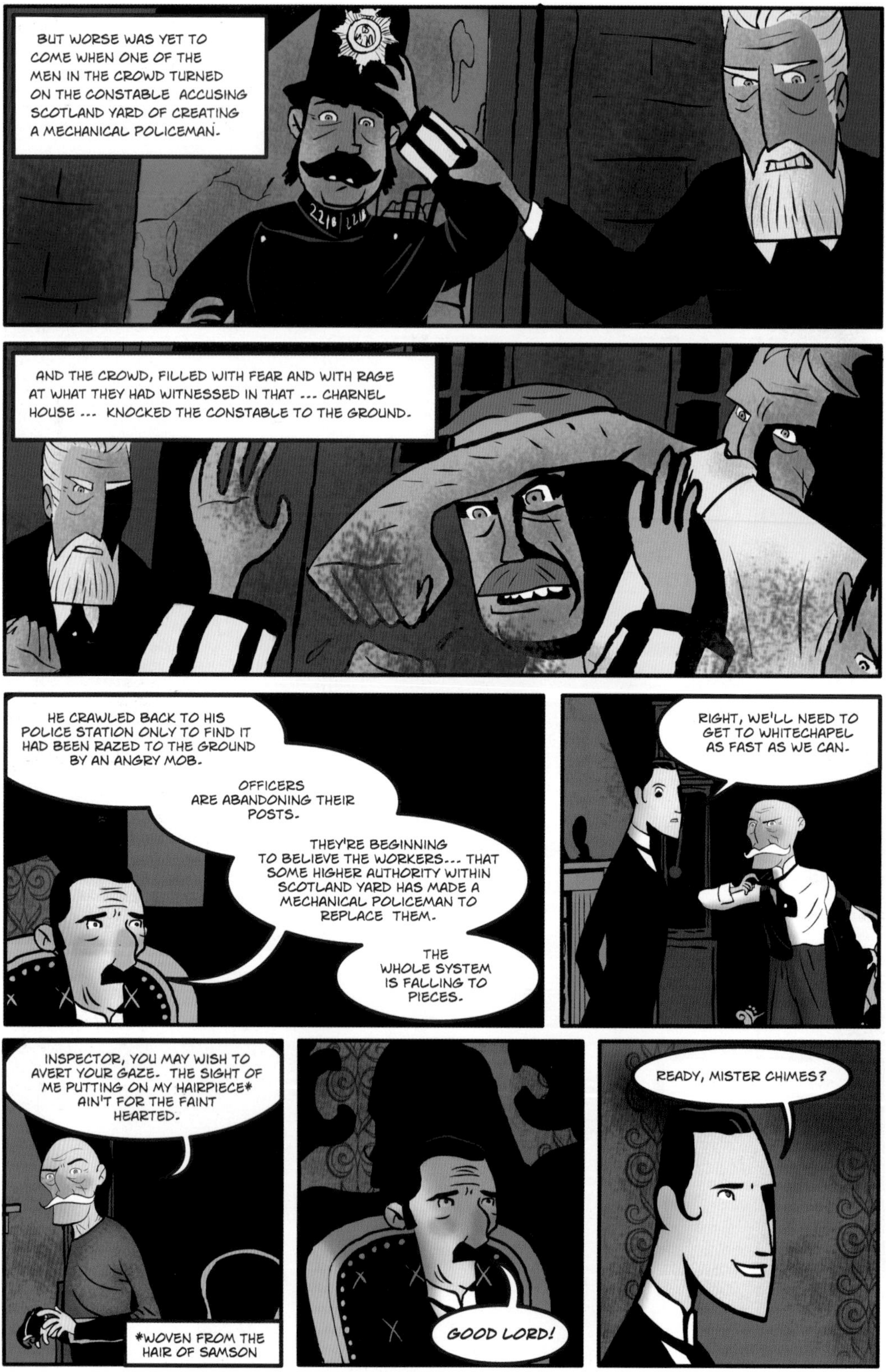
BUT WORSE WAS YET TO COME WHEN ONE OF THE MEN IN THE CROWD TURNED ON THE CONSTABLE ACCUSING SCOTLAND YARD OF CREATING A MECHANICAL POLICEMAN.
AND THE CROWD, FILLED WITH FEAR AND WITH RAGE AT WHAT THEY HAD WITNESSED IN THAT ... CHARNEL HOUSE ... KNOCKED THE CONSTABLE TO THE GROUND.
HE CRAWLED BACK TO HIS POLICE STATION ONLY TO FIND IT HAD BEEN RAZED TO THE GROUND BY AN ANGRY MOB.
OFFICERS ARE ABANDONING THEIR POSTS.
THEY'RE BEGINNING TO BELIEVE THE WORKERS... THAT SOME HIGHER AUTHORITY WITHIN SCOTLAND YARD HAS MADE A MECHANICAL POLICEMAN TO REPLACE THEM.
THE WHOLE SYSTEM IS FALLING TO PIECES.
RIGHT, WE'LL NEED TO GET TO WHITECHAPEL AS FAST AS WE CAN.
INSPECTOR, YOU MAY WISH TO AVERT YOUR GAZE. THE SIGHT OF ME PUTTING ON MY HAIRPIECE* AIN'T FOR THE FAINT HEARTED.
*WOVEN FROM THE HAIR OF SAMSON
GOOD LORD!
READY, MISTER CHIMES?

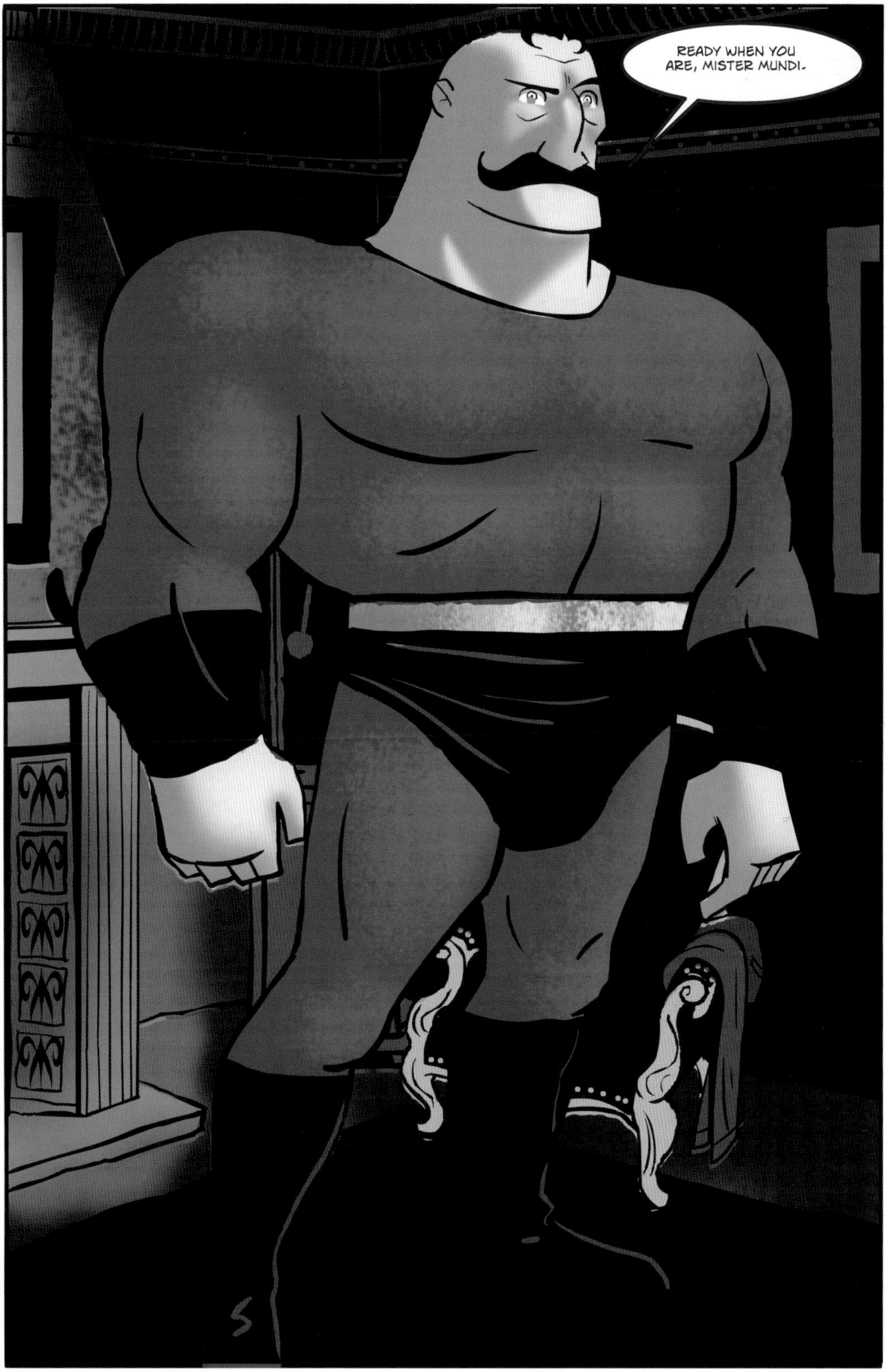
READY WHEN YOU ARE, MISTER MUNDI.

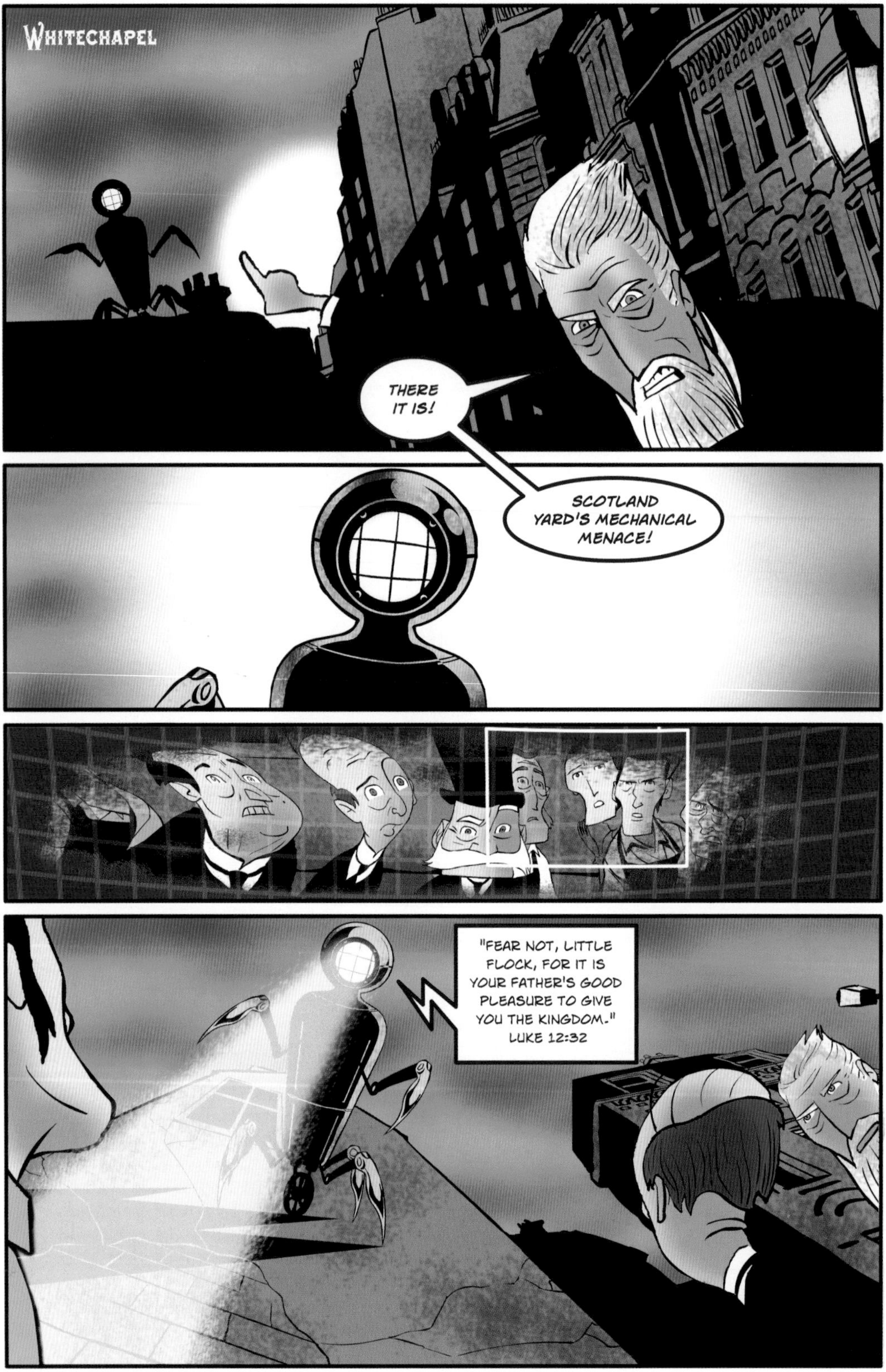
WHITECHAPEL
THERE IT IS!
SCOTLAND YARD'S MECHANICAL MENACE!
"FEAR NOT, LITTLE FLOCK, FOR IT IS YOUR FATHER'S GOOD PLEASURE TO GIVE YOU THE KINGDOM." LUKE 12:32

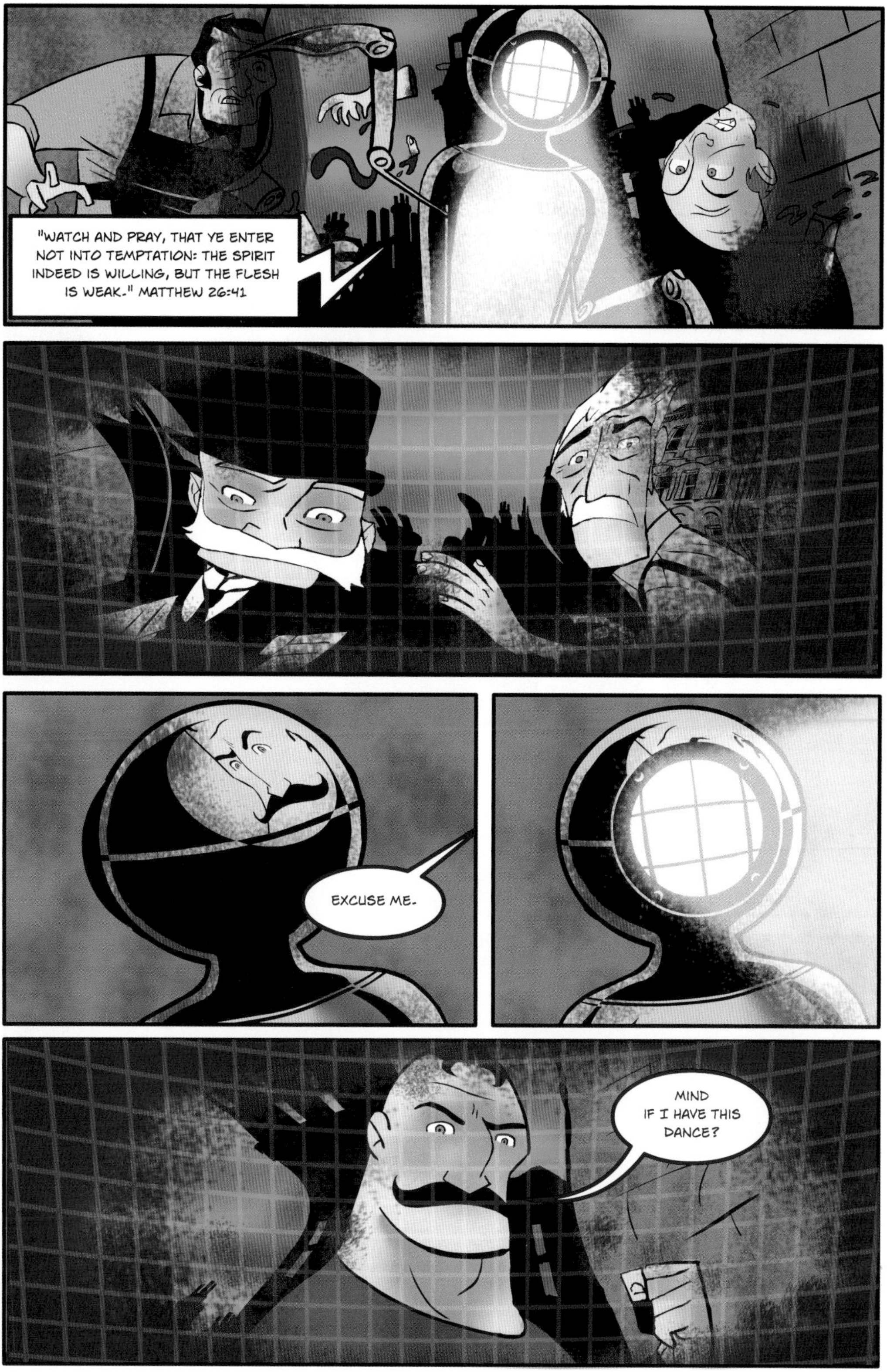
"WATCH AND PRAY, THAT YE ENTER NOT INTO TEMPTATION: THE SPIRIT INDEED IS WILLING, BUT THE FLESH IS WEAK." MATTHEW 26:41
EXCUSE ME.
MIND IF I HAVE THIS DANCE?

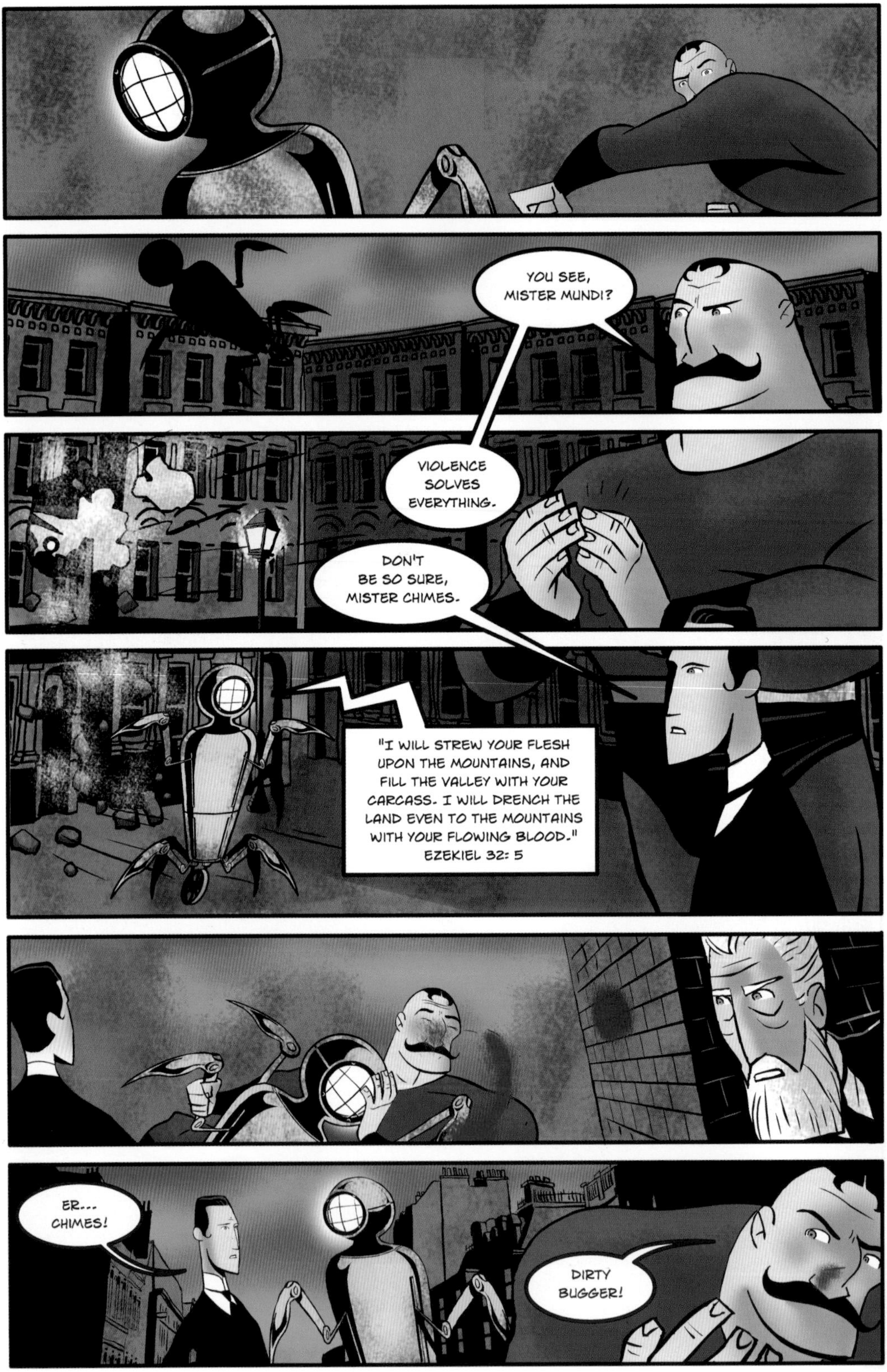
YOU SEE,
MISTER MUNDI?
VIOLENCE
SOLVES
EVERYTHING.
DON'T
BE SO SURE,
MISTER CHIMES.
"I WILL STREW YOUR FLESH
UPON THE MOUNTAINS, AND
FILL THE VALLEY WITH YOUR
CARCASS. I WILL DRENCH THE
LAND EVEN TO THE MOUNTAINS
WITH YOUR FLOWING BLOOD."
EZEKIEL 32: 5
ER...
CHIMES!
DIRTY
BUGGER!

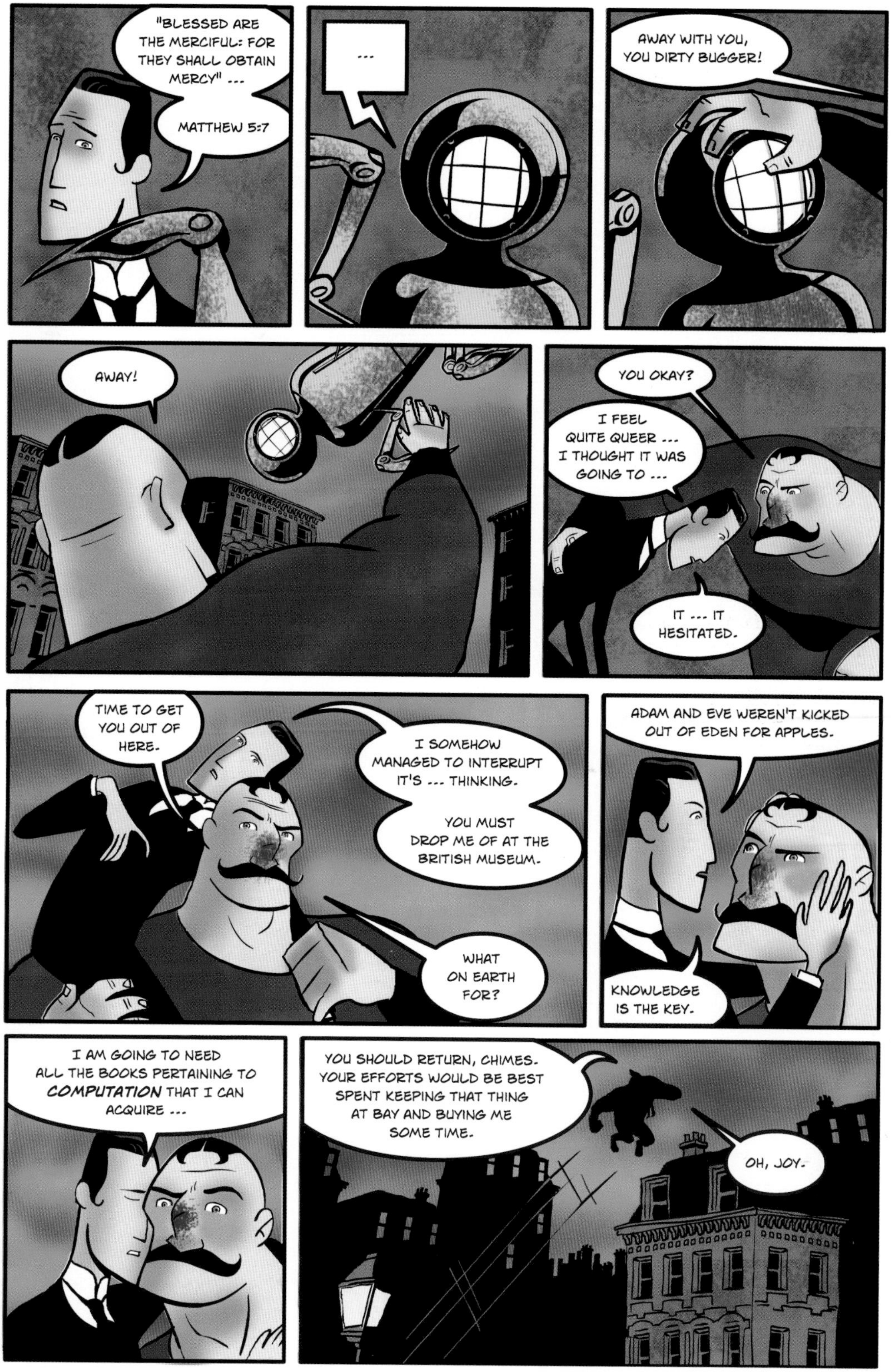
"BLESSED ARE THE MERCIFUL: FOR THEY SHALL OBTAIN MERCY" ...
MATTHEW 5:7
...
AWAY WITH YOU, YOU DIRTY BUGGER!
AWAY!
YOU OKAY?
I FEEL QUITE QUEER ... I THOUGHT IT WAS GOING TO ...
IT ... IT HESITATED.
TIME TO GET YOU OUT OF HERE.
I SOMEHOW MANAGED TO INTERRUPT IT'S ... THINKING.
YOU MUST DROP ME OF AT THE BRITISH MUSEUM.
WHAT ON EARTH FOR?
ADAM AND EVE WEREN'T KICKED OUT OF EDEN FOR APPLES.
KNOWLEDGE IS THE KEY.
I AM GOING TO NEED ALL THE BOOKS PERTAINING TO COMPUTATION THAT I CAN ACQUIRE ...
YOU SHOULD RETURN, CHIMES. YOUR EFFORTS WOULD BE BEST SPENT KEEPING THAT THING AT BAY AND BUYING ME SOME TIME.
OH, JOY.

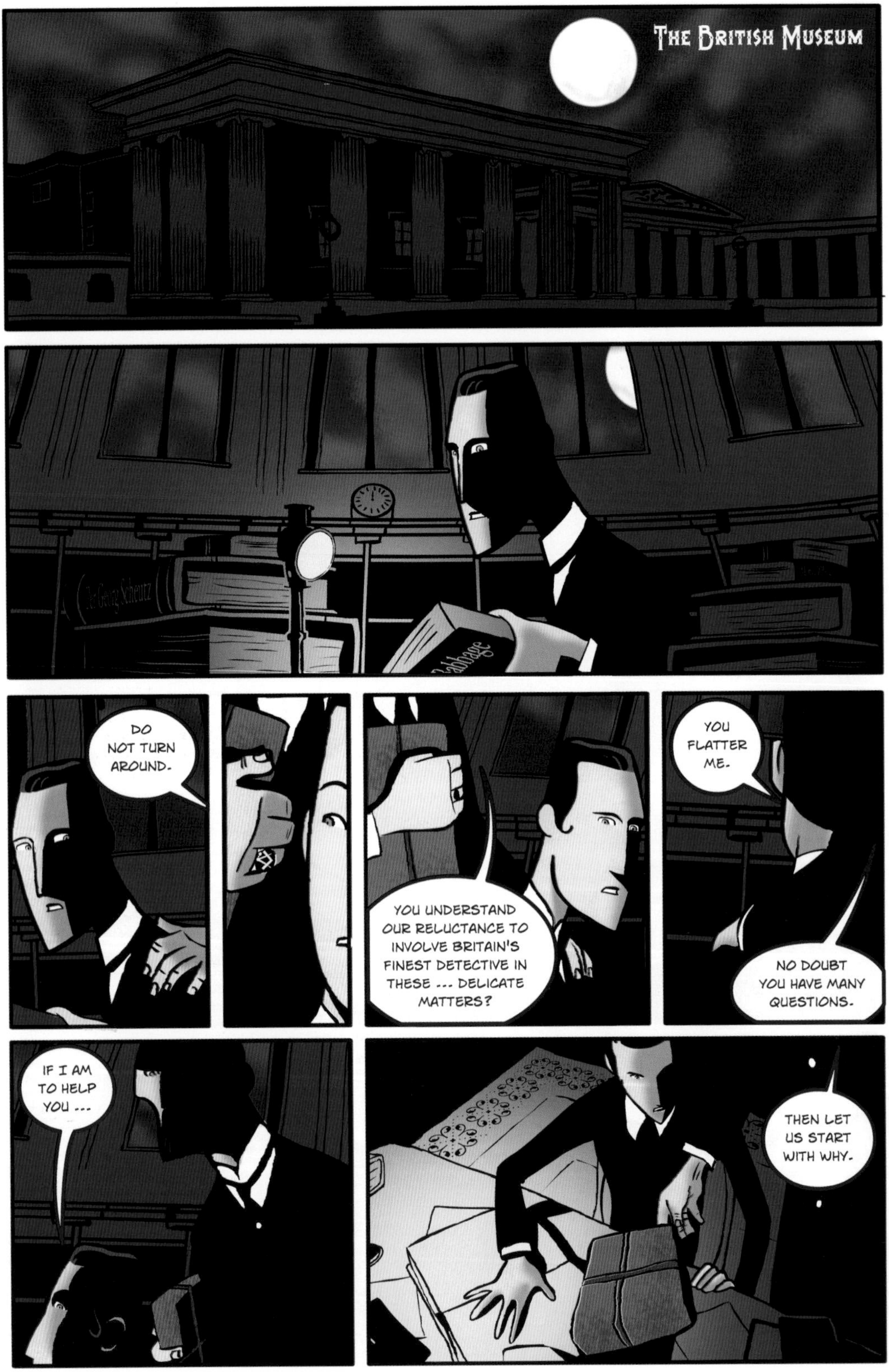
THE BRITISH MUSEUM
Babbage
DO NOT TURN AROUND.
YOU UNDERSTAND OUR RELUCTANCE TO INVOLVE BRITAIN'S FINEST DETECTIVE IN THESE ... DELICATE MATTERS?
YOU FLATTER ME.
NO DOUBT YOU HAVE MANY QUESTIONS.
IF I AM TO HELP YOU ...
THEN LET US START WITH WHY.

THIS IS BELIEVED TO BE THE WORK OF DOCTOR MIRABILIS, A THIRTEENTH CENTURY FRANCISCAN FRIAR ... A GENIUS ... AN ALCHEMIST ... A HERETIC.

IN 1267 HE WAS SECRETLY COMMISSIONED TO COMPILE A COMPENDIUM OF ALL KNOWLEDGE FOR POPE CLEMENT IV.

THE COMPENDIUM WAS WRITTEN ENTIRELY IN CODE.

MIRABILIS FELL OUT OF FAVOUR WITH THE PONTIF'S SUCCESSOR.

HE FOUND HIMSELF IMPRISONED UNDER SUSPICION OF WITCHCRAFT.

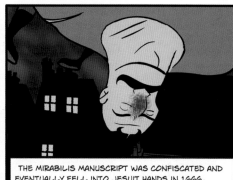

THE MIRABILIS MANUSCRIPT WAS CONFISCATED AND EVENTUALLY FELL INTO JESUIT HANDS IN 1666.

THEY'VE BEEN TRYING TO DECRYPT IT EVER SINCE.

BEFORE HE WAS IMPRISONED, MIRABILIS HAD MANAGED TO HIDE THE COMPENDIUM'S CYPHER. THE KNIGHTS TEMPLAR BURIED IT UNDER SOLOMON'S TEMPLE IN JERUSALEM WHERE THEY HAD BEEN EXCAVATING.

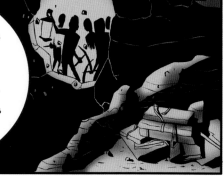

IN 1867, SIX HUNDRED YEARS, SIX MONTHS AND SIX DAYS AFTER THE MANUSCRIPT WAS COMMISSIONED, THE TUNNELS BENEATH THE TEMPLE WERE EXCAVATED ONCE MORE BY THE PALESTINE EXPLORATION FUND, HEADED BY SIR CHARLES WARREN. WE DISCOVERED A SECRET ROOM WHEREIN WE FOUND THE MIRABILIS CYPHER AND A COMPREHENSIVE INDEX OF THE MIRABILIS MANUSCRIPT.

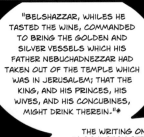

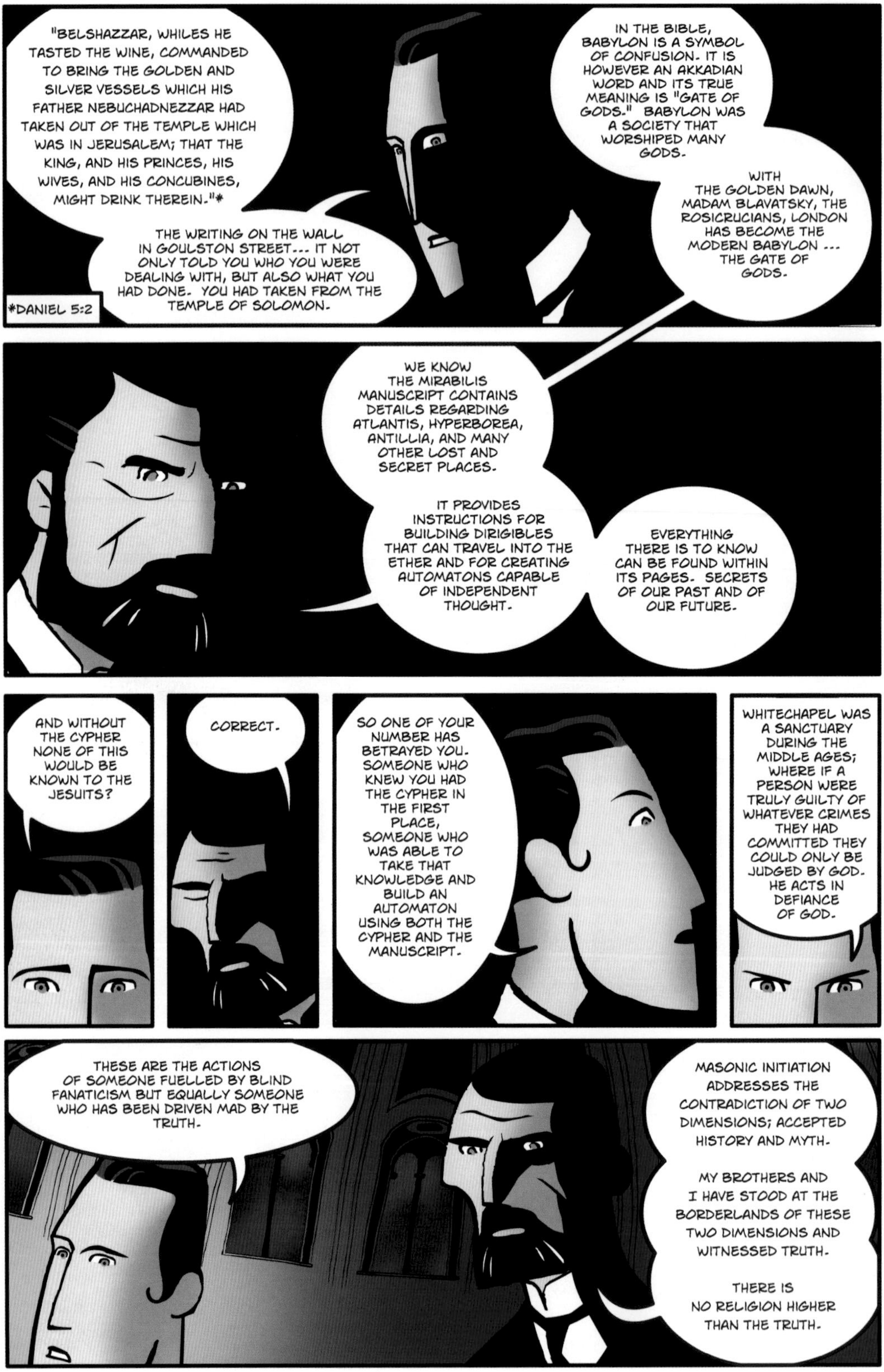

"BELSHAZZAR, WHILES HE TASTED THE WINE, COMMANDED TO BRING THE GOLDEN AND SILVER VESSELS WHICH HIS FATHER NEBUCHADNEZZAR HAD TAKEN OUT OF THE TEMPLE WHICH WAS IN JERUSALEM; THAT THE KING, AND HIS PRINCES, HIS WIVES, AND HIS CONCUBINES, MIGHT DRINK THEREIN."*

THE WRITING ON THE WALL IN GOULSTON STREET... IT NOT ONLY TOLD YOU WHO YOU WERE DEALING WITH, BUT ALSO WHAT YOU HAD DONE. YOU HAD TAKEN FROM THE TEMPLE OF SOLOMON.

*DANIEL 5:2

IN THE BIBLE, BABYLON IS A SYMBOL OF CONFUSION. IT IS HOWEVER AN AKKADIAN WORD AND ITS TRUE MEANING IS "GATE OF GODS." BABYLON WAS A SOCIETY THAT WORSHIPED MANY GODS.

WITH THE GOLDEN DAWN, MADAM BLAVATSKY, THE ROSICRUCIANS, LONDON HAS BECOME THE MODERN BABYLON ... THE GATE OF GODS.

WE KNOW THE MIRABILIS MANUSCRIPT CONTAINS DETAILS REGARDING ATLANTIS, HYPERBOREA, ANTILLIA, AND MANY OTHER LOST AND SECRET PLACES.

IT PROVIDES INSTRUCTIONS FOR BUILDING DIRIGIBLES THAT CAN TRAVEL INTO THE ETHER AND FOR CREATING AUTOMATONS CAPABLE OF INDEPENDENT THOUGHT.

EVERYTHING THERE IS TO KNOW CAN BE FOUND WITHIN ITS PAGES. SECRETS OF OUR PAST AND OF OUR FUTURE.

AND WITHOUT THE CYPHER NONE OF THIS WOULD BE KNOWN TO THE JESUITS?

CORRECT.

SO ONE OF YOUR NUMBER HAS BETRAYED YOU. SOMEONE WHO KNEW YOU HAD THE CYPHER IN THE FIRST PLACE, SOMEONE WHO WAS ABLE TO TAKE THAT KNOWLEDGE AND BUILD AN AUTOMATON USING BOTH THE CYPHER AND THE MANUSCRIPT.

WHITECHAPEL WAS A SANCTUARY DURING THE MIDDLE AGES; WHERE IF A PERSON WERE TRULY GUILTY OF WHATEVER CRIMES THEY HAD COMMITTED THEY COULD ONLY BE JUDGED BY GOD. HE ACTS IN DEFIANCE OF GOD.

THESE ARE THE ACTIONS OF SOMEONE FUELLED BY BLIND FANATICISM BUT EQUALLY SOMEONE WHO HAS BEEN DRIVEN MAD BY THE TRUTH.

MASONIC INITIATION ADDRESSES THE CONTRADICTION OF TWO DIMENSIONS; ACCEPTED HISTORY AND MYTH.

MY BROTHERS AND I HAVE STOOD AT THE BORDERLANDS OF THESE TWO DIMENSIONS AND WITNESSED TRUTH.

THERE IS NO RELIGION HIGHER THAN THE TRUTH.

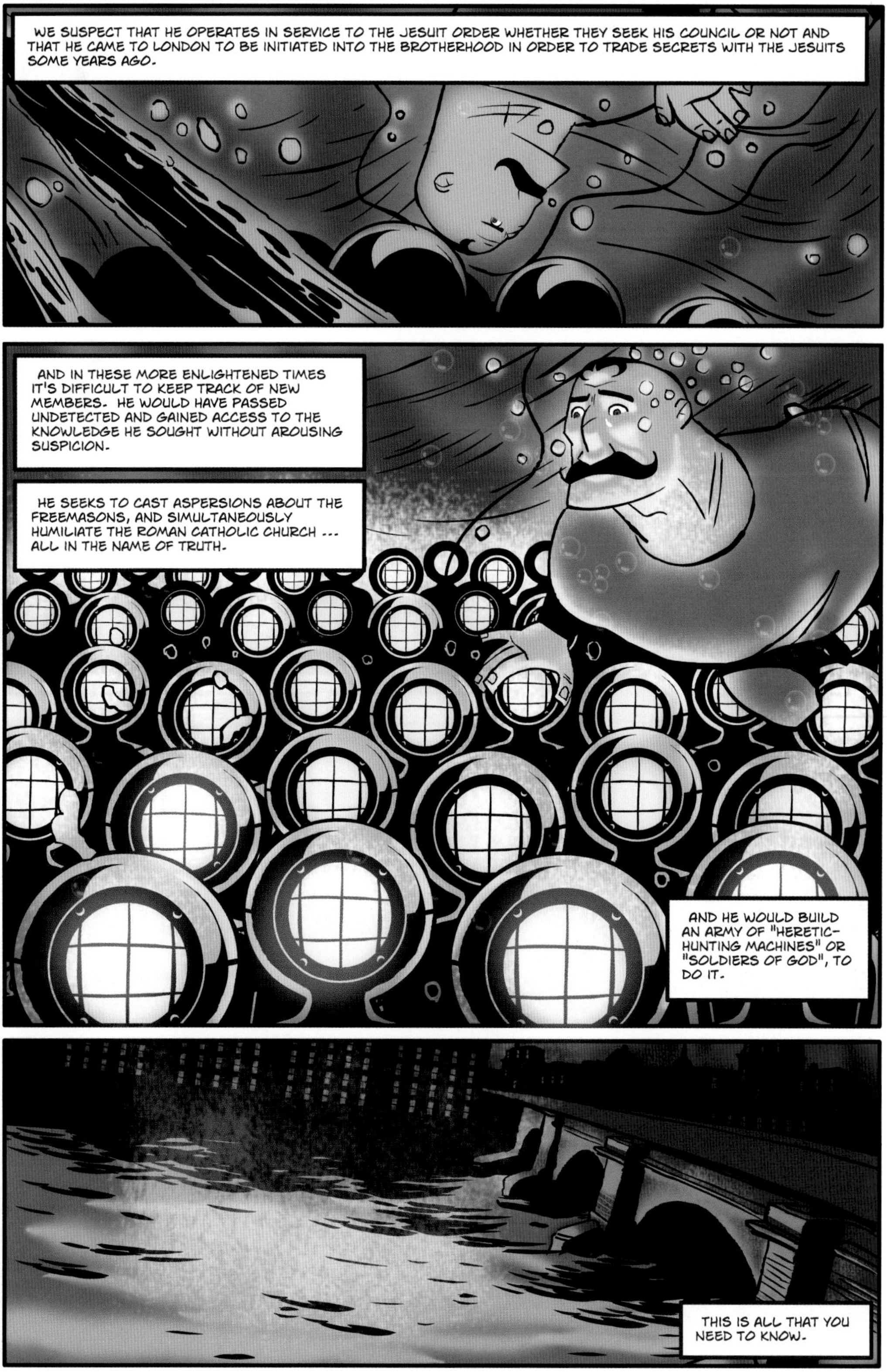
WE SUSPECT THAT HE OPERATES IN SERVICE TO THE JESUIT ORDER WHETHER THEY SEEK HIS COUNCIL OR NOT AND THAT HE CAME TO LONDON TO BE INITIATED INTO THE BROTHERHOOD IN ORDER TO TRADE SECRETS WITH THE JESUITS SOME YEARS AGO.
AND IN THESE MORE ENLIGHTENED TIMES IT'S DIFFICULT TO KEEP TRACK OF NEW MEMBERS. HE WOULD HAVE PASSED UNDETECTED AND GAINED ACCESS TO THE KNOWLEDGE HE SOUGHT WITHOUT AROUSING SUSPICION.
HE SEEKS TO CAST ASPERSIONS ABOUT THE FREEMASONS, AND SIMULTANEOUSLY HUMILIATE THE ROMAN CATHOLIC CHURCH ... ALL IN THE NAME OF TRUTH.
AND HE WOULD BUILD AN ARMY OF "HERETIC-HUNTING MACHINES" OR "SOLDIERS OF GOD", TO DO IT.
THIS IS ALL THAT YOU NEED TO KNOW.

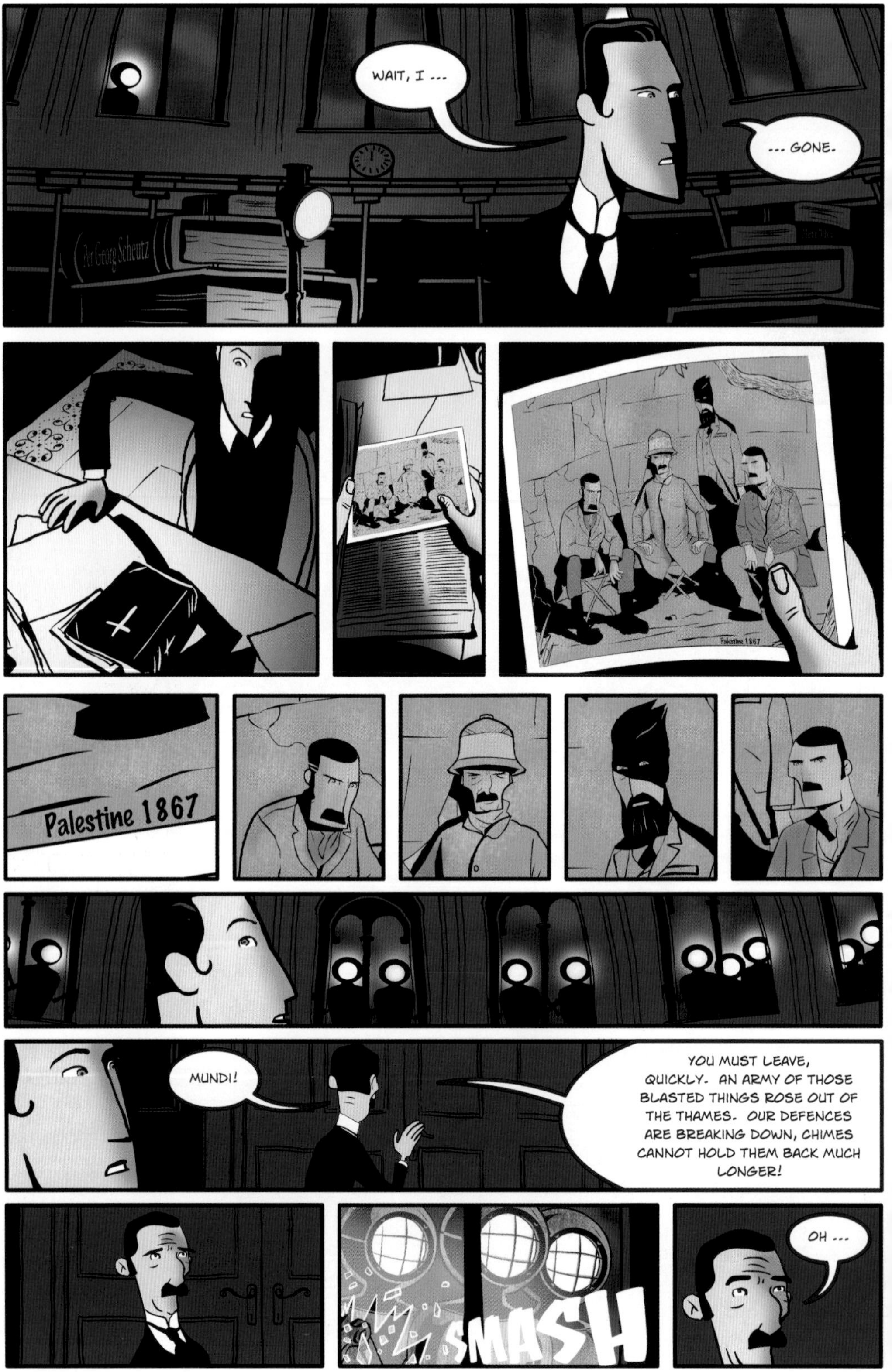
WAIT, I ...
... GONE.
Per Georg Scheutz
Palestine 1867
Palestine 1867
MUNDI!
YOU MUST LEAVE, QUICKLY. AN ARMY OF THOSE BLASTED THINGS ROSE OUT OF THE THAMES. OUR DEFENCES ARE BREAKING DOWN, CHIMES CANNOT HOLD THEM BACK MUCH LONGER!
SMASH
OH ...

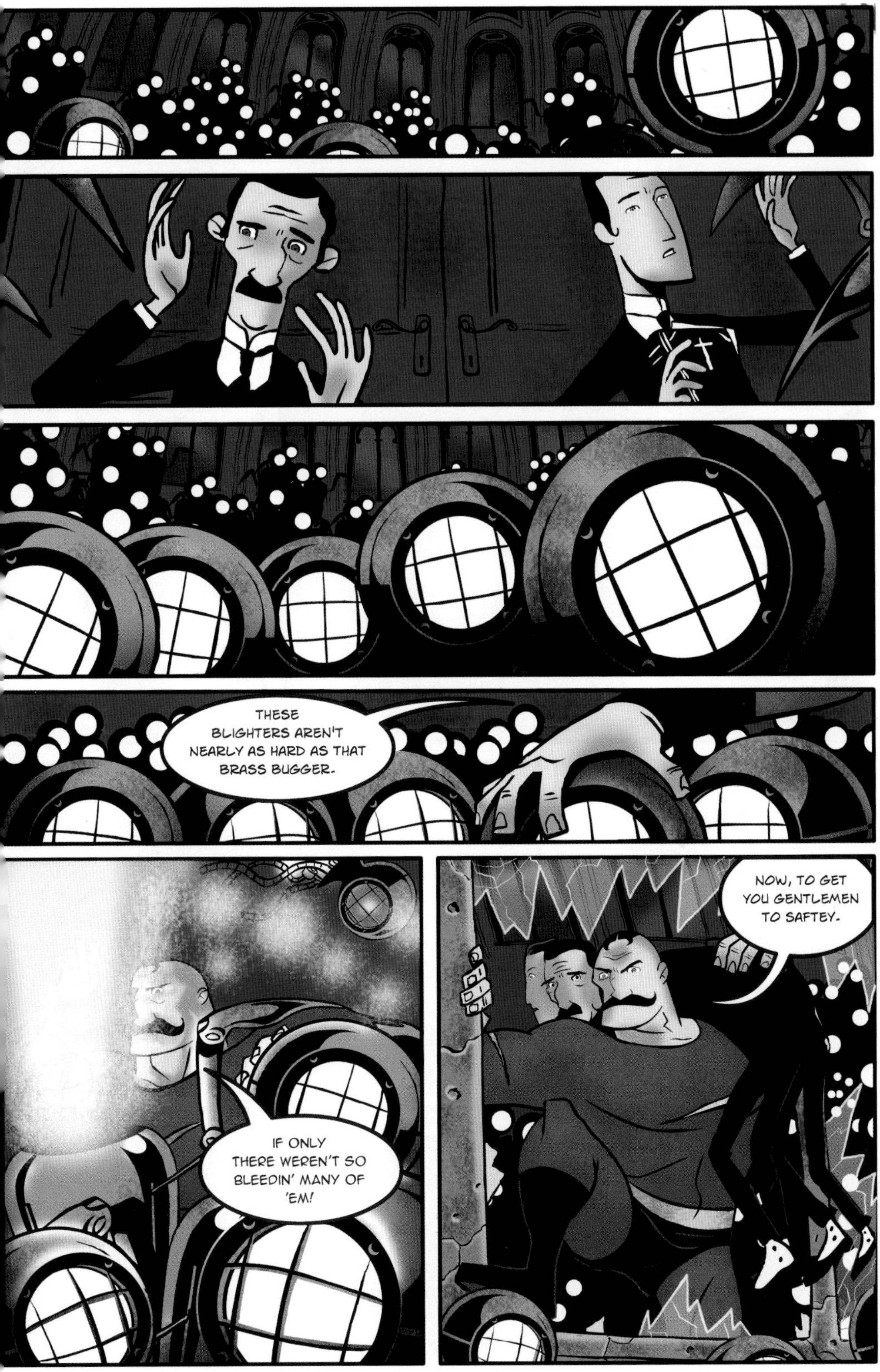
THESE BLIGHTERS AREN'T NEARLY AS HARD AS THAT BRASS BUGGER.
IF ONLY THERE WEREN'T SO BLEEDIN' MANY OF 'EM!
NOW, TO GET YOU GENTLEMEN TO SAFTEY.

ARE YOU ALL RIGHT?

MY HANDS, THEY... THEY WON'T STOP SHAKING.

THERE... THERE ARE SO MANY OF THEM! WHAT ARE WE GOING TO DO?

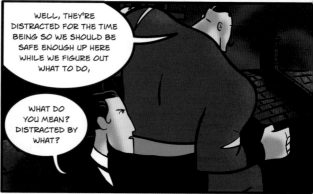

GOOD QUESTION ... WHAT ARE WE GOING TO DO, MUNDI? WE CAN'T JUST LEAVE LONDON LIKE THIS.

THE MACHINE OPERATES USING THE TEN COMMANDMENTS TO GOVERN IT'S PRIMARY FUNCTIONS. ONE TO TEN.

IT'S SECONDARY FUNCTIONS ARE PASSAGES FROM THE BIBLE. CHAPTER AND VERSE ... THINK, MUNDI, THINK—

WELL, THEY'RE DISTRACTED FOR THE TIME BEING SO WE SHOULD BE SAFE ENOUGH UP HERE WHILE WE FIGURE OUT WHAT TO DO,

WHAT DO YOU MEAN? DISTRACTED BY WHAT?

THEY STARTED BUILDING A COUPLE OF HOURS AGO.

BUILDING?

26

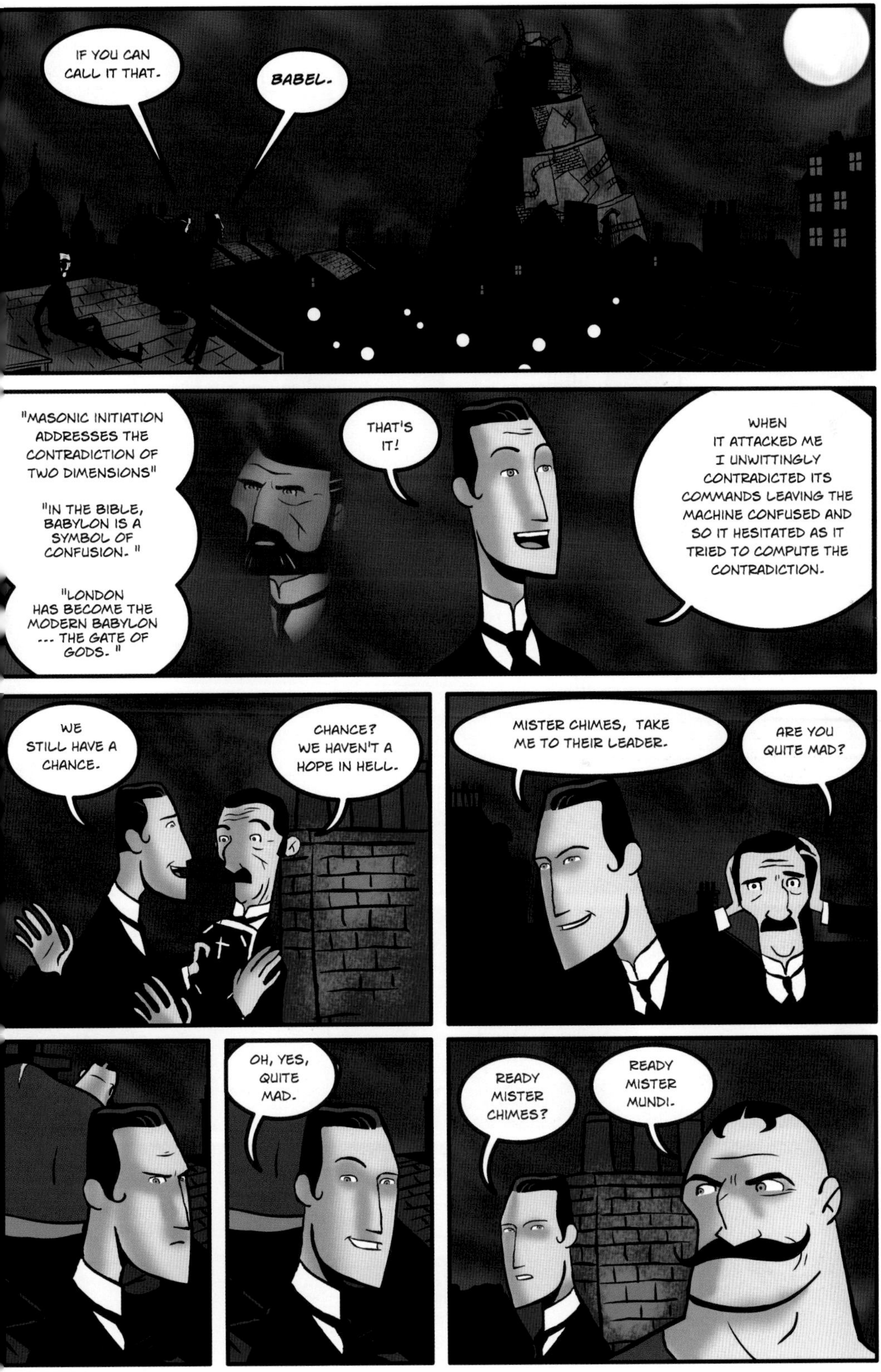
IF YOU CAN CALL IT THAT.
BABEL.
"MASONIC INITIATION ADDRESSES THE CONTRADICTION OF TWO DIMENSIONS"
"IN THE BIBLE, BABYLON IS A SYMBOL OF CONFUSION."
"LONDON HAS BECOME THE MODERN BABYLON --- THE GATE OF GODS."
THAT'S IT!
WHEN IT ATTACKED ME I UNWITTINGLY CONTRADICTED ITS COMMANDS LEAVING THE MACHINE CONFUSED AND SO IT HESITATED AS IT TRIED TO COMPUTE THE CONTRADICTION.
WE STILL HAVE A CHANCE.
CHANCE? WE HAVEN'T A HOPE IN HELL.
MISTER CHIMES, TAKE ME TO THEIR LEADER.
ARE YOU QUITE MAD?
OH, YES, QUITE MAD.
READY MISTER CHIMES?
READY MISTER MUNDI.

KNOCK KNOCK.

THAT GOT IT'S ATTENTION.

"AND THE LORD APPEARED TO SOLOMON BY NIGHT, AND SAID UNTO HIM, I HAVE HEARD THY PRAYER, AND HAVE CHOSEN THIS PLACE TO MYSELF FOR AN HOUSE OF SACRIFICE."
2 CHRONICLES 7:12

"FOOLISHNESS IS BOUND IN THE HEART OF A CHILD; BUT THE ROD OF CORRECTION SHALL DRIVE IT FAR FROM HIM."
PROVERBS 22:15

"THOUGH THOU SHOULDEST BRAY A FOOL IN A MORTAR AMONG WHEAT WITH A PESTLE, YET WILL NOT HIS FOOLISHNESS DEPART FROM HIM."
PROVERBS 27:22

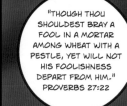

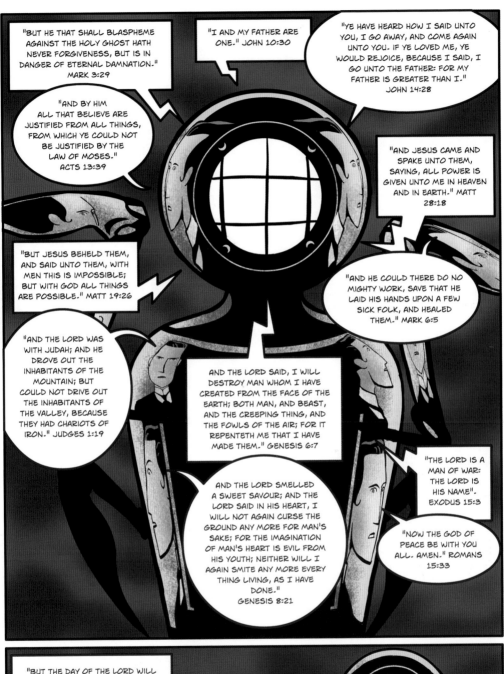

"BUT HE THAT SHALL BLASPHEME AGAINST THE HOLY GHOST HATH NEVER FORGIVENESS, BUT IS IN DANGER OF ETERNAL DAMNATION." MARK 3:29

"I AND MY FATHER ARE ONE." JOHN 10:30

"YE HAVE HEARD HOW I SAID UNTO YOU, I GO AWAY, AND COME AGAIN UNTO YOU. IF YE LOVED ME, YE WOULD REJOICE, BECAUSE I SAID, I GO UNTO THE FATHER: FOR MY FATHER IS GREATER THAN I." JOHN 14:28

"AND BY HIM ALL THAT BELIEVE ARE JUSTIFIED FROM ALL THINGS, FROM WHICH YE COULD NOT BE JUSTIFIED BY THE LAW OF MOSES." ACTS 13:39

"AND JESUS CAME AND SPAKE UNTO THEM, SAYING, ALL POWER IS GIVEN UNTO ME IN HEAVEN AND IN EARTH." MATT 28:18

"BUT JESUS BEHELD THEM, AND SAID UNTO THEM, WITH MEN THIS IS IMPOSSIBLE; BUT WITH GOD ALL THINGS ARE POSSIBLE." MATT 19:26

"AND HE COULD THERE DO NO MIGHTY WORK, SAVE THAT HE LAID HIS HANDS UPON A FEW SICK FOLK, AND HEALED THEM." MARK 6:5

"AND THE LORD WAS WITH JUDAH; AND HE DROVE OUT THE INHABITANTS OF THE MOUNTAIN; BUT COULD NOT DRIVE OUT THE INHABITANTS OF THE VALLEY, BECAUSE THEY HAD CHARIOTS OF IRON." JUDGES 1:19

AND THE LORD SAID, I WILL DESTROY MAN WHOM I HAVE CREATED FROM THE FACE OF THE EARTH; BOTH MAN, AND BEAST, AND THE CREEPING THING, AND THE FOWLS OF THE AIR; FOR IT REPENTETH ME THAT I HAVE MADE THEM." GENESIS 6:7

"THE LORD IS A MAN OF WAR: THE LORD IS HIS NAME"- EXODUS 15:3

AND THE LORD SMELLED A SWEET SAVOUR; AND THE LORD SAID IN HIS HEART, I WILL NOT AGAIN CURSE THE GROUND ANY MORE FOR MAN'S SAKE; FOR THE IMAGINATION OF MAN'S HEART IS EVIL FROM HIS YOUTH; NEITHER WILL I AGAIN SMITE ANY MORE EVERY THING LIVING, AS I HAVE DONE." GENESIS 8:21

"NOW THE GOD OF PEACE BE WITH YOU ALL. AMEN." ROMANS 15:33

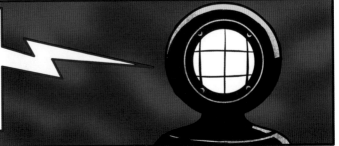

"BUT THE DAY OF THE LORD WILL COME AS A THIEF IN THE NIGHT; IN THE WHICH THE HEAVENS SHALL PASS AWAY WITH A GREAT NOISE, AND THE ELEMENTS SHALL MELT WITH FERVENT HEAT, THE EARTH ALSO AND THE WORKS THAT ARE THEREIN SHALL BE BURNED UP." PETER 3:10

"ONE GENERATION PASSETH AWAY, AND ANOTHER GENERATION COMETH: BUT THE EARTH ABIDETH FOR EVER." ECCLESIASTES 1:
THOU ... SHALL... NOT ...
...
CONTRADICT?
THAT'S IT?
NO FANCY FINALE? NO DUEL TO THE DEATH? NO HUGE EXPLOSION?
CAN YOU HEAR THAT?
SOUNDS LIKE...
TICKING?
HANG ON!

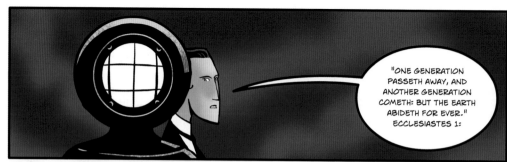

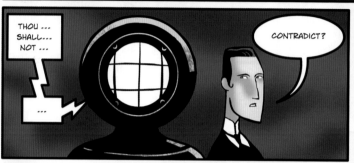

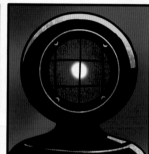

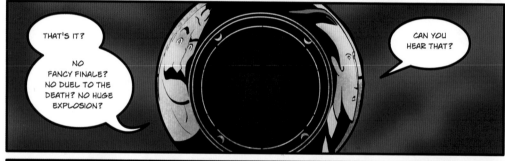

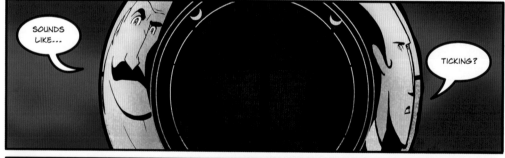

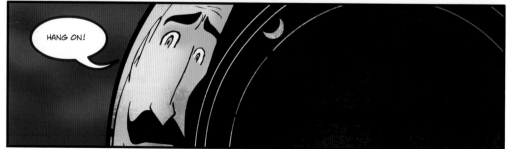

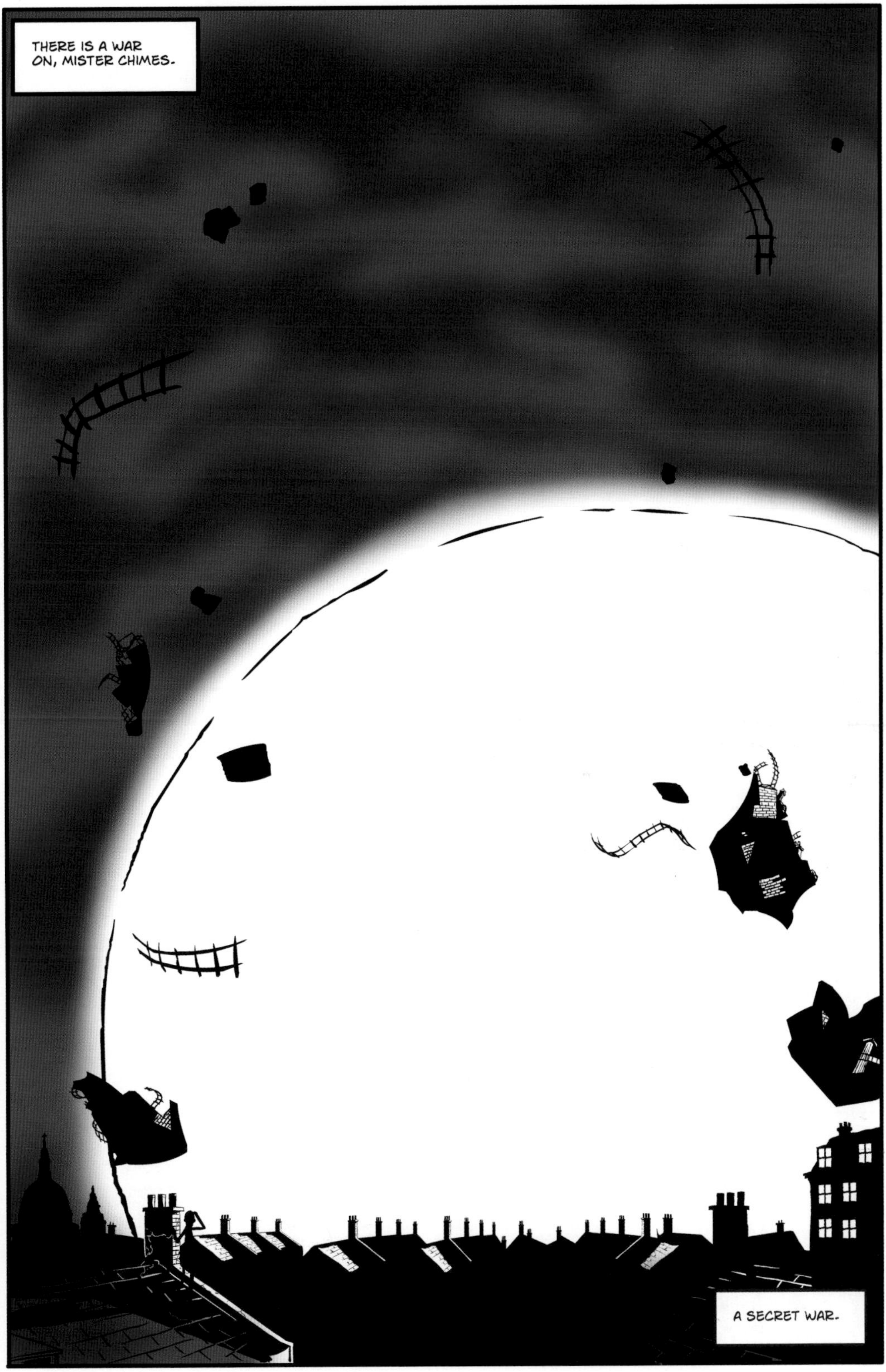
THERE IS A WAR
ON, MISTER CHIMES.
A SECRET WAR.

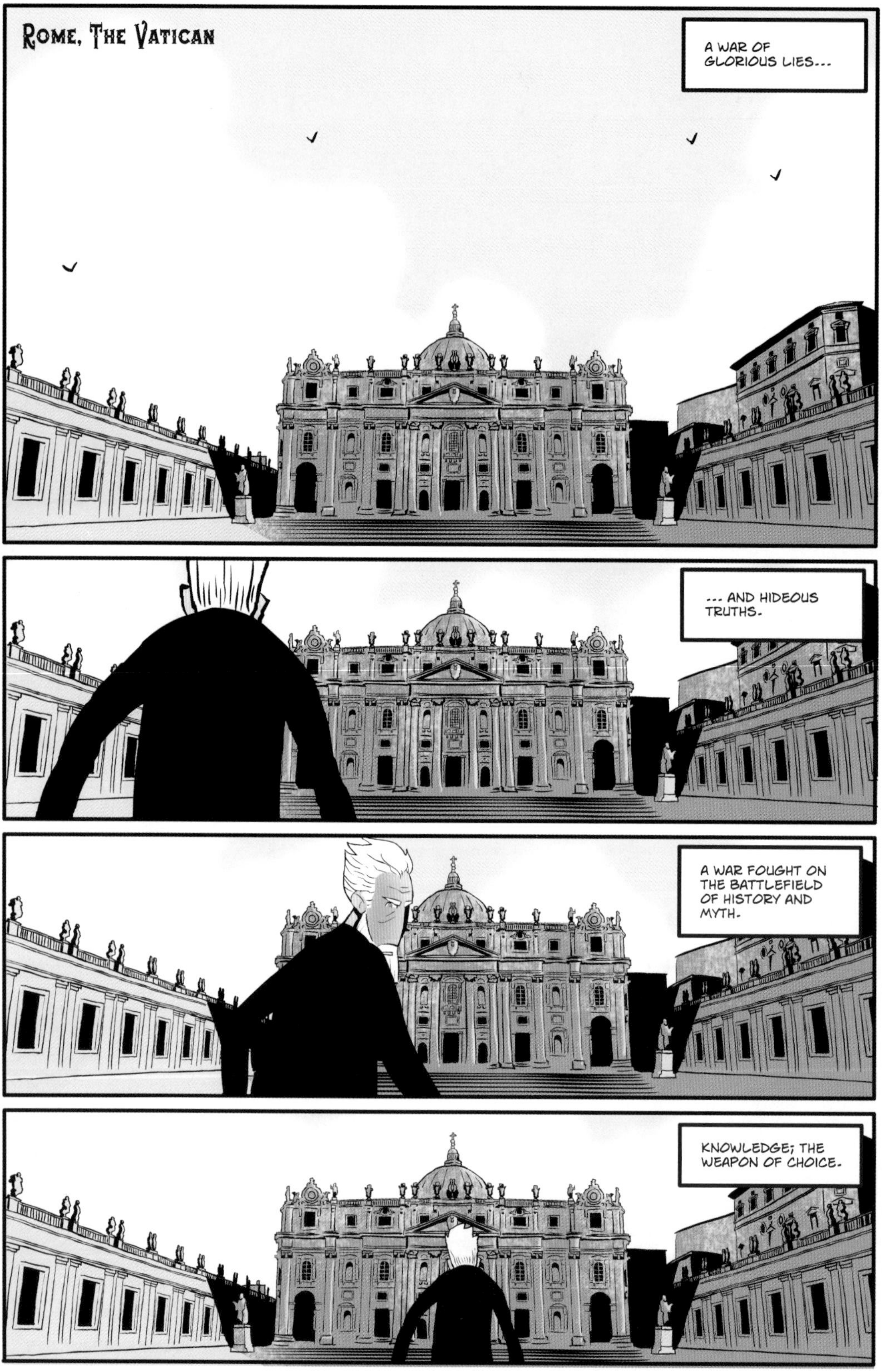
ROME, THE VATICAN
A WAR OF GLORIOUS LIES...
... AND HIDEOUS TRUTHS.
A WAR FOUGHT ON THE BATTLEFIELD OF HISTORY AND MYTH.
KNOWLEDGE; THE WEAPON OF CHOICE.

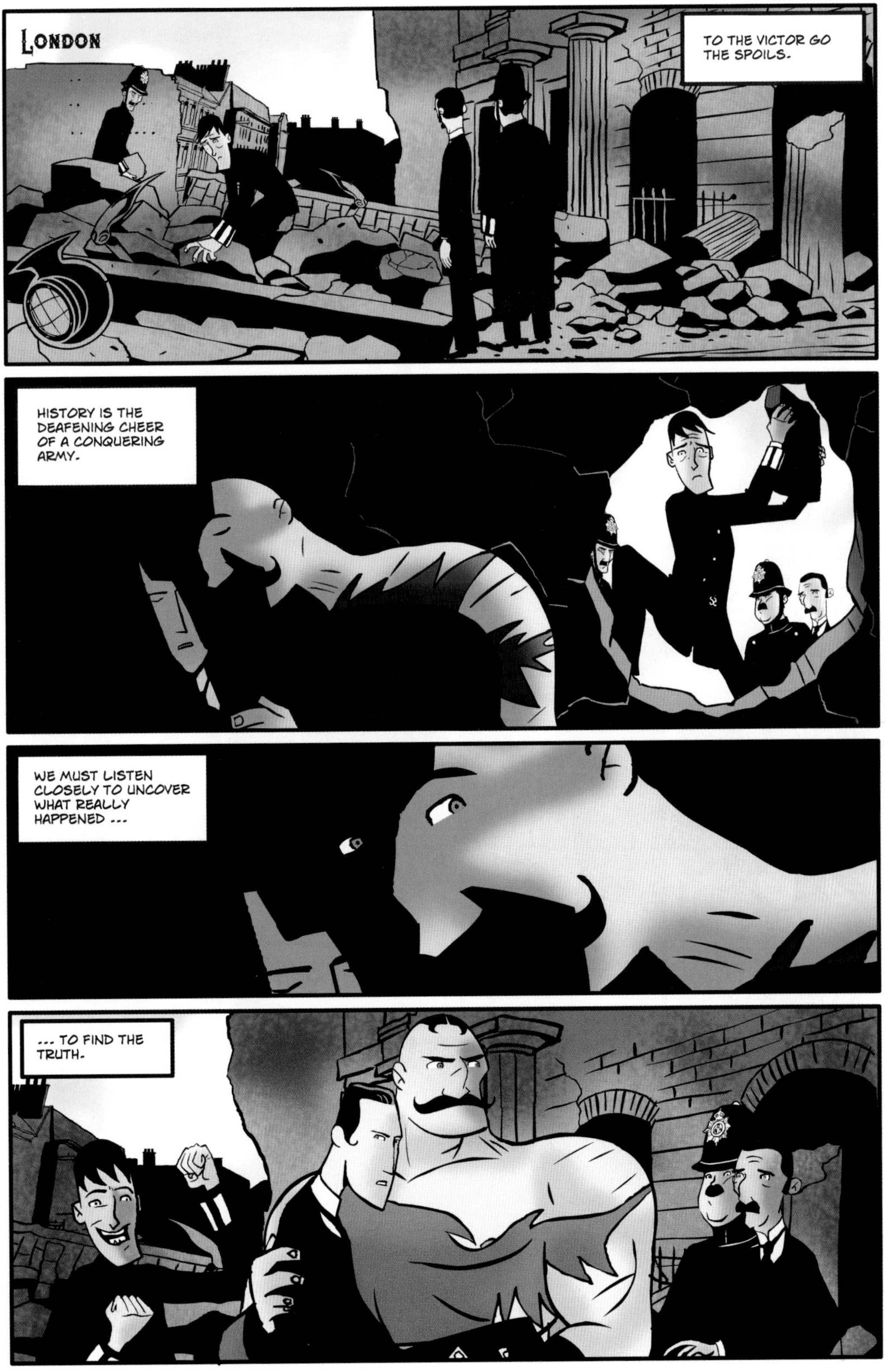
LONDON
TO THE VICTOR GO THE SPOILS.
HISTORY IS THE DEAFENING CHEER OF A CONQUERING ARMY.
WE MUST LISTEN CLOSELY TO UNCOVER WHAT REALLY HAPPENED ...
... TO FIND THE TRUTH.

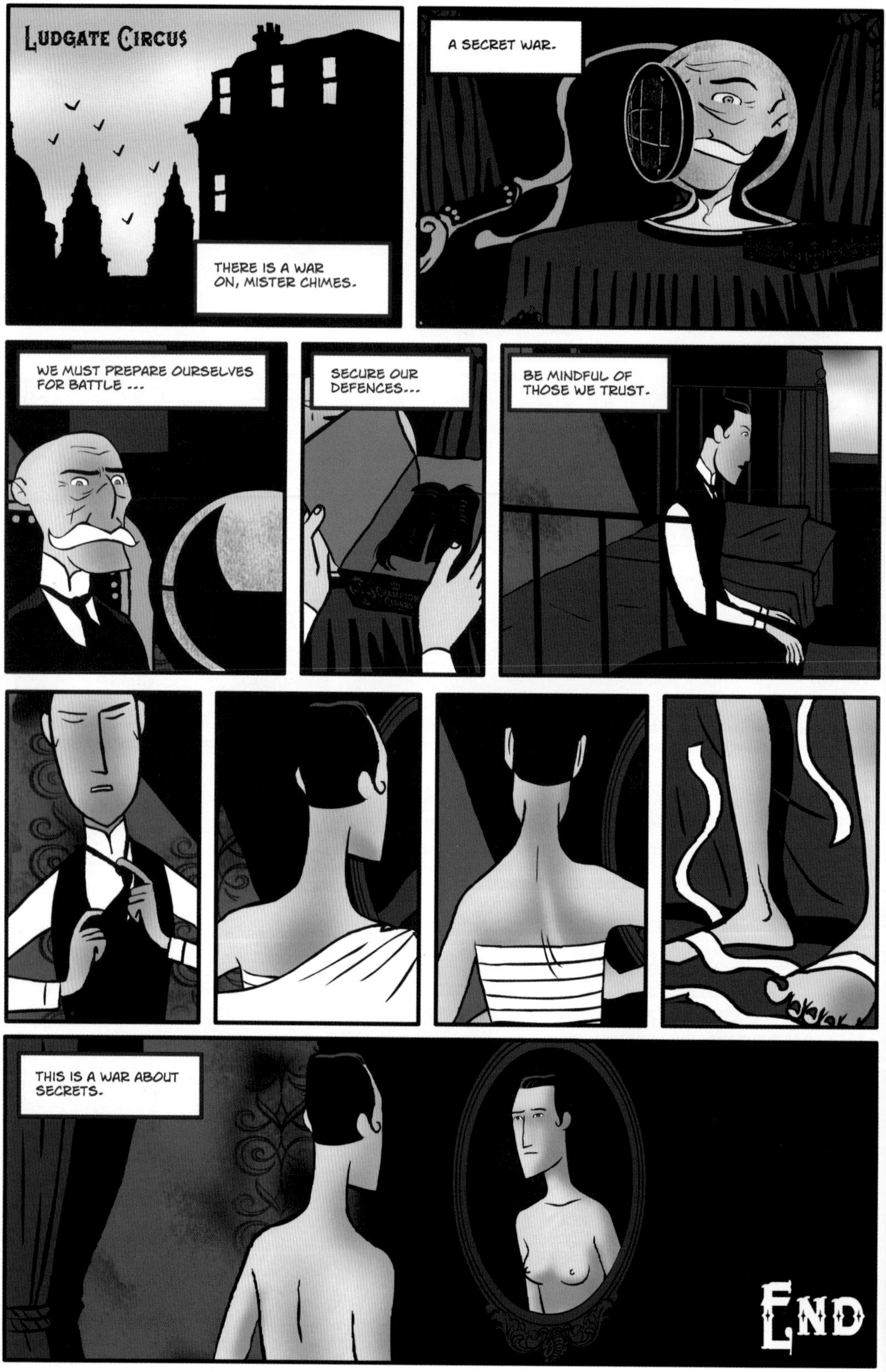
LUDGATE CIRCUS
THERE IS A WAR ON, MISTER CHIMES.
A SECRET WAR.
WE MUST PREPARE OURSELVES FOR BATTLE ...
SECURE OUR DEFENCES...
BE MINDFUL OF THOSE WE TRUST.
THIS IS A WAR ABOUT SECRETS.
END

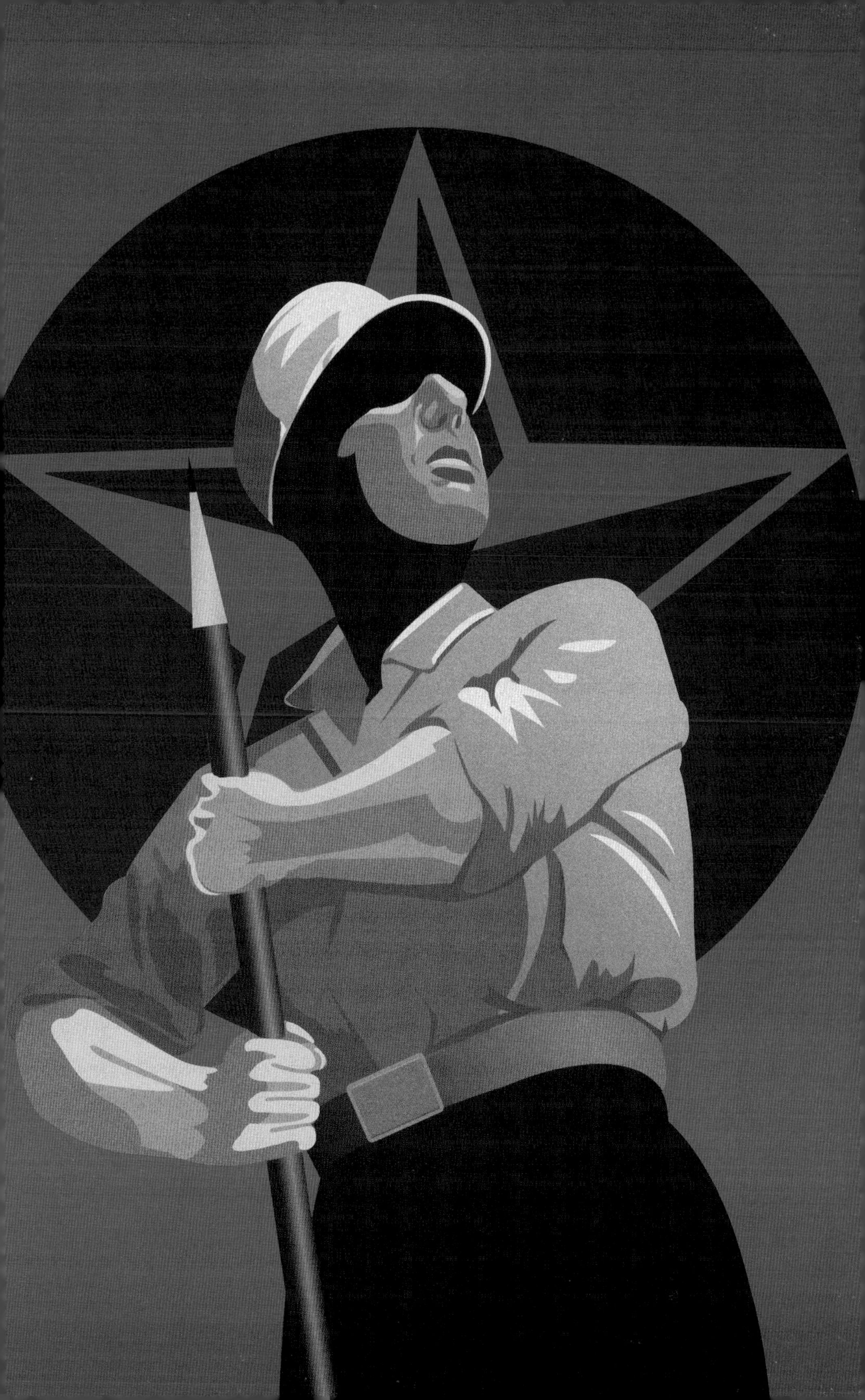

Nick Plumber is a screenwriter, independent film-maker, singer for the band Barstool Messiah, and staff writer for *Modern Drunkard Magazine*. He has a degree in Anthropology from Metropolitan State College of Denver and prides himself on being a high school and graduate school drop out. He has worked as a bouncer, bar-tender, DJ, archaeologist, health insurance salesman, chef, stage hand, banquet waiter, and ice cream truck driver. Currently he works part-time as an administra-tive assistant for the Denver chapter of SCORE, coun-selors to America's small businesses.

Adam Adamowicz grew up in New York and got his Psychology degree in Colorado. A former tattooist and ice cream truck driver, he has spent over 7 years as a Concept Artist for such publishers as Microsoft and the now defunct Psygnosis. Past forays in comics include cover illustration for Malibu Graphics (*Men in Black*), in-teriors for Fantagraphics Books (*Duplex Planet*) and spot illustrations for the *SF Bay Guardian*. His favorite sport is extreme outdoor patio surfing.

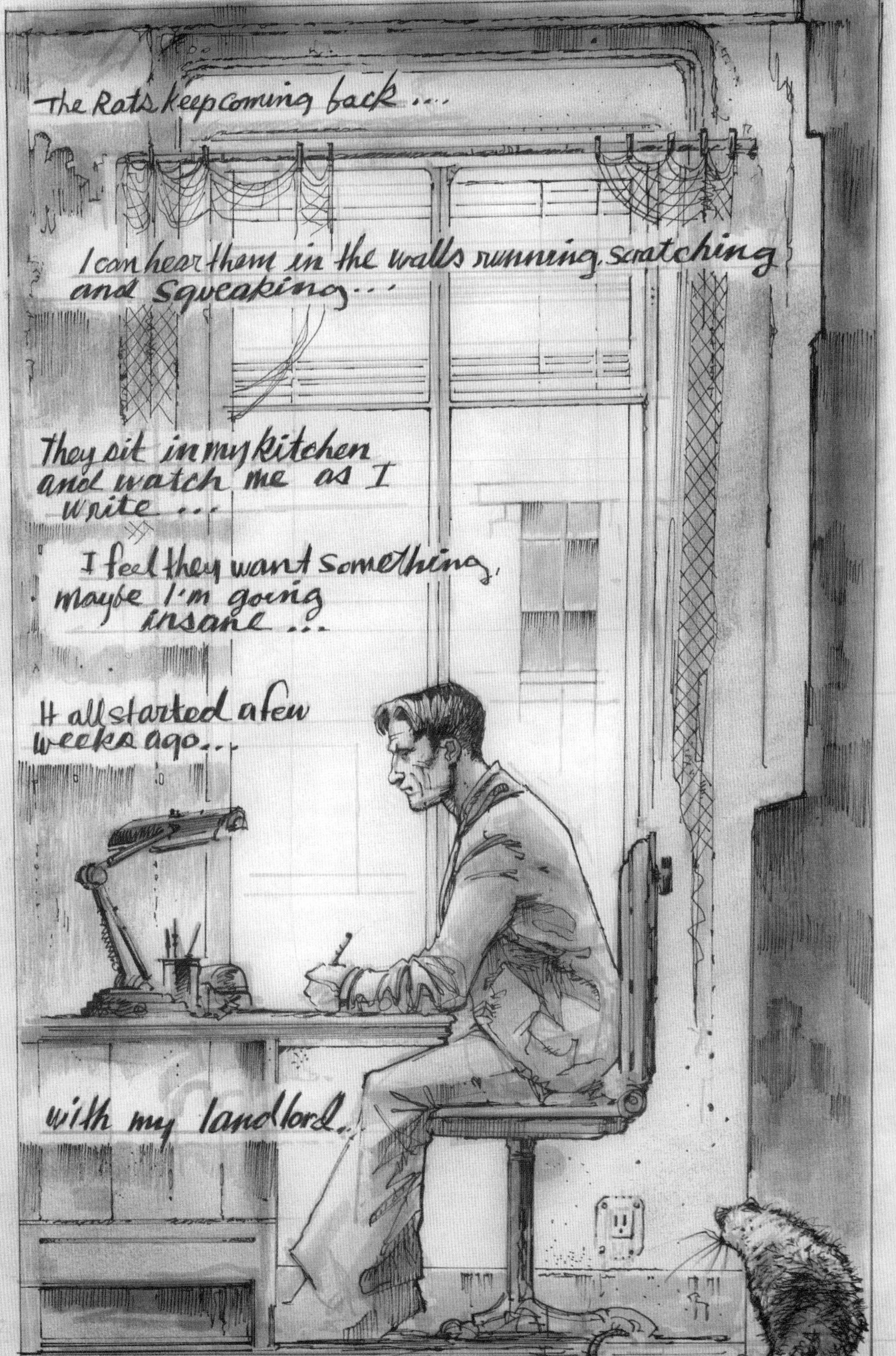

The Rats keep coming back...
I can hear them in the walls running, scratching and squeaking...
They sit in my kitchen and watch me as I write...
I feel they want something, maybe I'm going insane...
It all started a few weeks ago...
with my landlord...

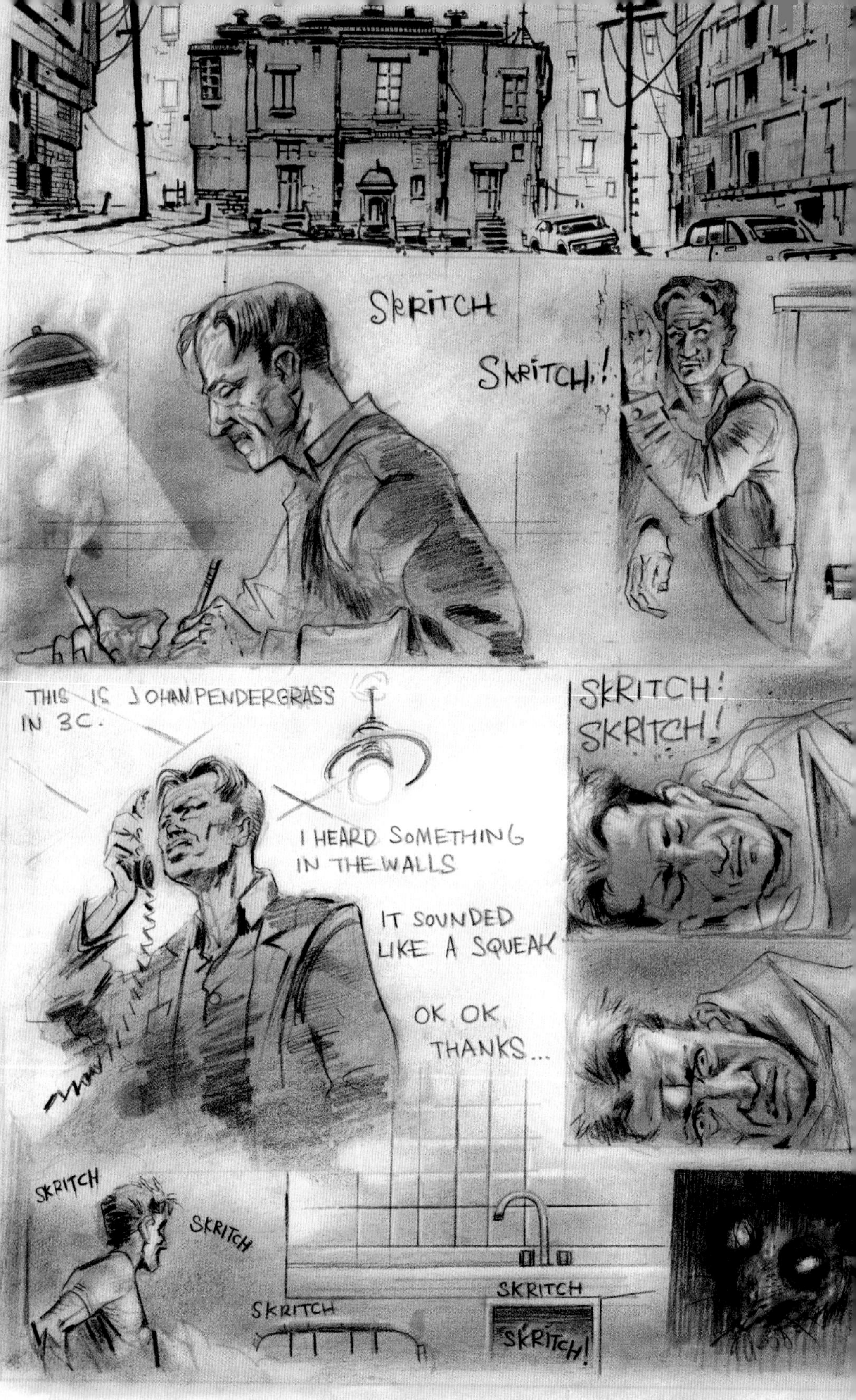
SKRITCH
SKRITCH!
THIS IS JOHAN PENDERGRASS IN 3C.
I HEARD SOMETHING IN THE WALLS
IT SOUNDED LIKE A SQUEAK
OK OK THANKS...
SKRITCH! SKRITCH!
SKRITCH
SKRITCH
SKRITCH
SKRITCH
SKRITCH!

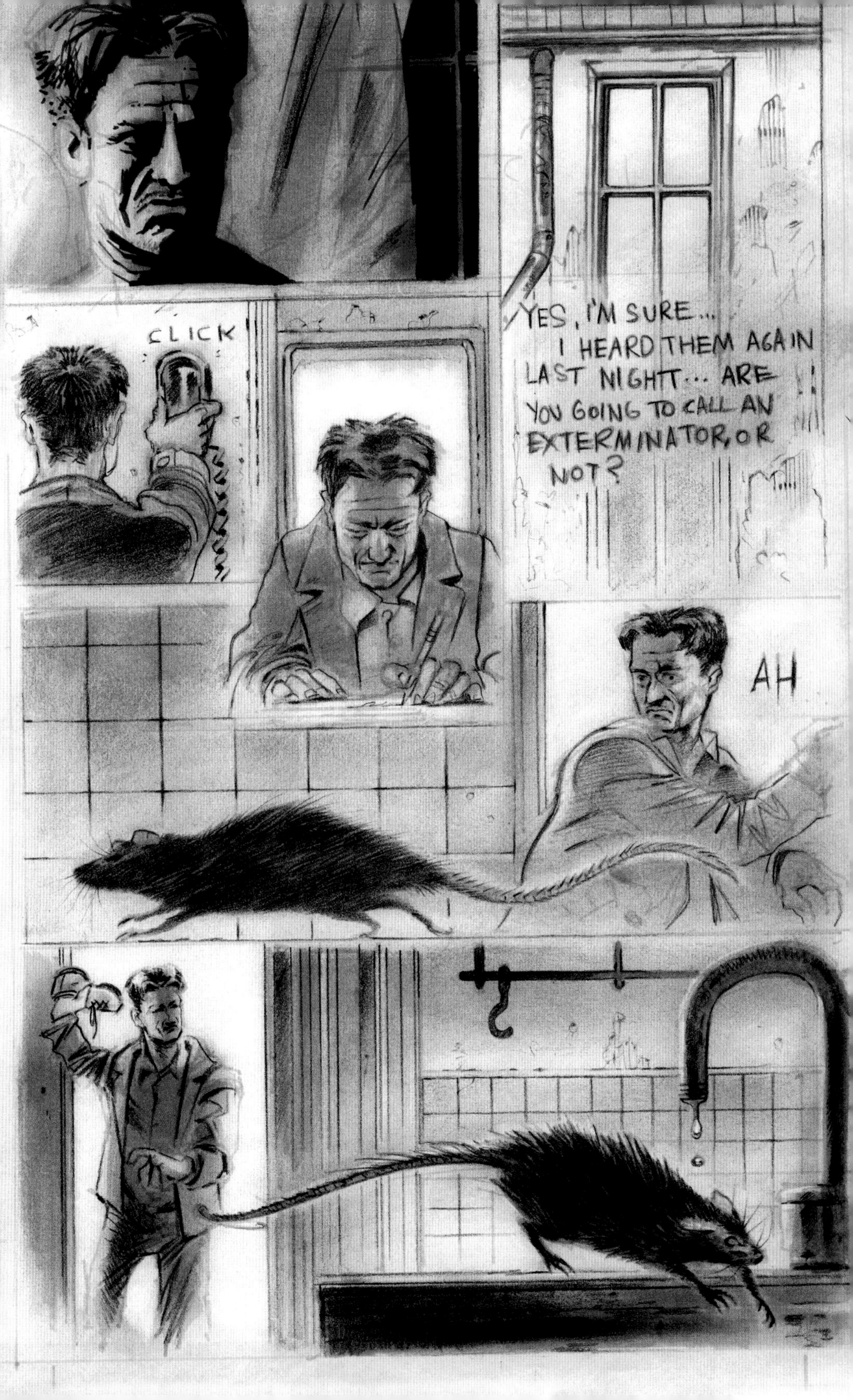
CLICK
YES, I'M SURE... I HEARD THEM AGAIN LAST NIGHT... ARE YOU GOING TO CALL AN EXTERMINATOR, OR NOT?
AH

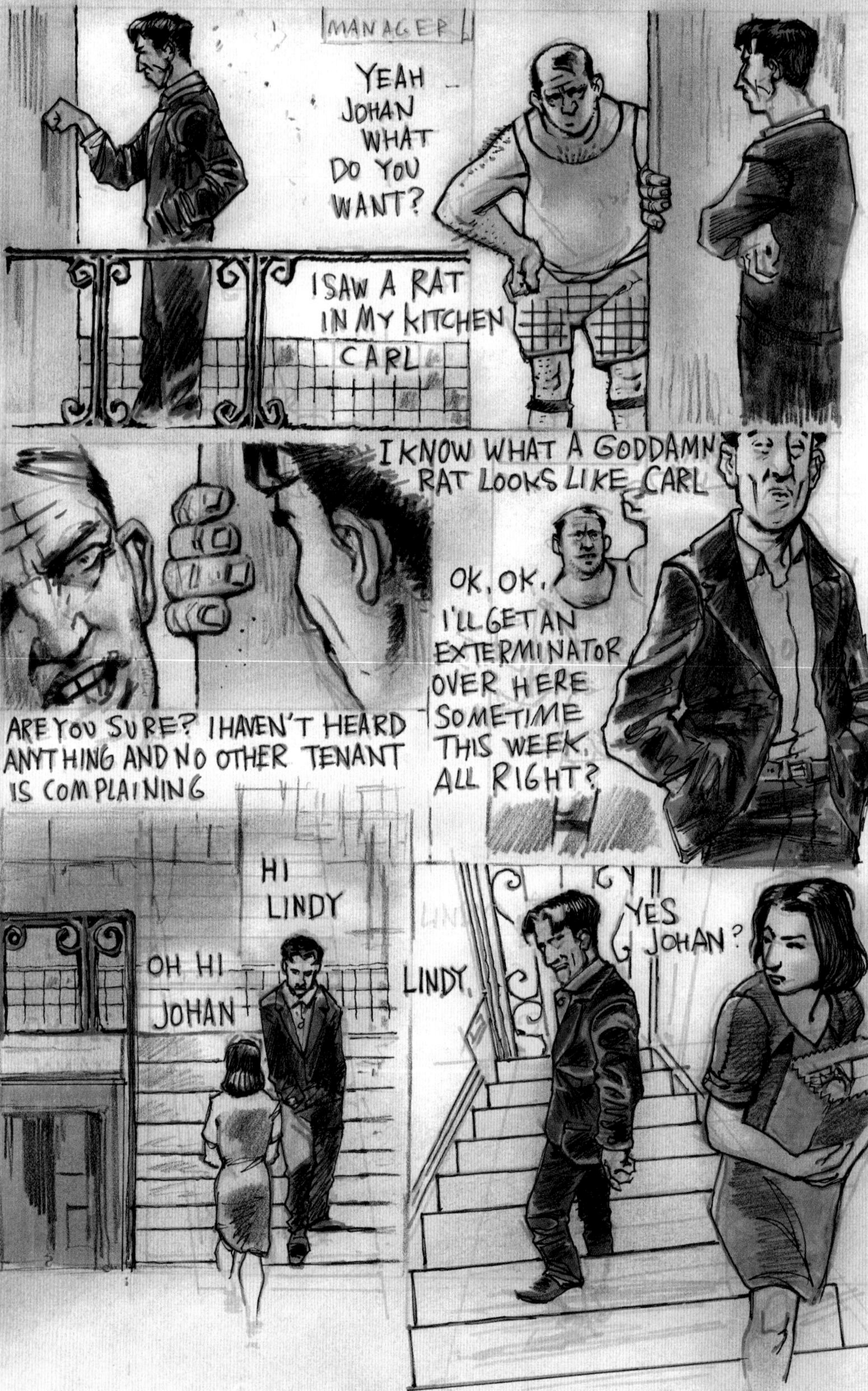
MANAGER
YEAH JOHAN WHAT DO YOU WANT?
I SAW A RAT IN MY KITCHEN CARL
I KNOW WHAT A GODDAMN RAT LOOKS LIKE CARL
ARE YOU SURE? I HAVEN'T HEARD ANYTHING AND NO OTHER TENANT IS COMPLAINING
OK, OK, I'LL GET AN EXTERMINATOR OVER HERE SOMETIME THIS WEEK, ALL RIGHT?
HI LINDY
OH HI JOHAN
LINDY.
YES JOHAN?

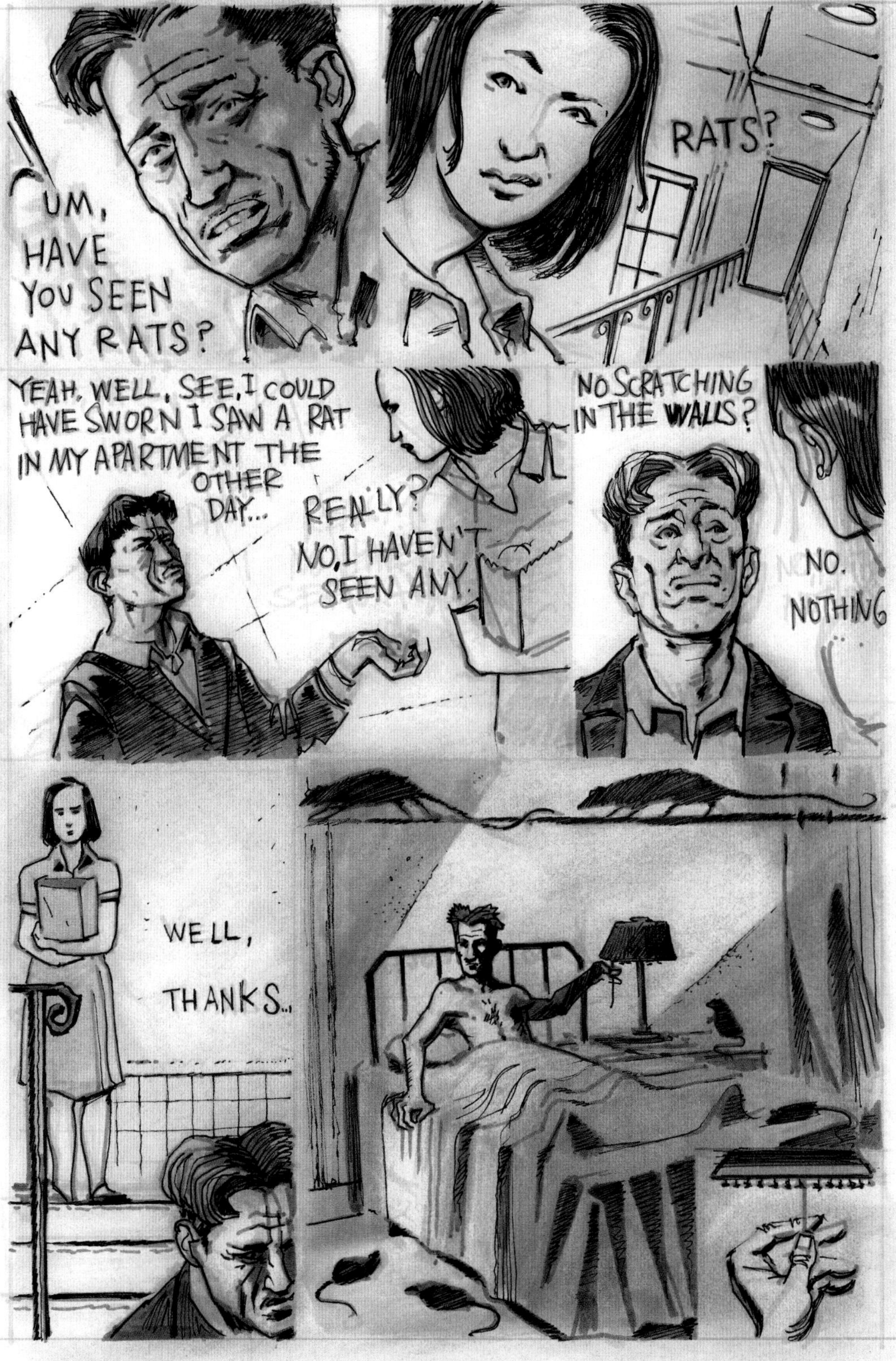
UM, HAVE YOU SEEN ANY RATS?
RATS?
YEAH, WELL, SEE, I COULD HAVE SWORN I SAW A RAT IN MY APARTMENT THE OTHER DAY...
REALLY? NO, I HAVEN'T SEEN ANY.
NO SCRATCHING IN THE WALLS?
NO. NOTHING...
WELL,
THANKS...

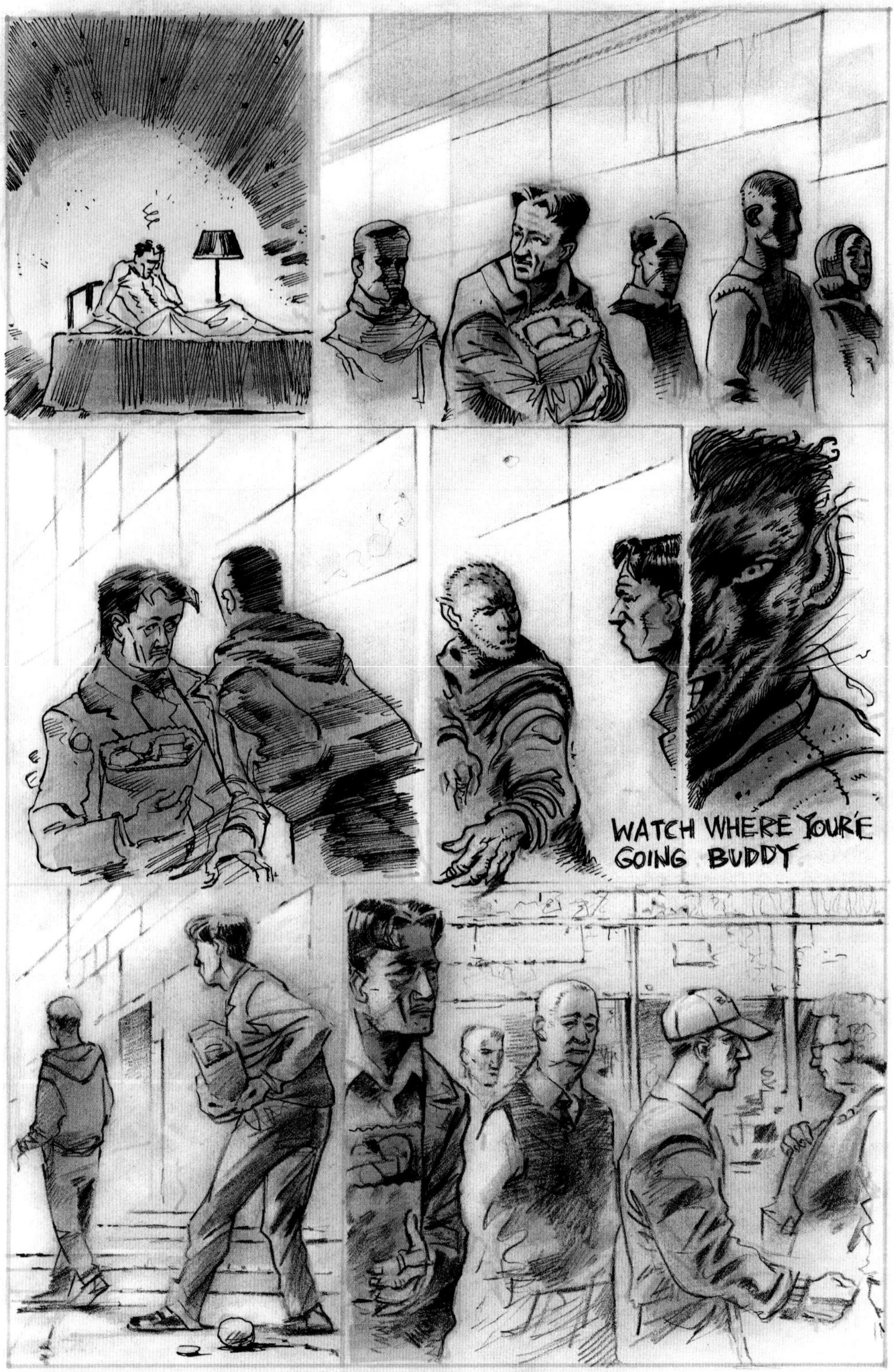
WATCH WHERE YOU'RE GOING BUDDY

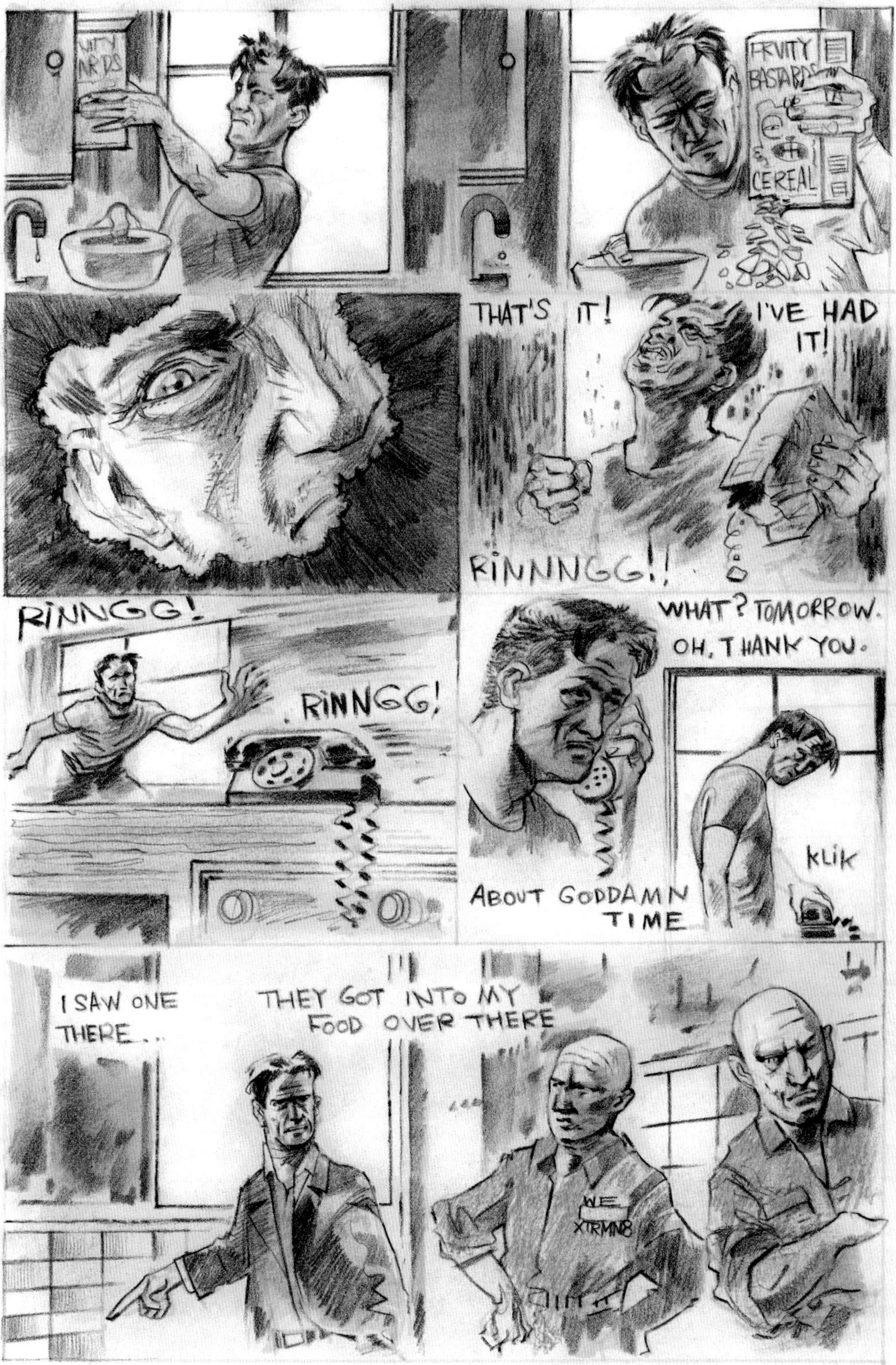
FRVITY BASTARDS CEREAL
THAT'S IT! I'VE HAD IT!
RINNNGG!!
RINNGG!
RINNGG!
WHAT? TOMORROW. OH, THANK YOU.
ABOUT GODDAMN TIME
KLIK
I SAW ONE THERE...
THEY GOT INTO MY FOOD OVER THERE
W.E. XTRMN8

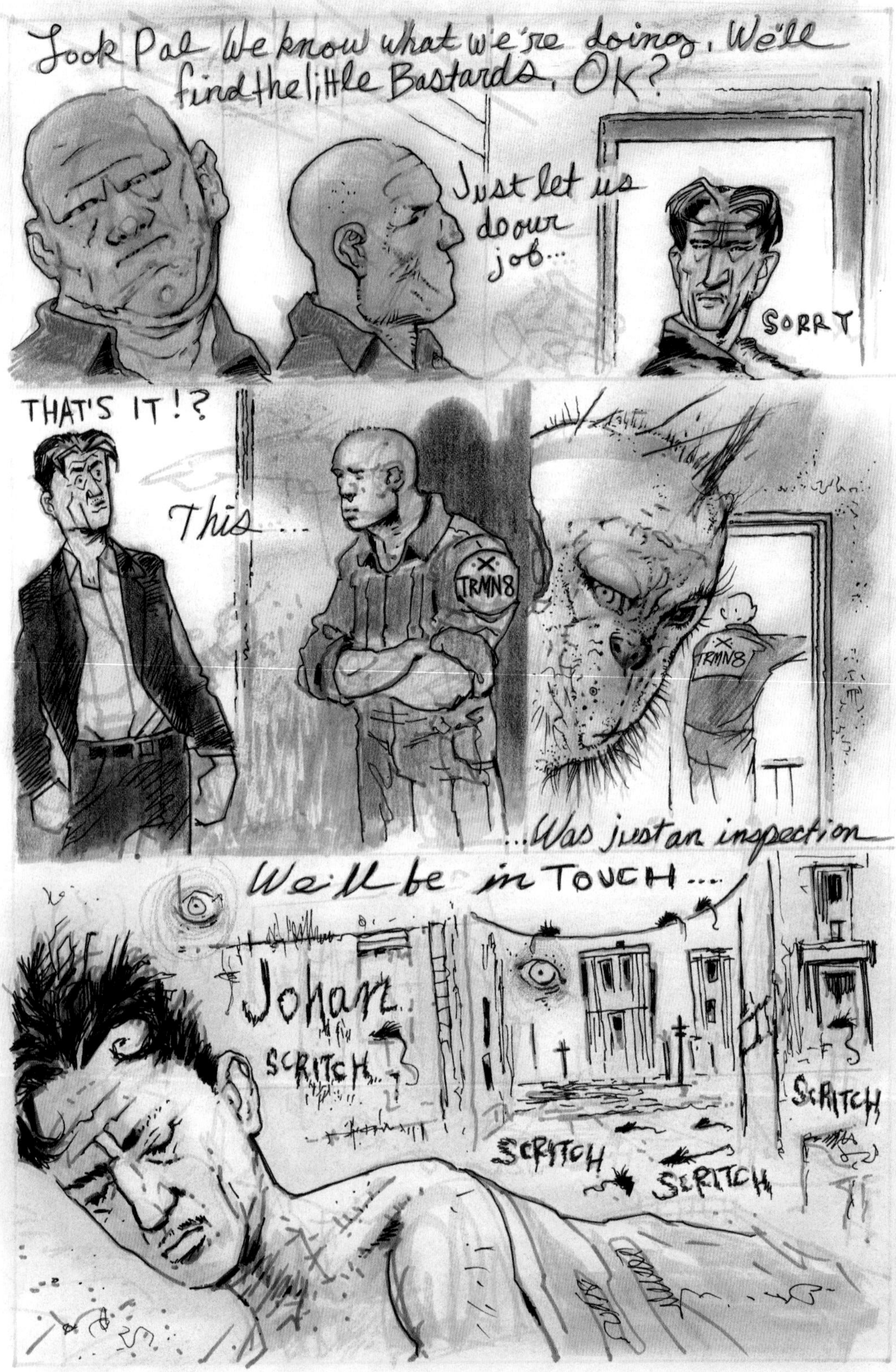
Look Pal We know what we're doing. We'll find the little Bastards. OK?
Just let us do our job...
SORRY
THAT'S IT!?
This...
...Was just an inspection
We'll be in TOUCH...
Johan
SCRITCH
SCRITCH
SCRITCH
SCRITCH

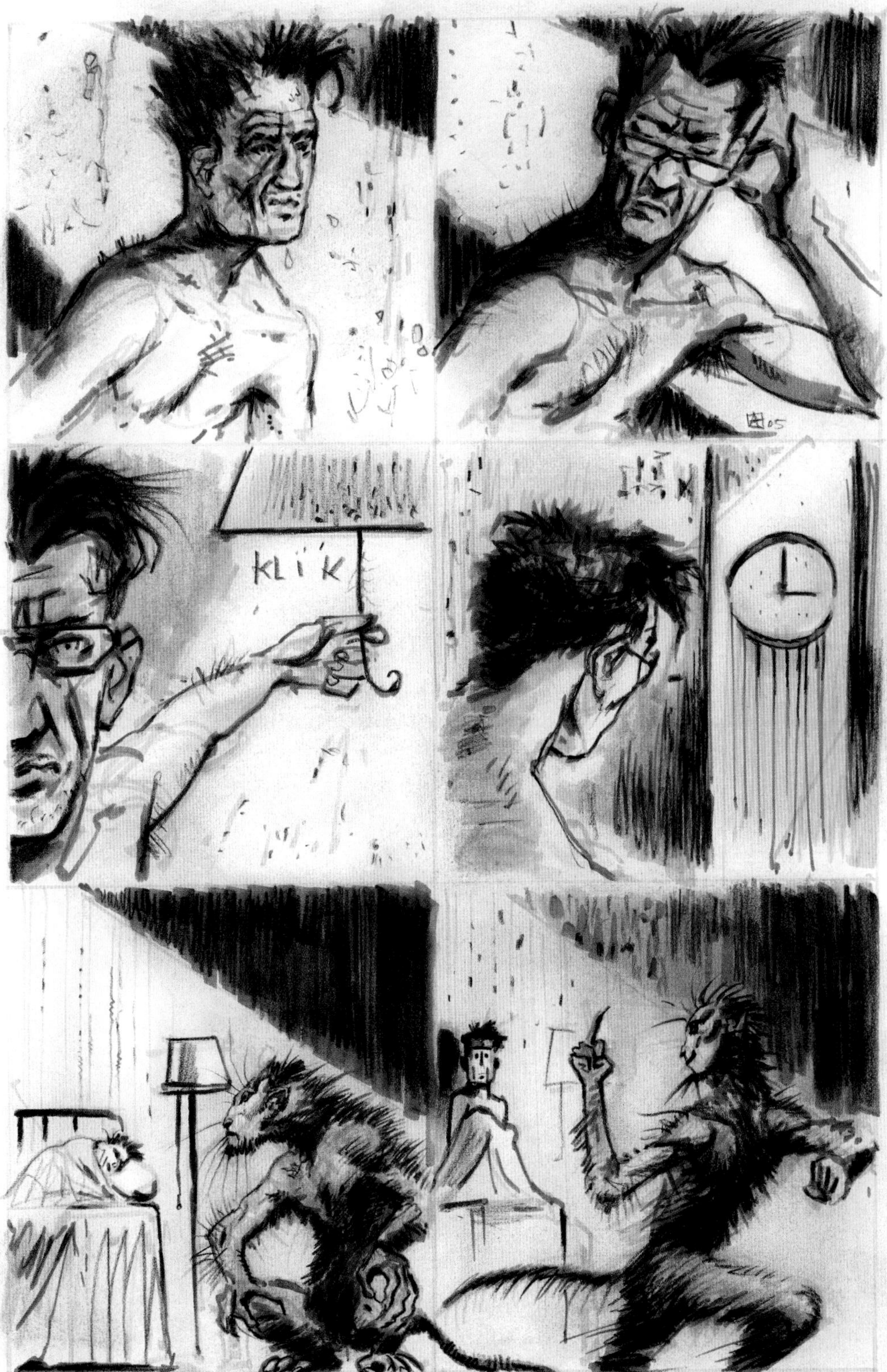
KLIK

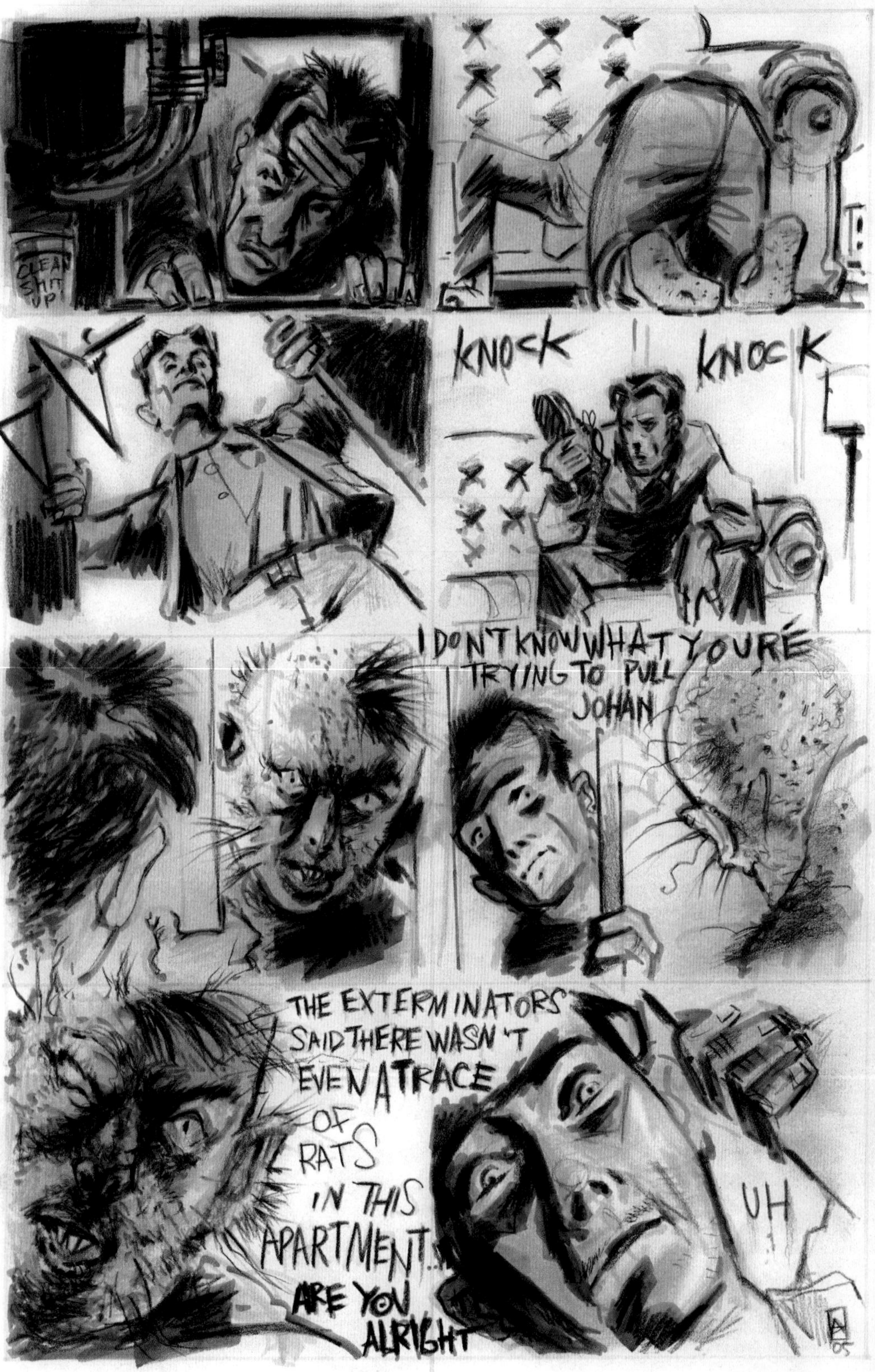
CLEAN SHIT UP
KNOCK
KNOCK
I DON'T KNOW WHAT YOU'RE TRYING TO PULL JOHAN
THE EXTERMINATORS SAID THERE WASN'T EVEN A TRACE OF RATS IN THIS APARTMENT... ARE YOU ALRIGHT
UH

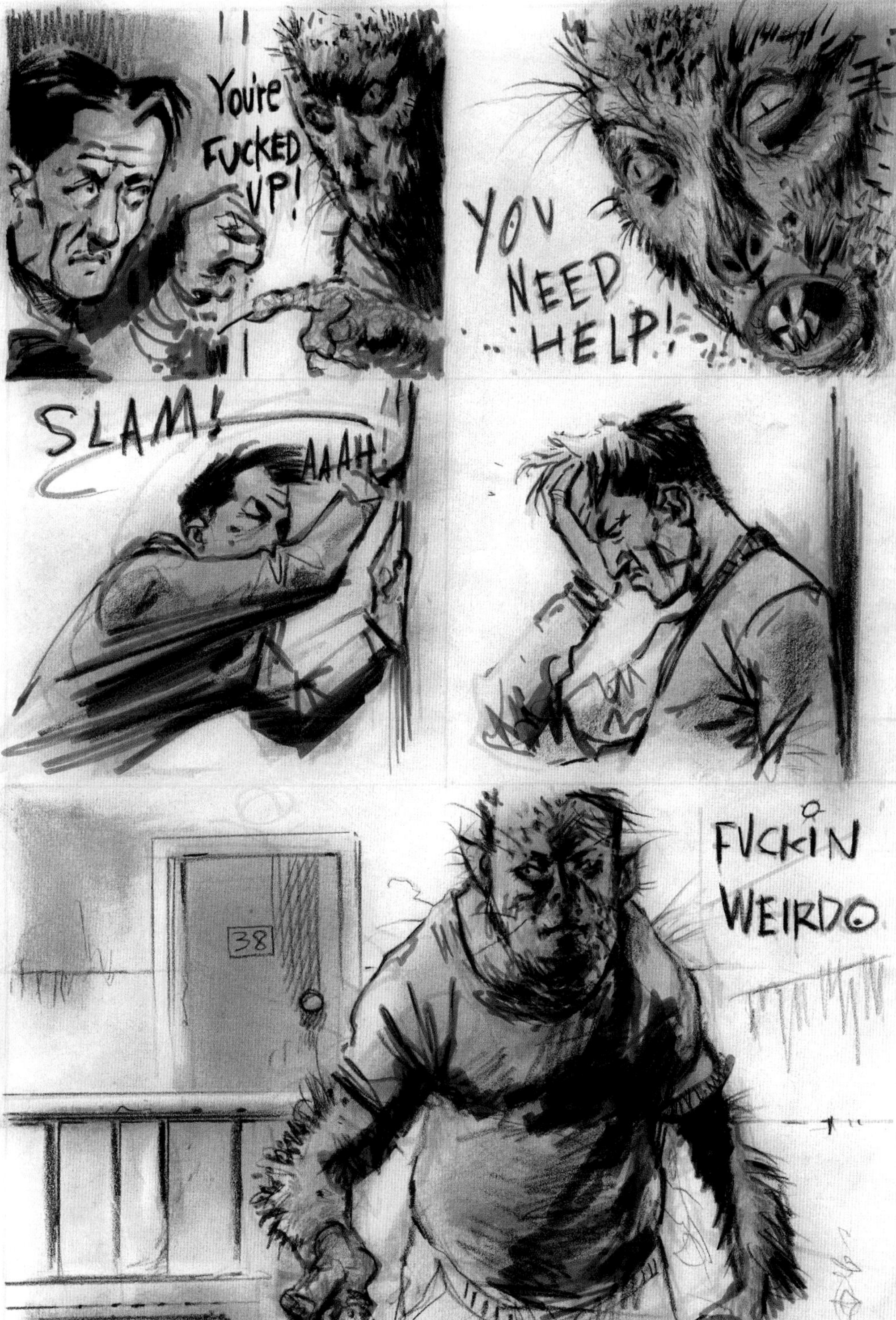
You're FUCKED UP!
YOU NEED HELP!
SLAM!
AAAH!
FUCKIN WEIRDO
38
TA 05

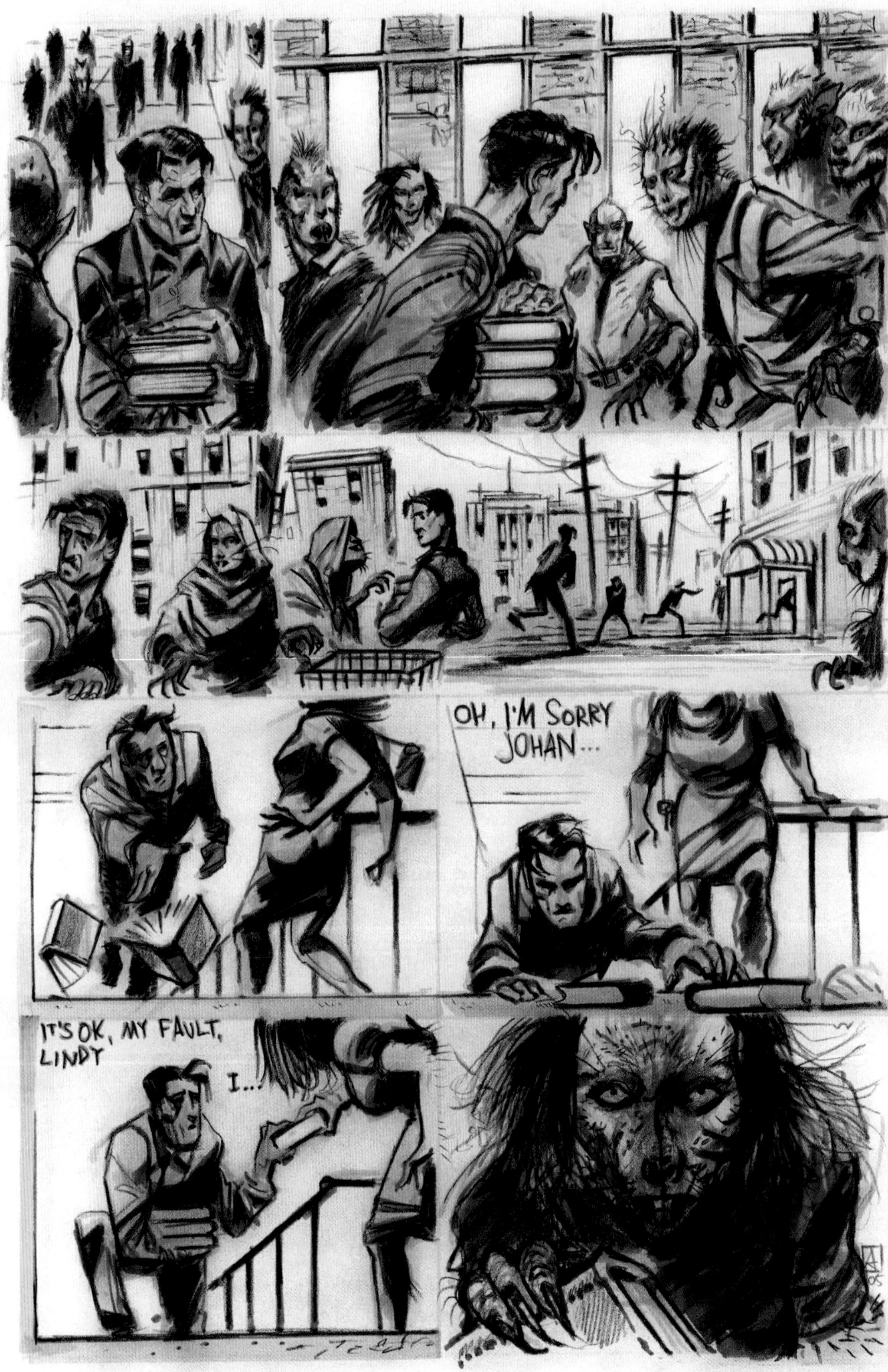
OH, I'M SORRY JOHAN...
IT'S OK, MY FAULT, LINDY
I...

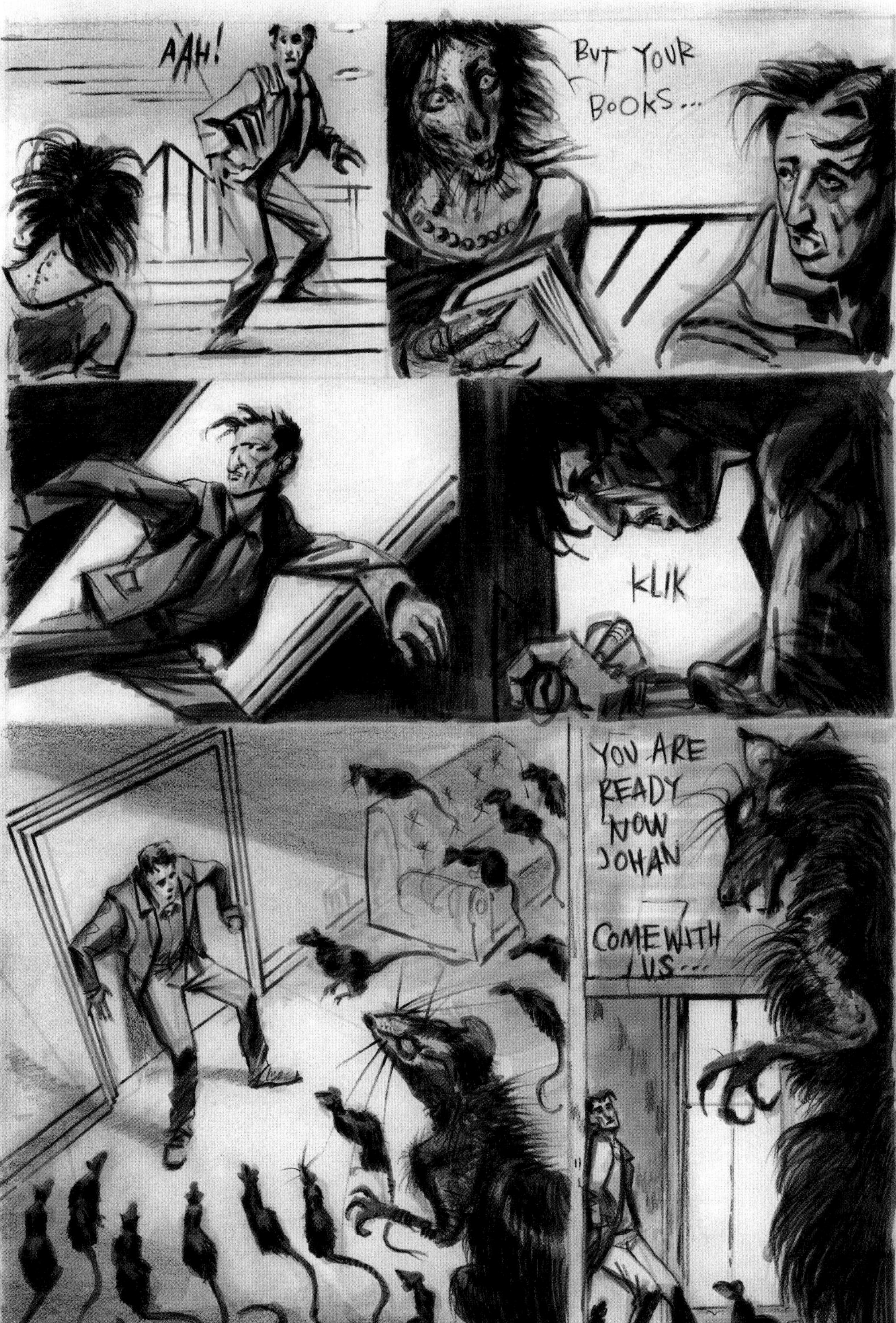
AAH!
BUT YOUR BOOKS...
KLIK
YOU ARE READY NOW JOHAN
COME WITH US...

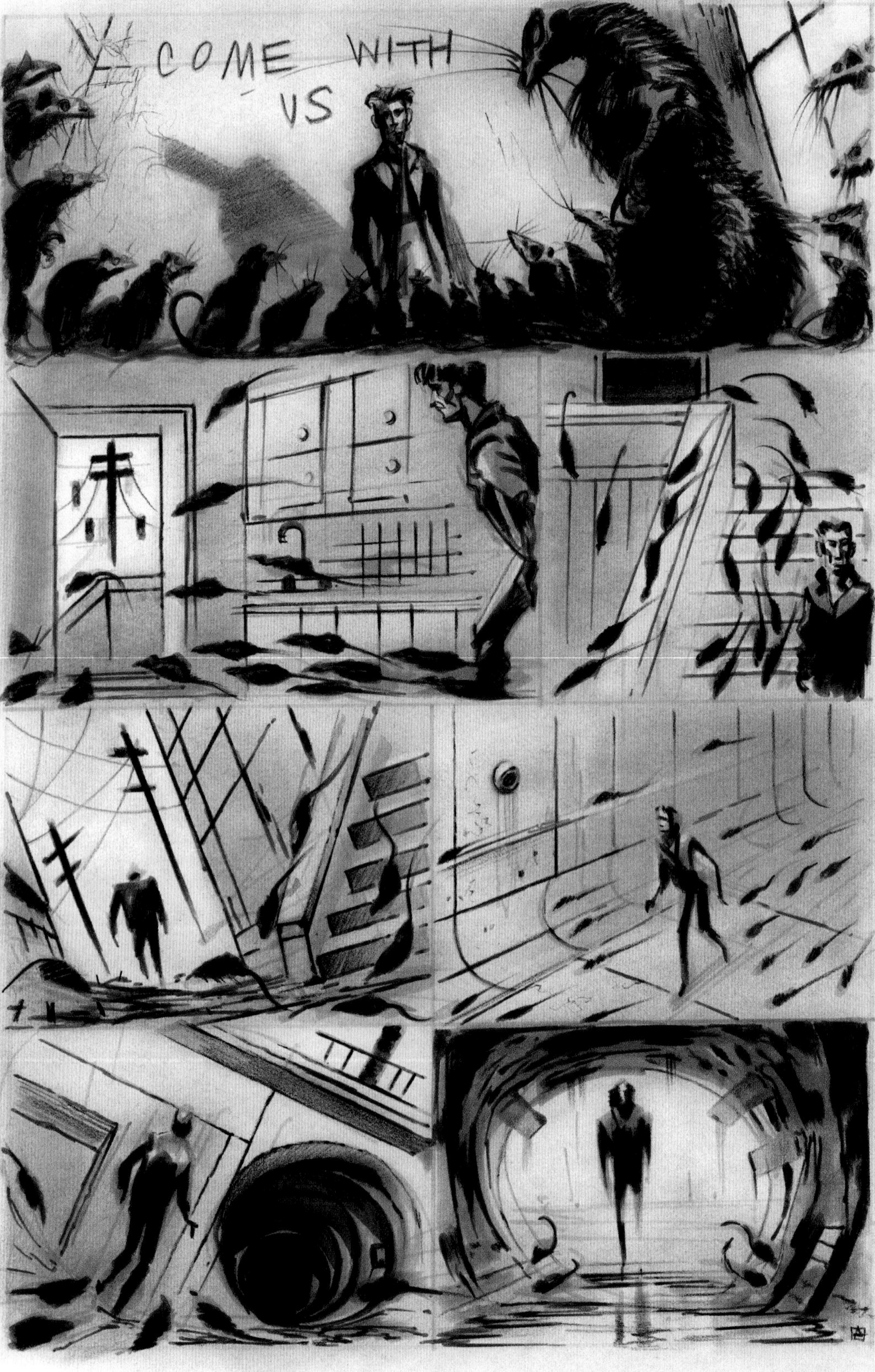
COME WITH US

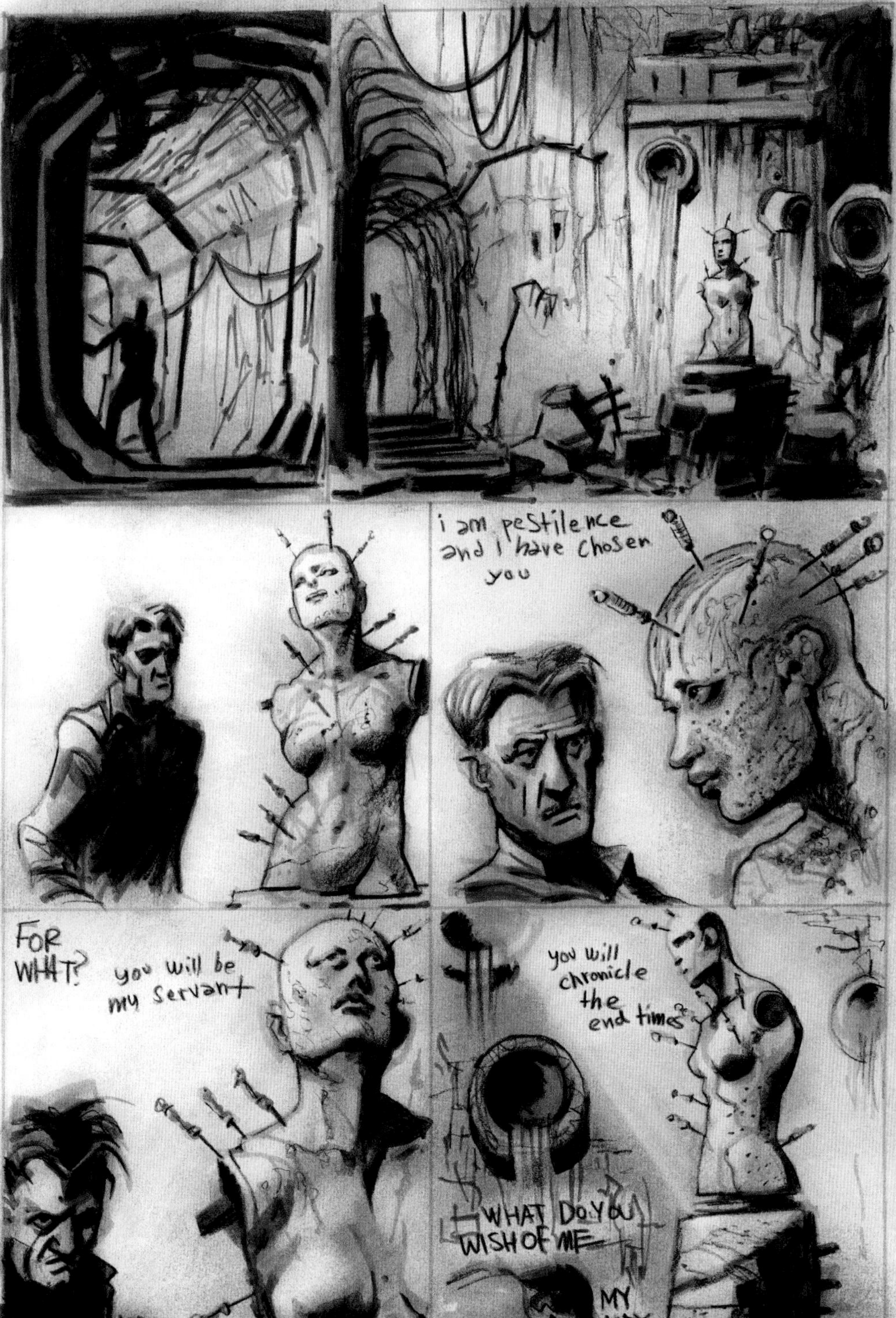
i am pestilence and I have chosen you
FOR WHAT?
you will be my servant
you will chronicle the end times
WHAT DO YOU WISH OF ME
MY LADY

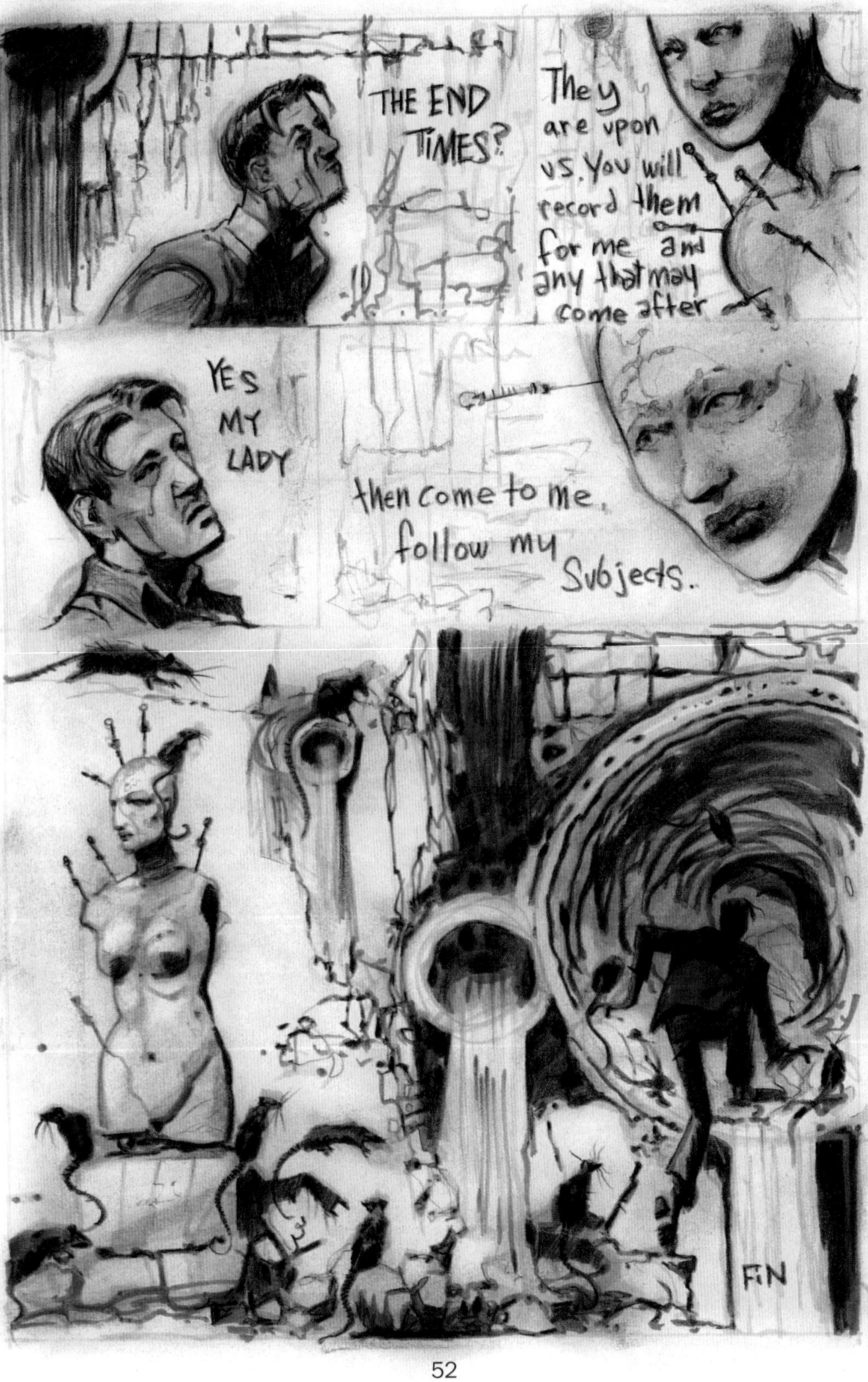
THE END TIMES?
They are upon us. You will record them for me and any that may come after
YES MY LADY
then come to me, follow my Subjects.
FIN

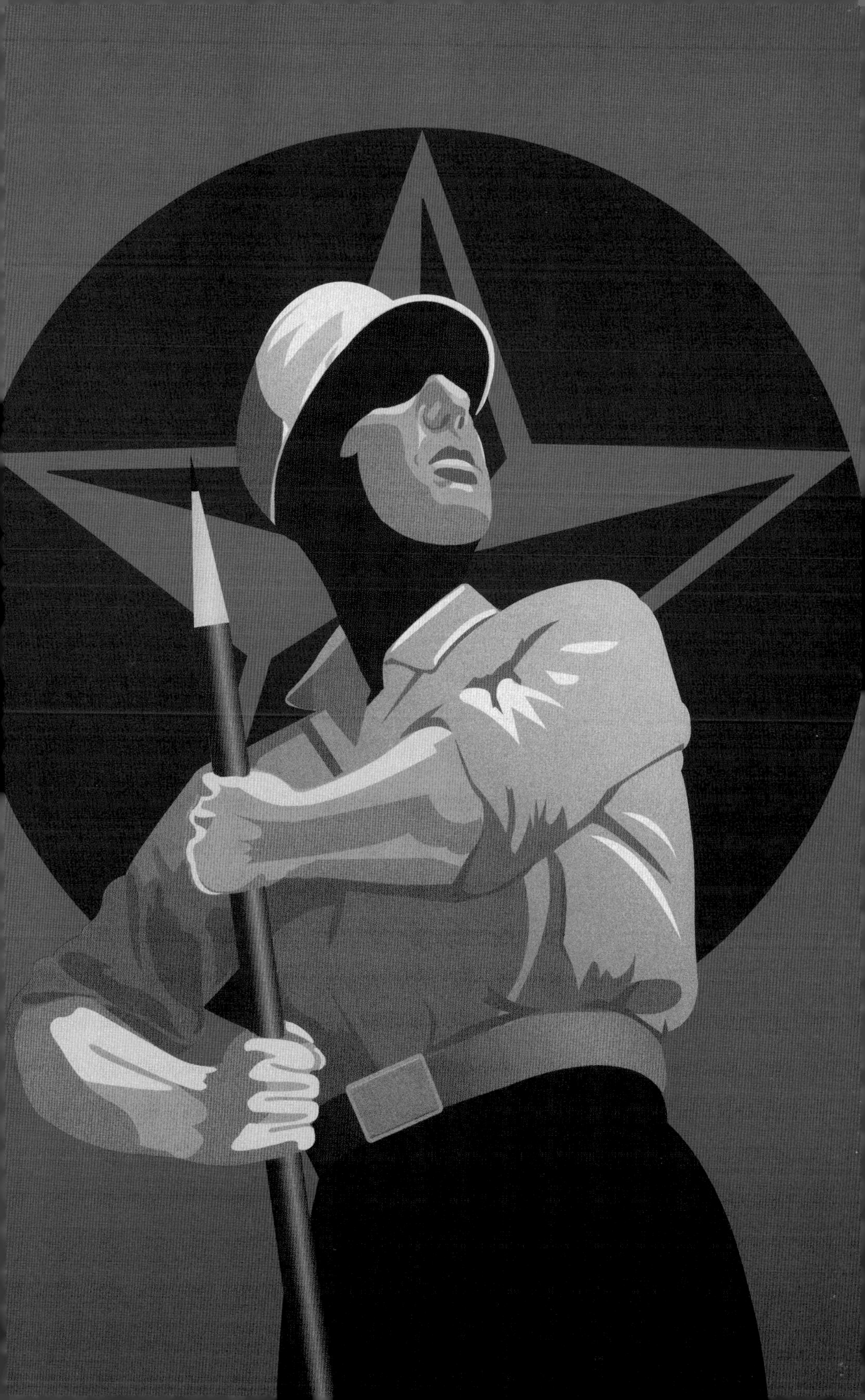

A self-taught artist, **RHS** has been publishing sequential art and illustrations in various Brazilian fanzines and comic books since he was 8 years old. This means that he has spent the last 19 years experimenting with language and different art techniques, searching for the perfect representation of his thoughts. He went from oil hand-made paintings to 100% digital. He studied anatomy just to make deformed bodies. He put surrealistic pop graphics together with the most depressive, sarcastic and acid scripts, creating a universe as fluffy as a puddle of blood. "Discreet Despair" is his longest story so far and showcases his world premiere work for a big publishing company. RHS´s plans for the future includes world domination and a magazine all of his own, where he could present all his eccentric ideas and characters.

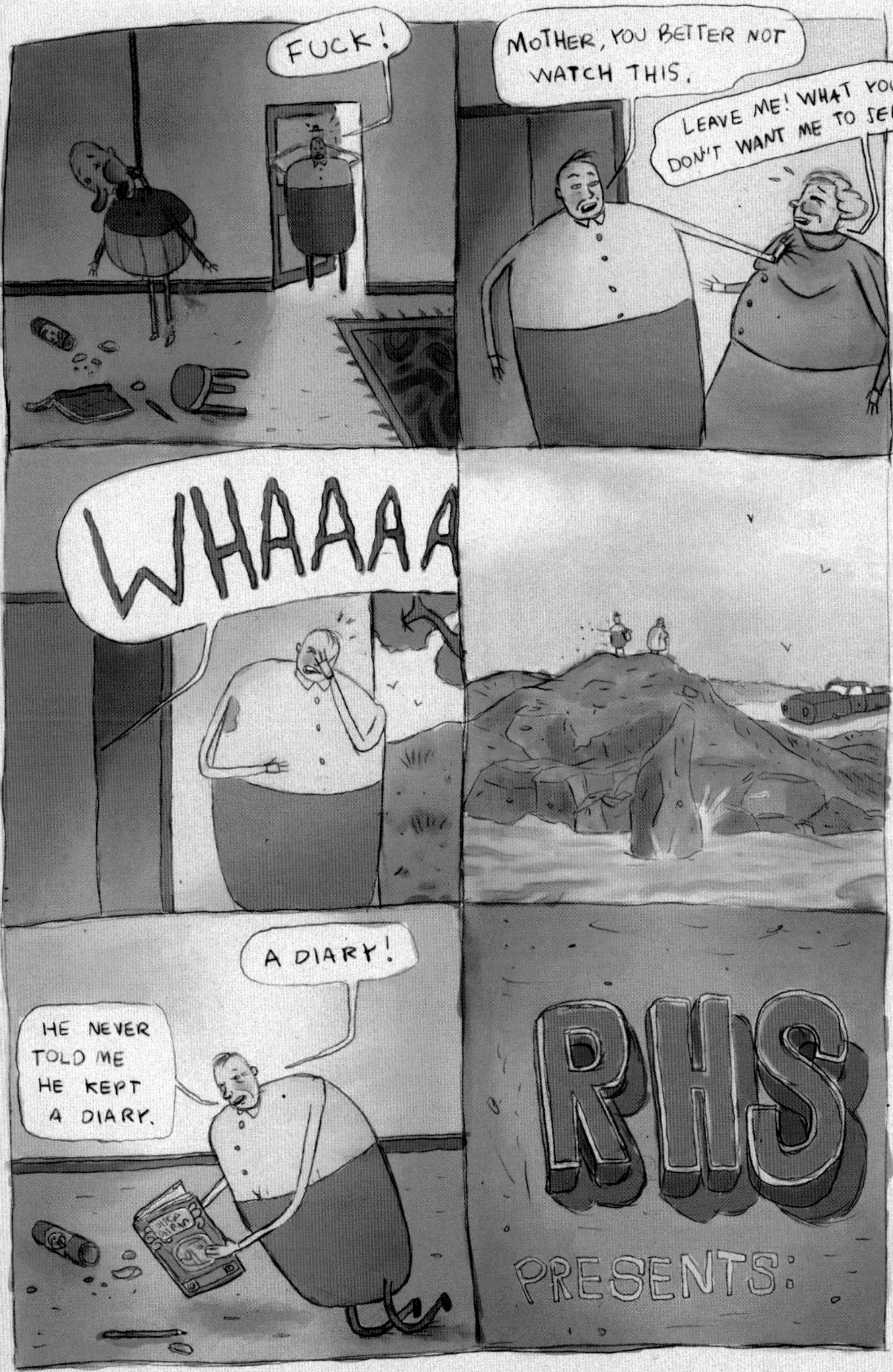
FUCK!
MOTHER, YOU BETTER NOT WATCH THIS.
LEAVE ME! WHAT YOU DON'T WANT ME TO SEE?
WHAAAA
A DIARY!
HE NEVER TOLD ME HE KEPT A DIARY.
RHS
PRESENTS:

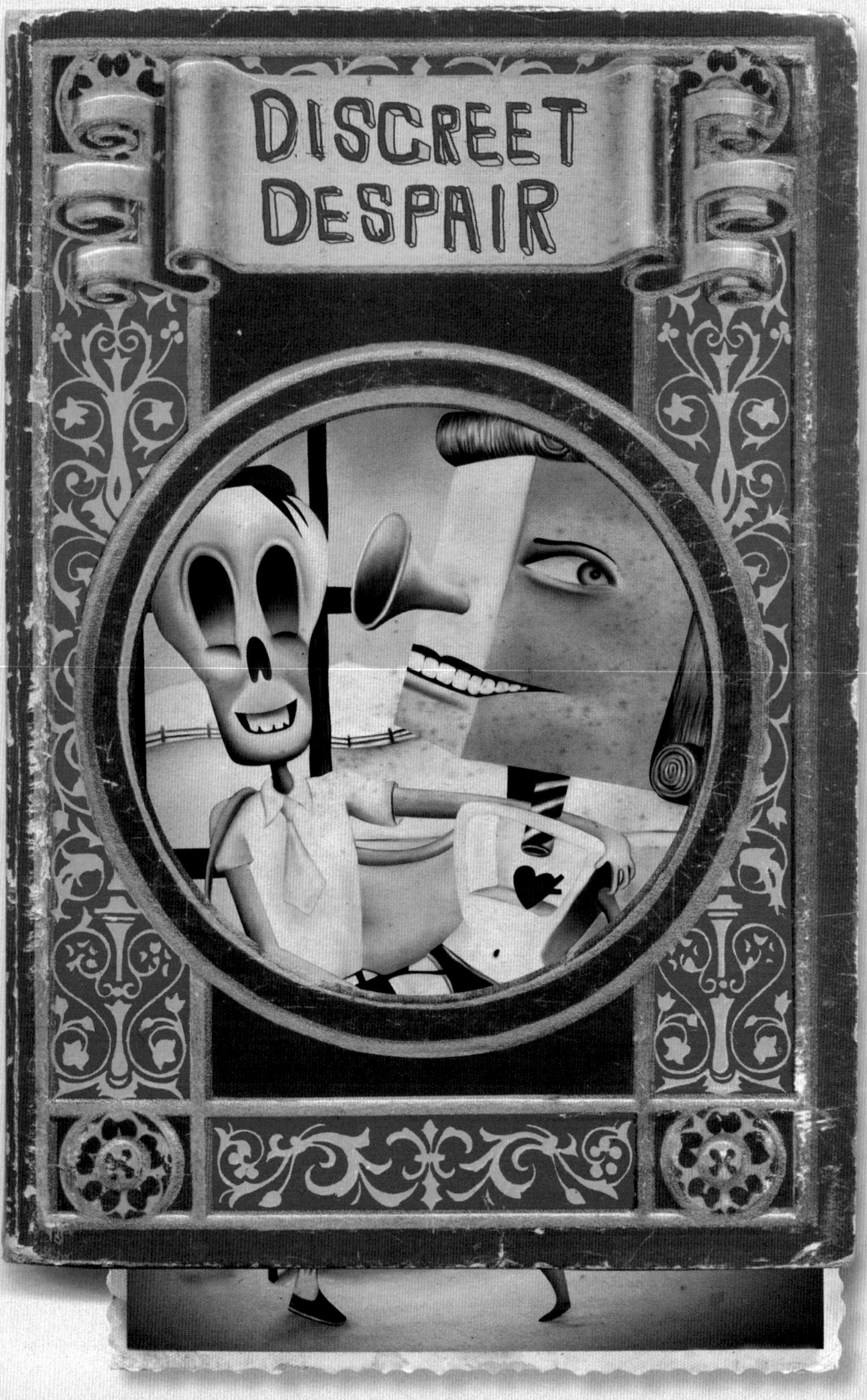
DISCREET
DESPAIR

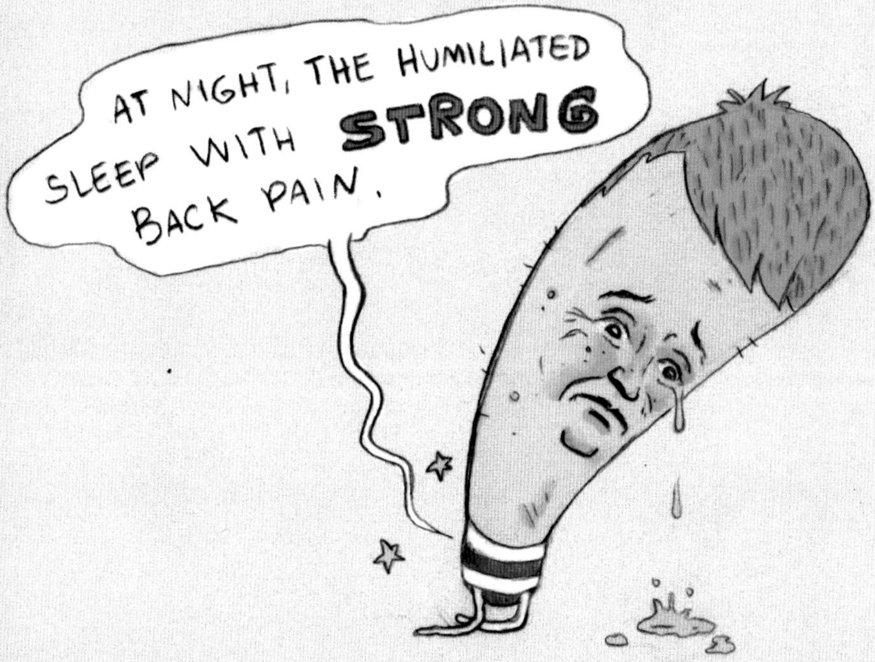
AT NIGHT, THE HUMILIATED SLEEP WITH **STRONG** BACK PAIN.

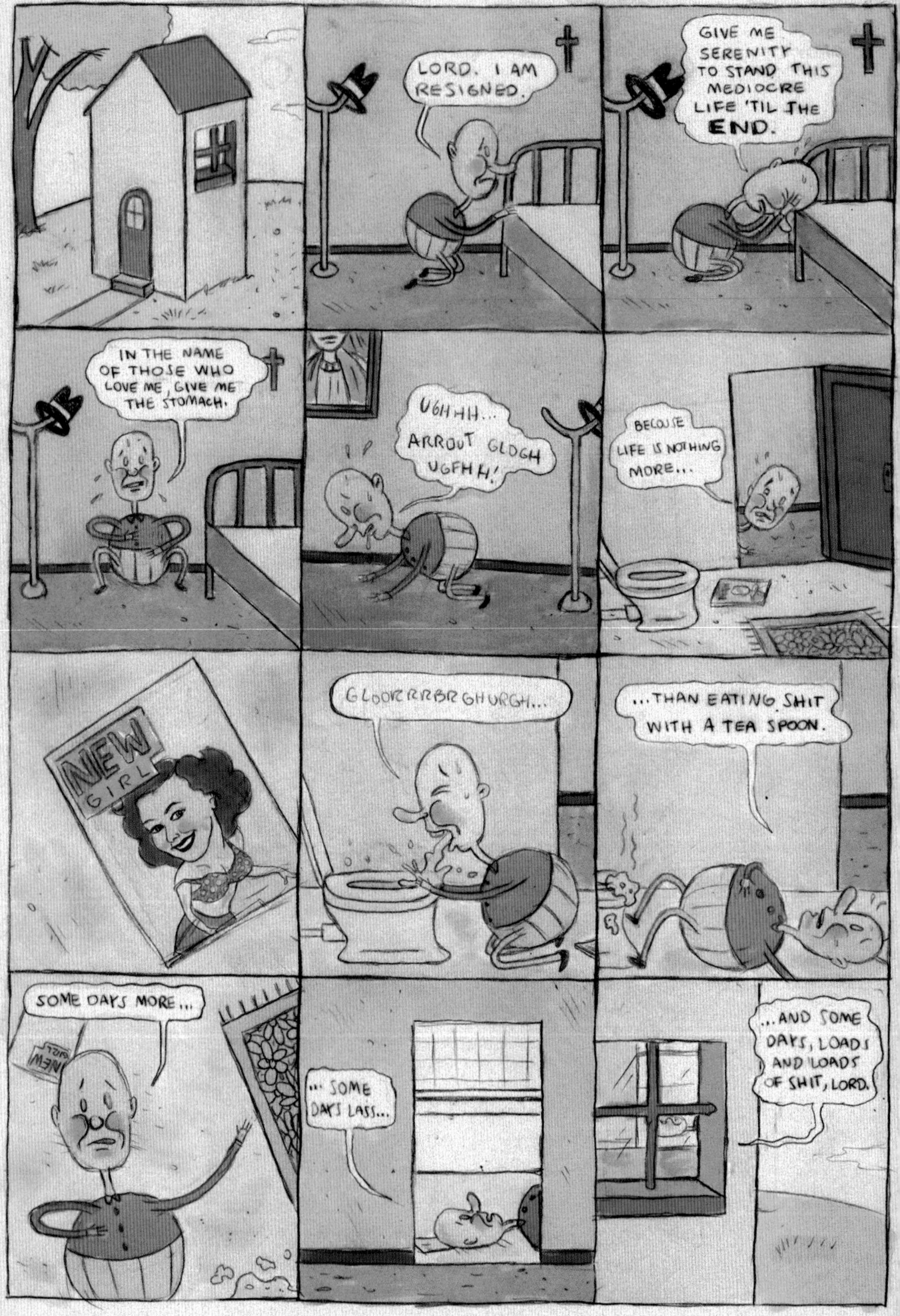
LORD. I AM RESIGNED.
GIVE ME SERENITY TO STAND THIS MEDIOCRE LIFE 'TIL THE END.
IN THE NAME OF THOSE WHO LOVE ME, GIVE ME THE STOMACH.
UGHHH... ARROUT GLOGH UGFHH!
BECOUSE LIFE IS NOTHING MORE...
NEW GIRL
GLOORRRBRGHURGH...
...THAN EATING SHIT WITH A TEA SPOON.
SOME DAYS MORE...
... SOME DAYS LASS...
...AND SOME DAYS, LOADS AND LOADS OF SHIT, LORD.

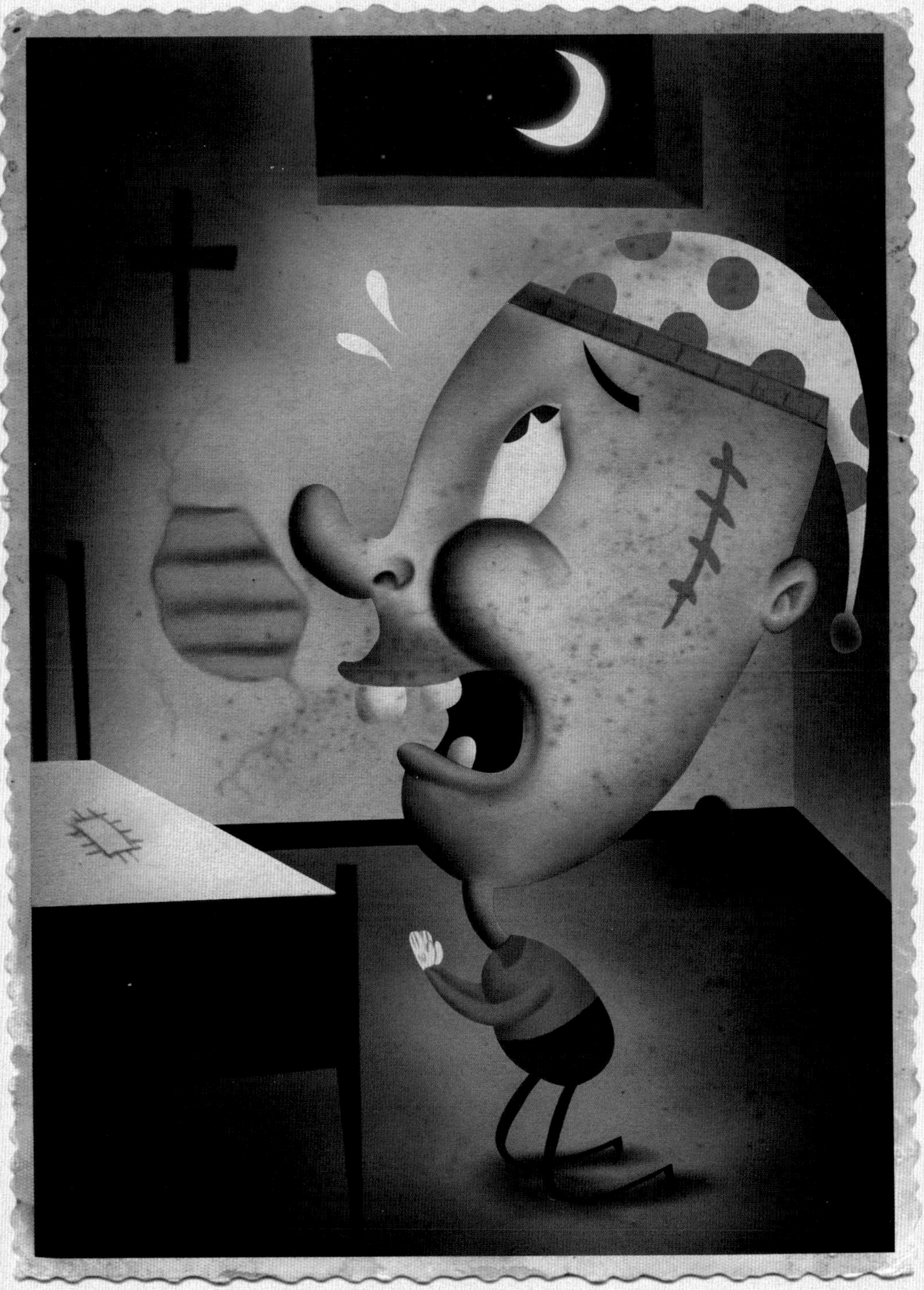

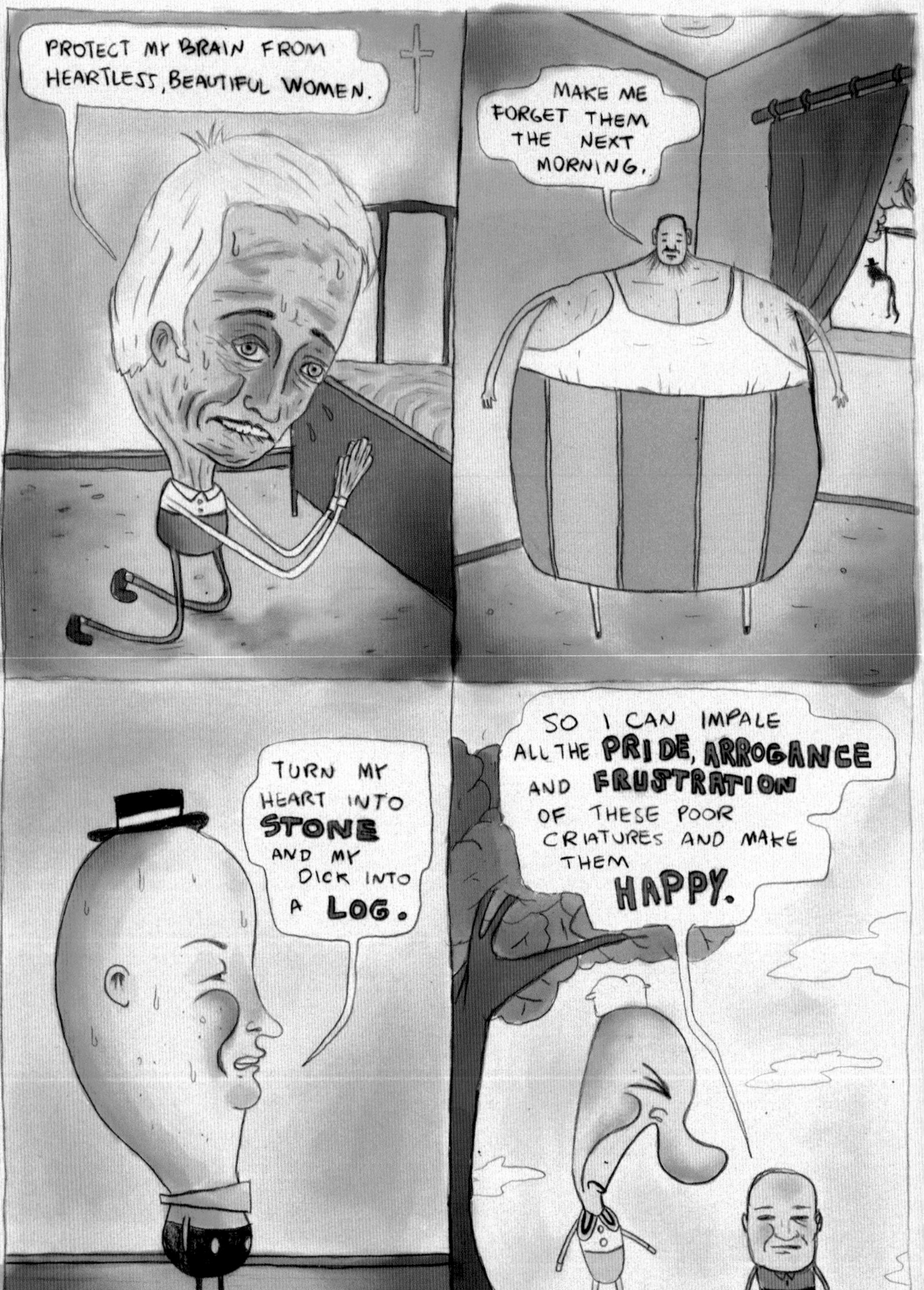
PROTECT MY BRAIN FROM HEARTLESS, BEAUTIFUL WOMEN.
MAKE ME FORGET THEM THE NEXT MORNING.
TURN MY HEART INTO STONE AND MY DICK INTO A LOG.
SO I CAN IMPALE ALL THE PRIDE, ARROGANCE AND FRUSTRATION OF THESE POOR CRIATURES AND MAKE THEM HAPPY.

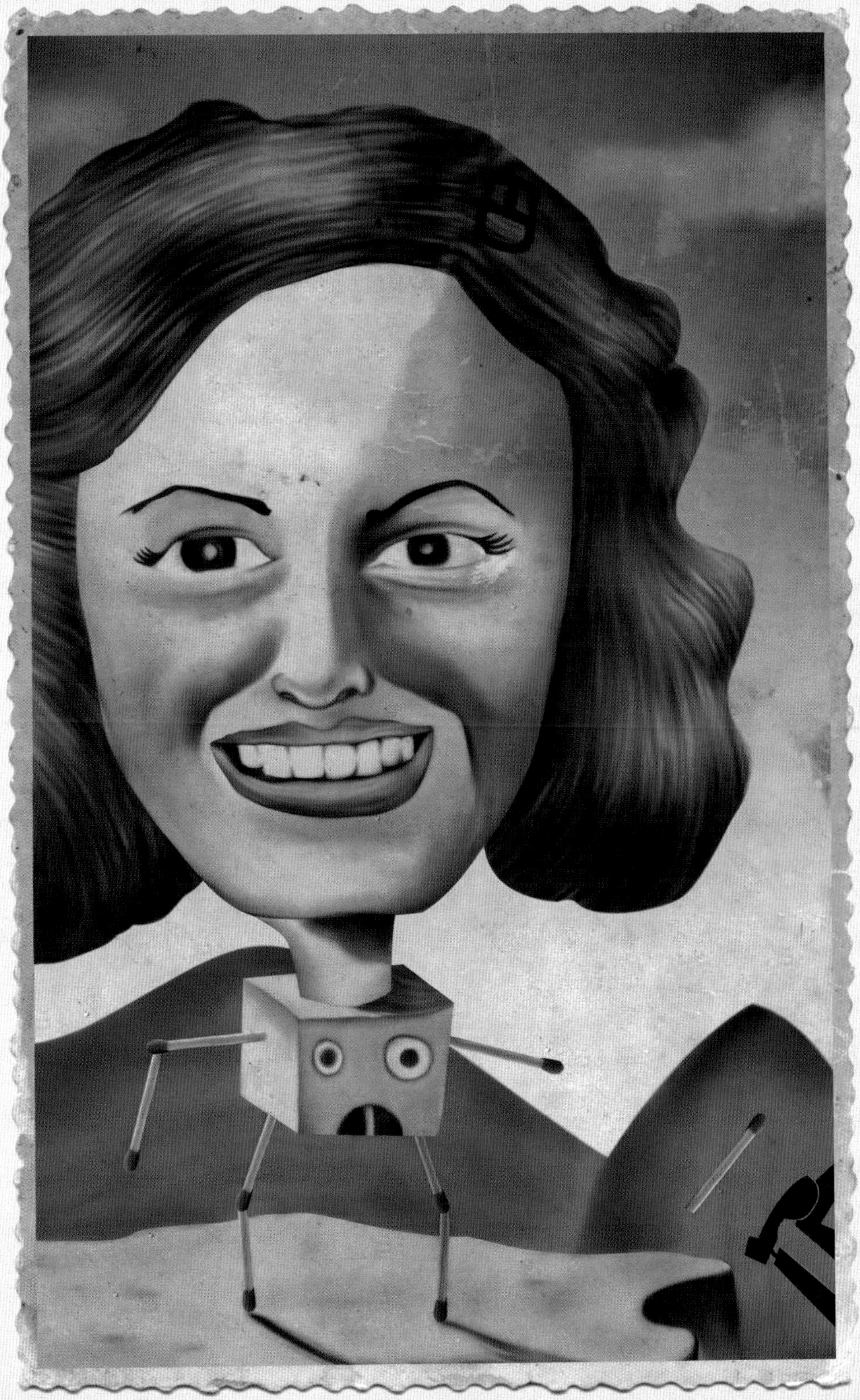

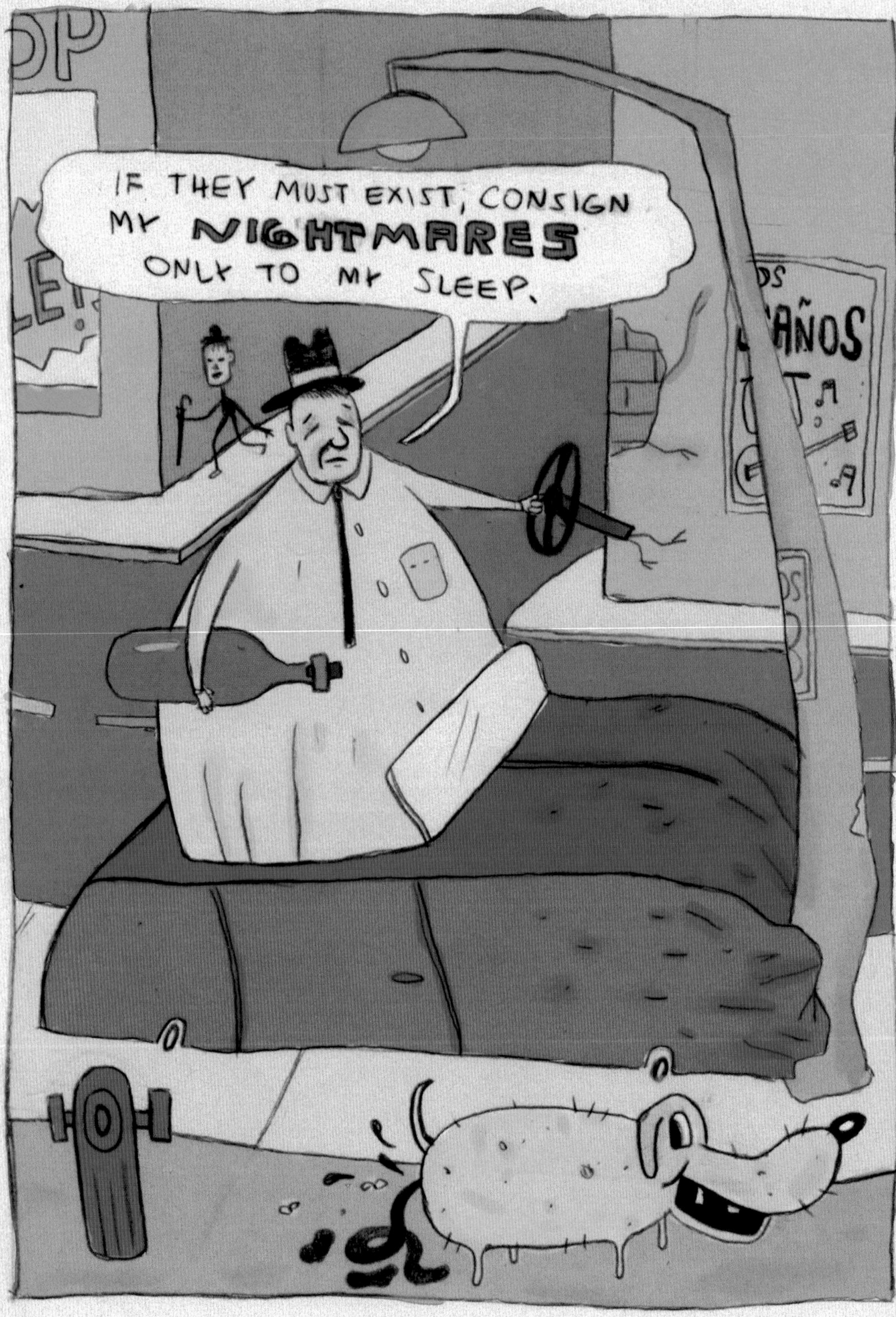
IF THEY MUST EXIST, CONSIGN MY NIGHTMARES ONLY TO MY SLEEP.

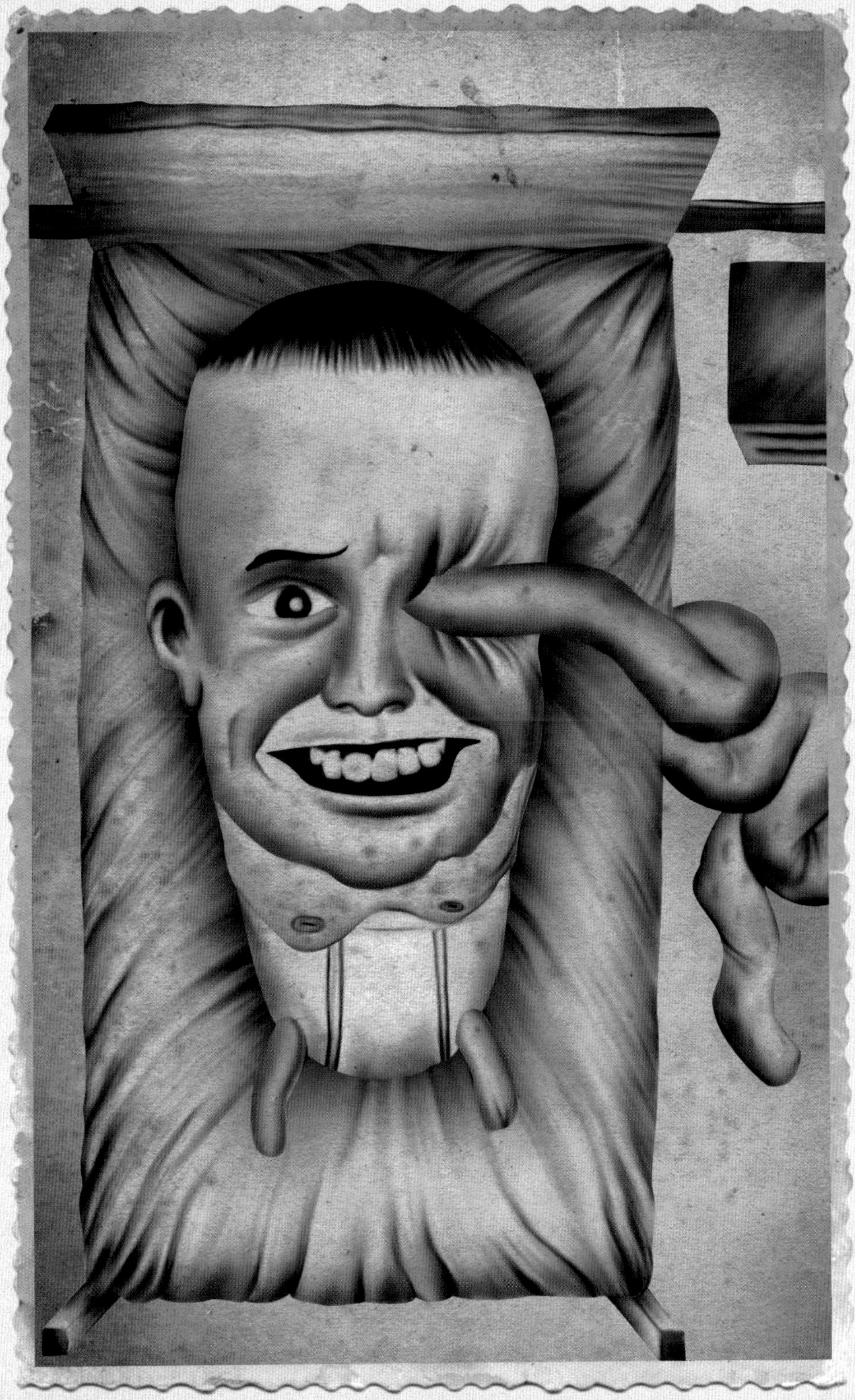

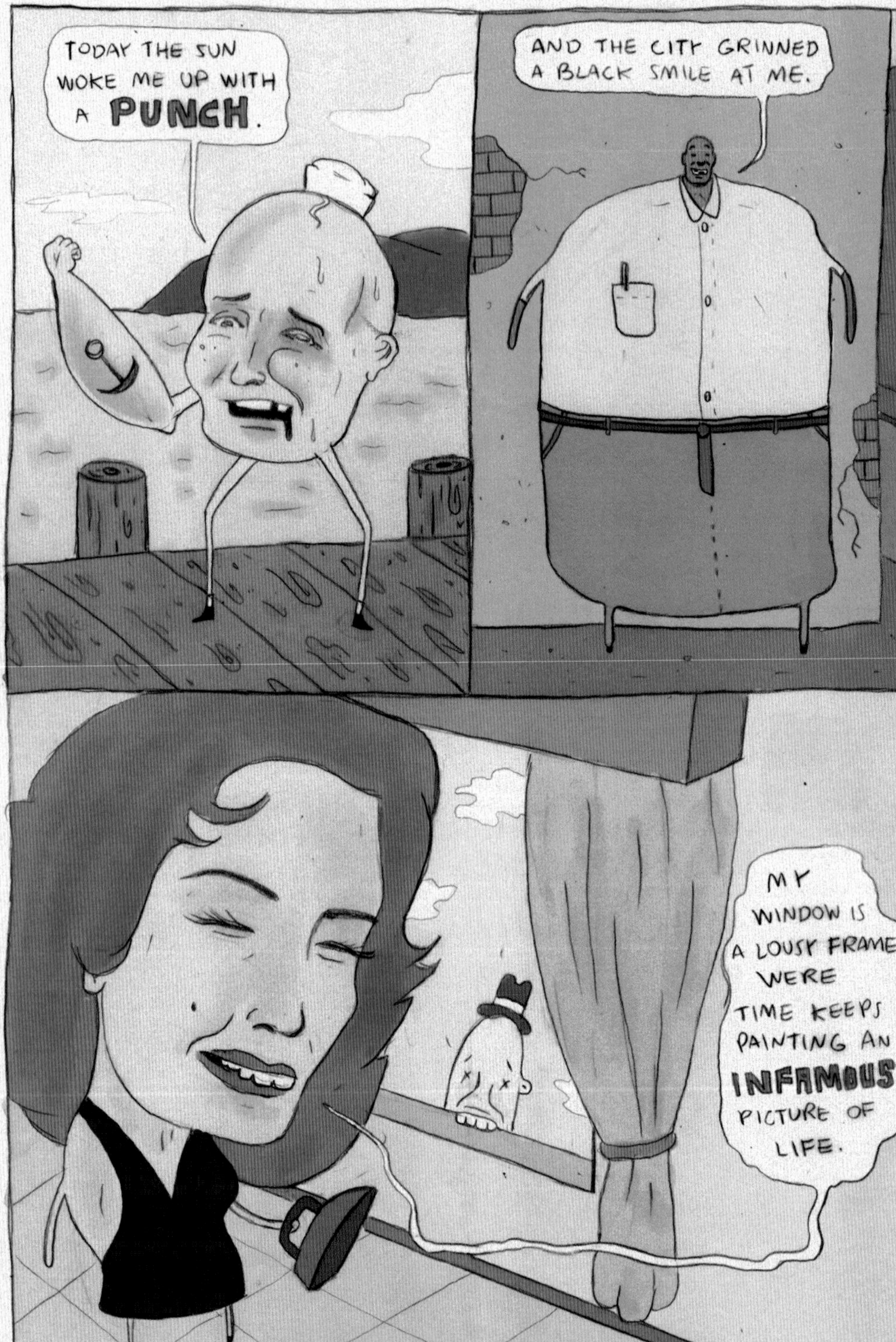
TODAY THE SUN WOKE ME UP WITH A PUNCH.
AND THE CITY GRINNED A BLACK SMILE AT ME.
MY WINDOW IS A LOUSY FRAME WERE TIME KEEPS PAINTING AN INFAMOUS PICTURE OF LIFE.

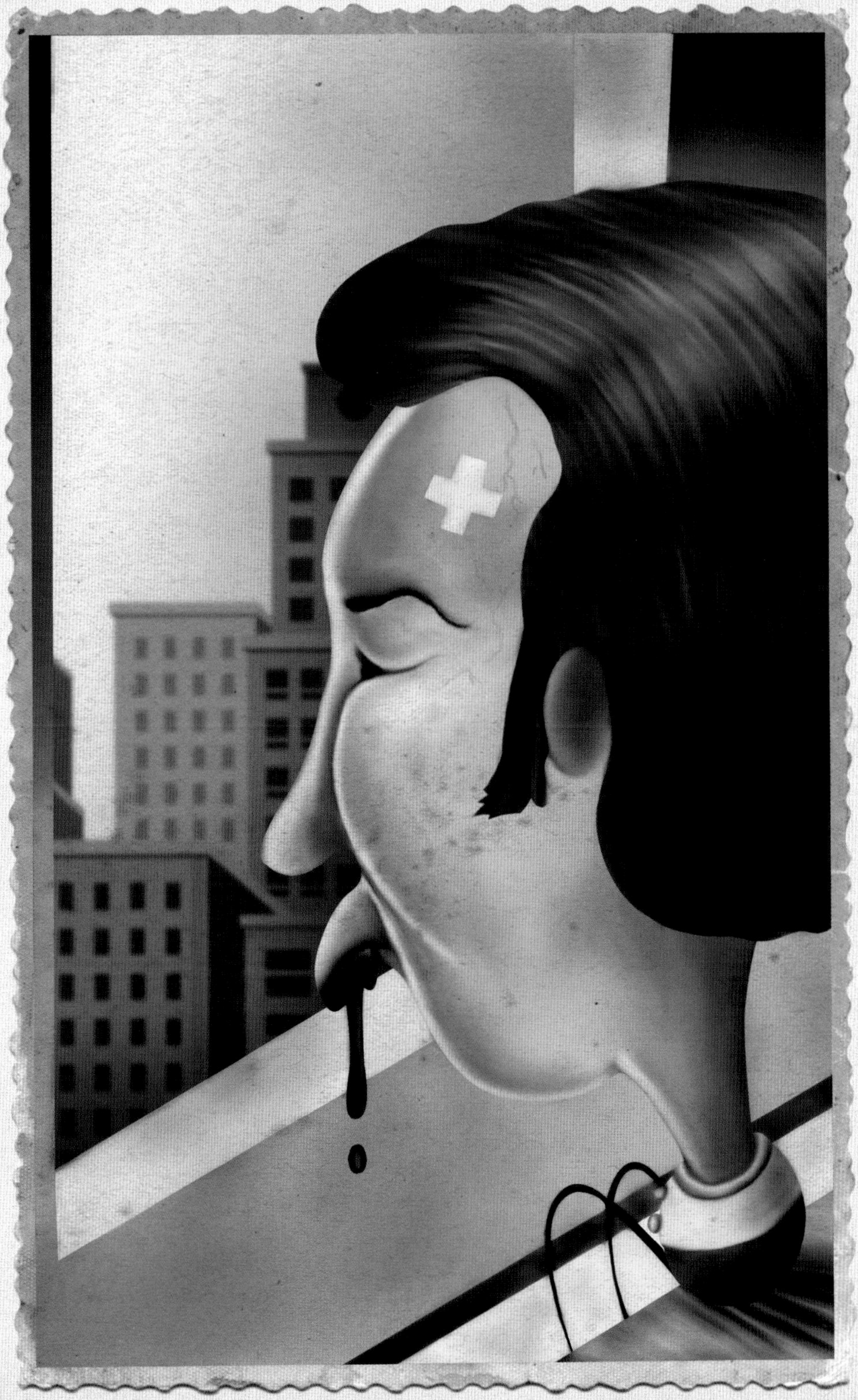

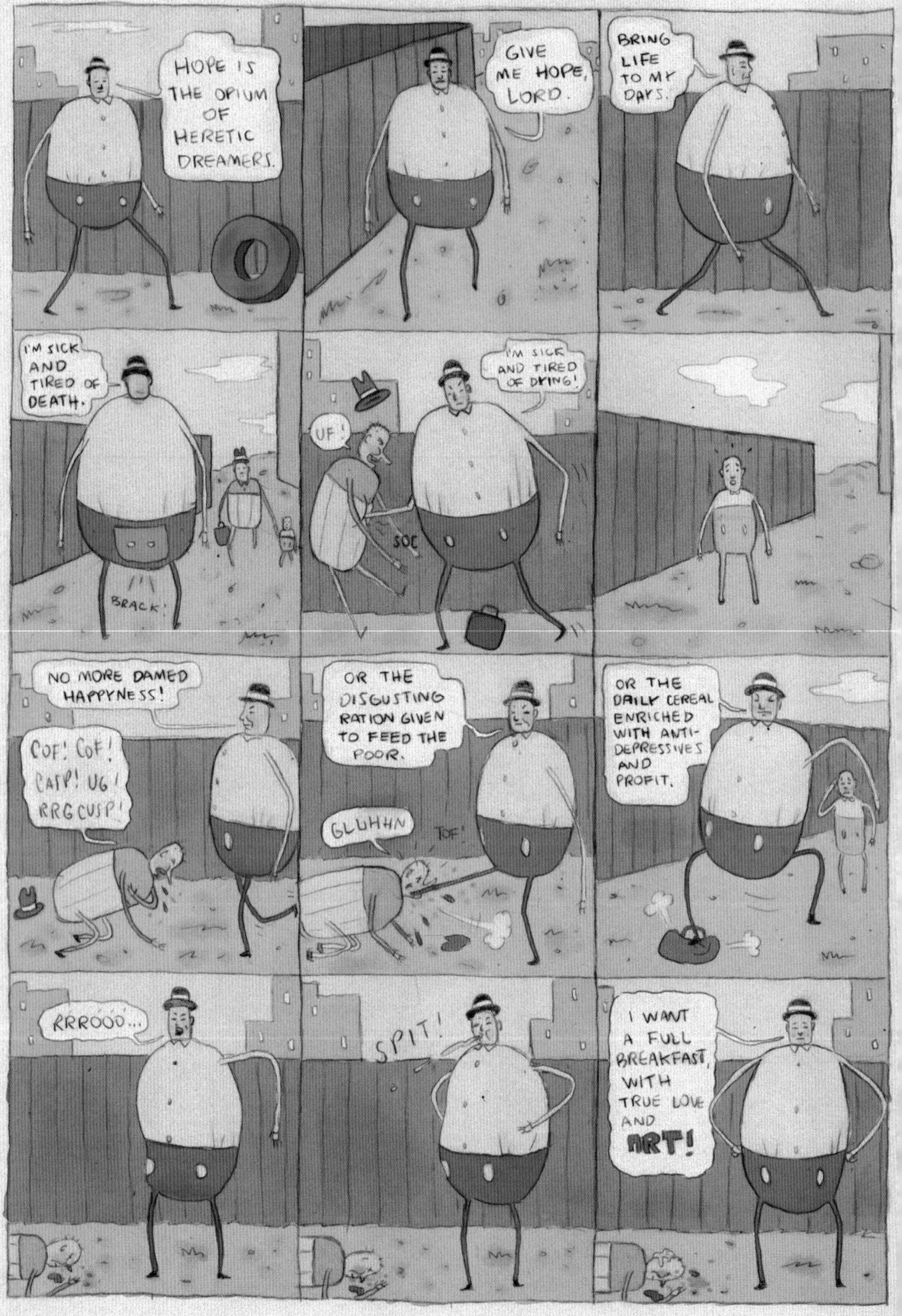
HOPE IS THE OPIUM OF HERETIC DREAMERS.
GIVE ME HOPE, LORD.
BRING LIFE TO MY DAYS.
I'M SICK AND TIRED OF DEATH.
BRACK!
I'M SICK AND TIRED OF DYING!
UF!
SOC
NO MORE DAMED HAPPYNESS!
COF! COF! GAFP! UG! RRG GUSP!
OR THE DISGUSTING RATION GIVEN TO FEED THE POOR.
GLUHHN
TOF!
OR THE DAILY CEREAL ENRICHED WITH ANTI-DEPRESSIVES AND PROFIT.
RRROOO...
SPIT!
I WANT A FULL BREAKFAST, WITH TRUE LOVE AND ART!

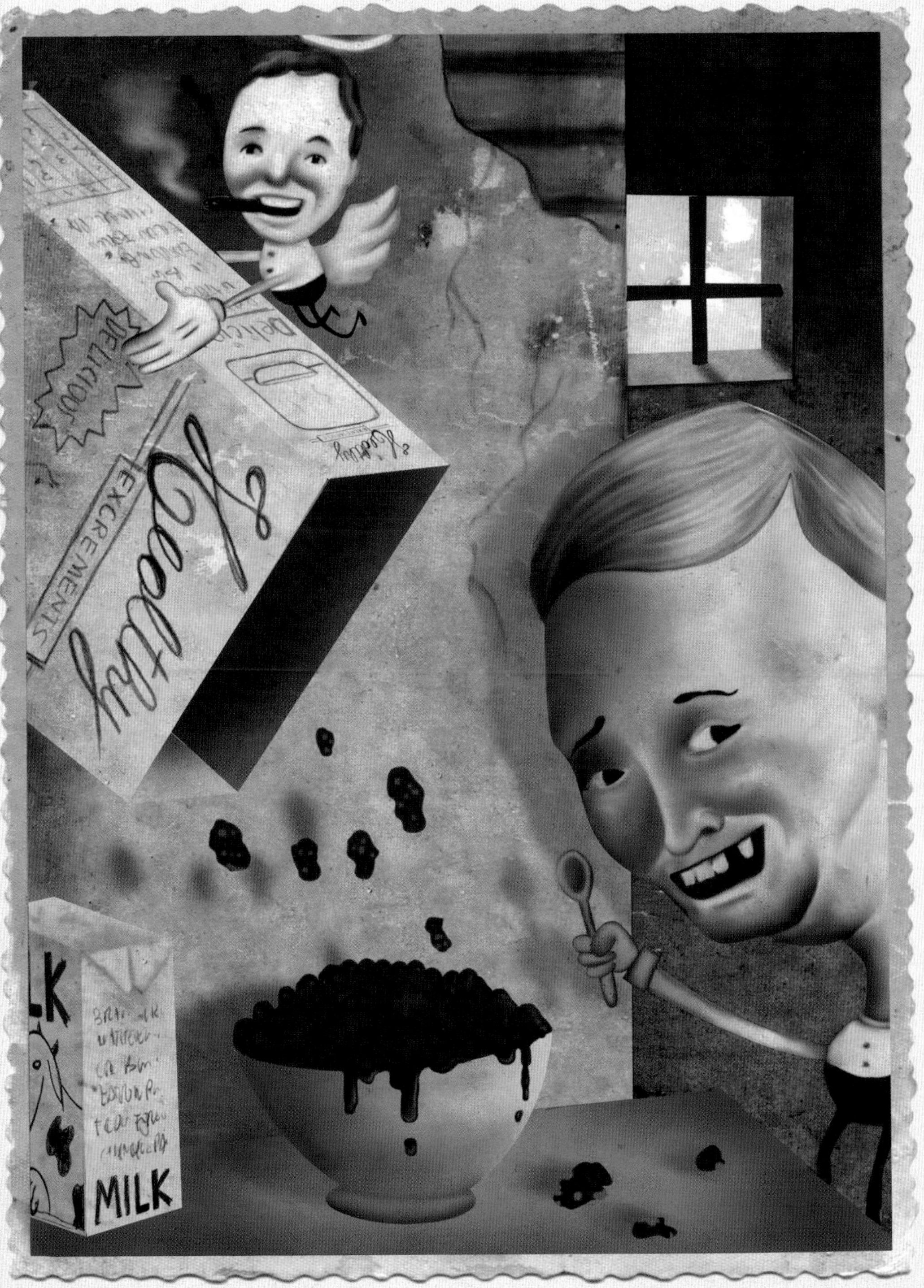
DELICIOUS
EXCREMENTS
MILK

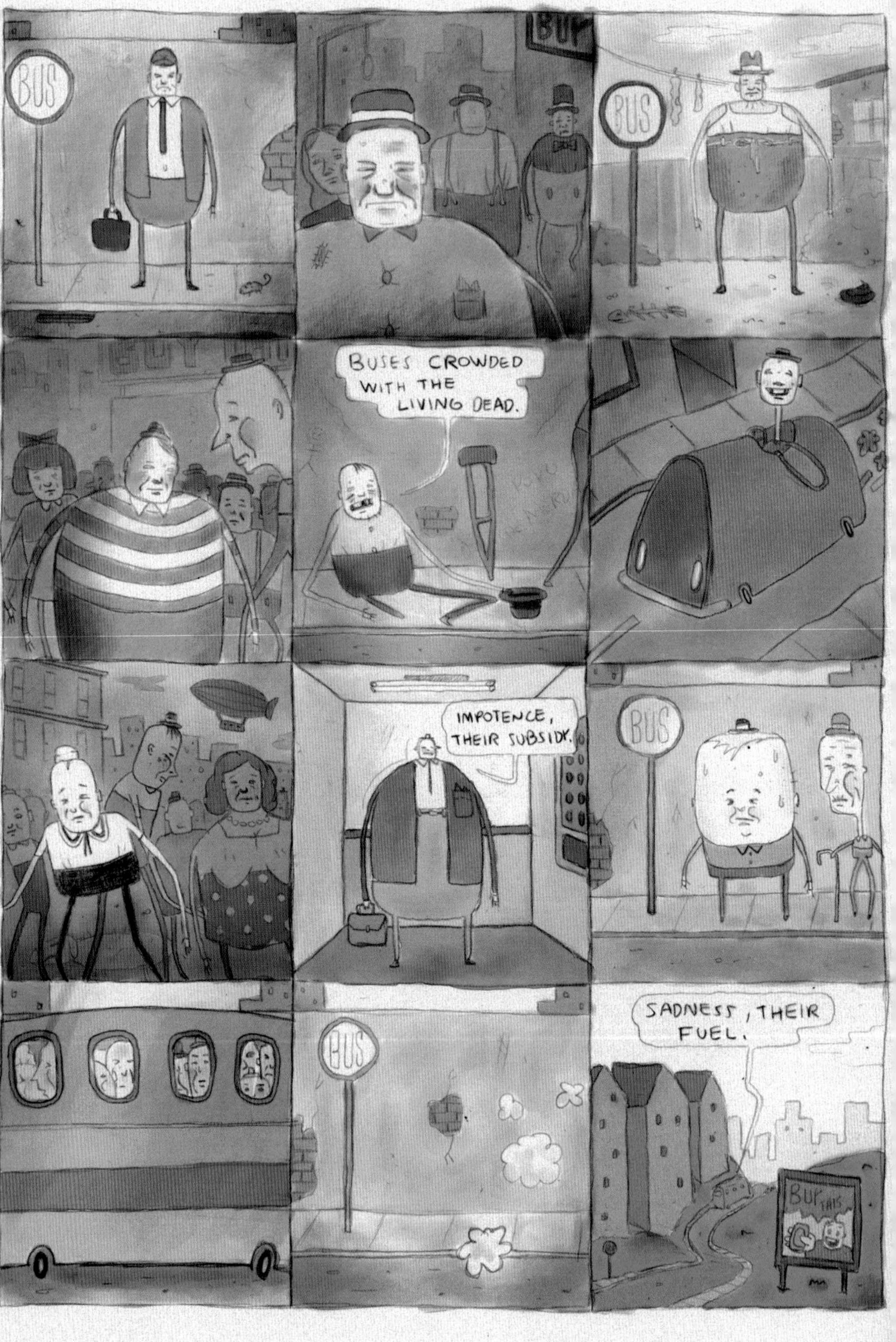
BUS
BUS
BUSES CROWDED WITH THE LIVING DEAD.
IMPOTENCE, THEIR SUBSIDY.
BUS
BUS
SADNESS, THEIR FUEL.

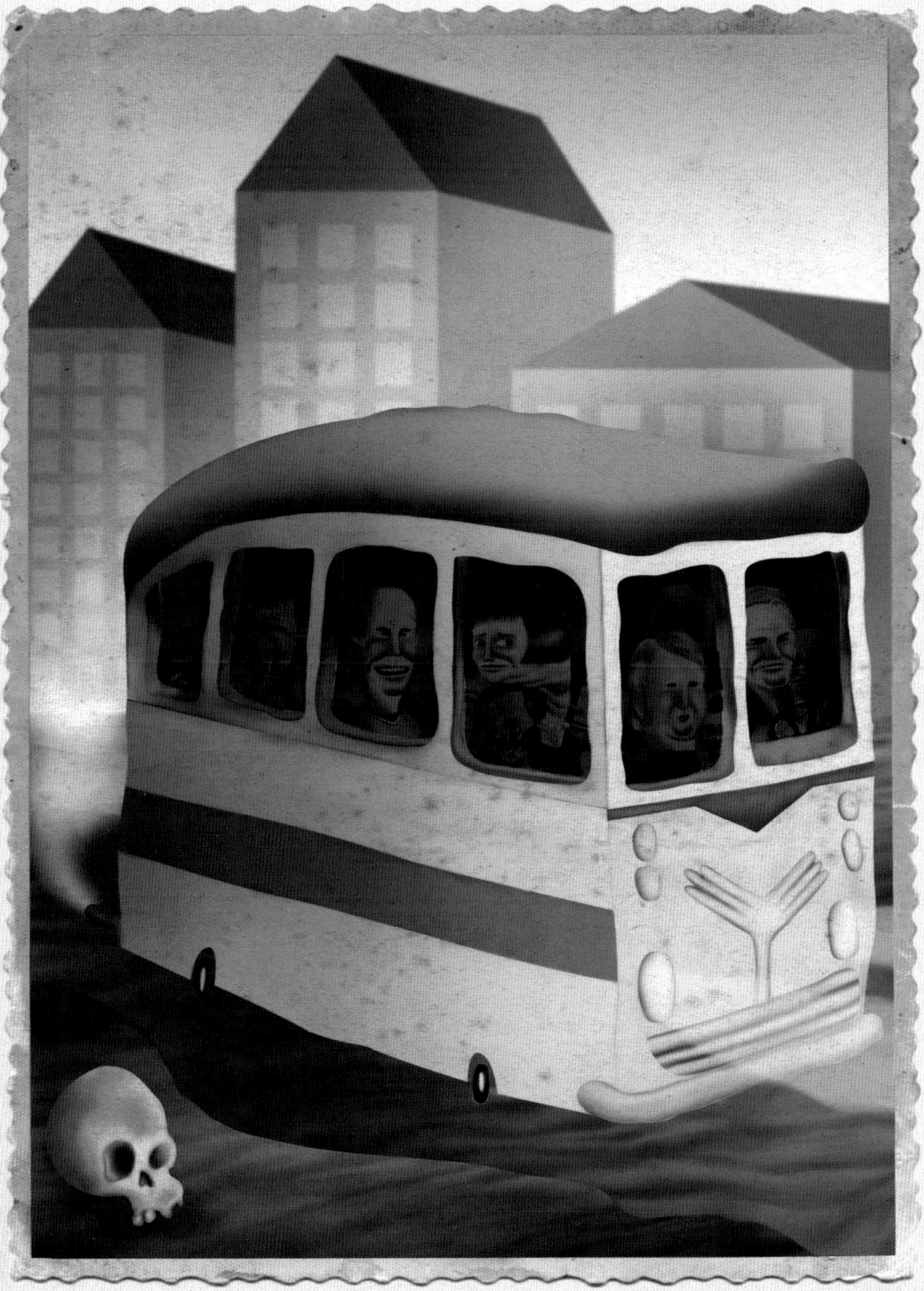

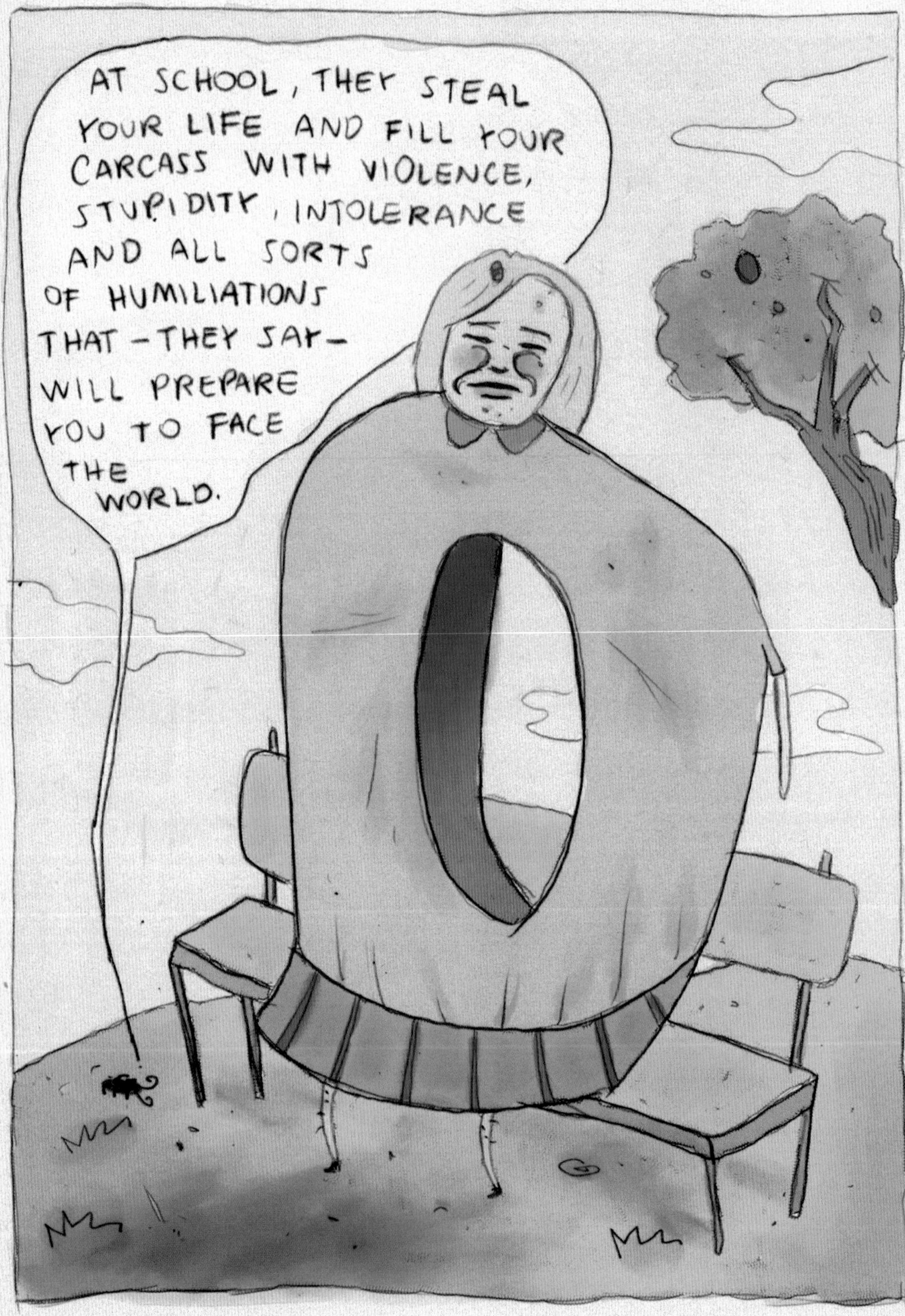
AT SCHOOL, THEY STEAL YOUR LIFE AND FILL YOUR CARCASS WITH VIOLENCE, STUPIDITY, INTOLERANCE AND ALL SORTS OF HUMILIATIONS THAT - THEY SAY - WILL PREPARE YOU TO FACE THE WORLD.

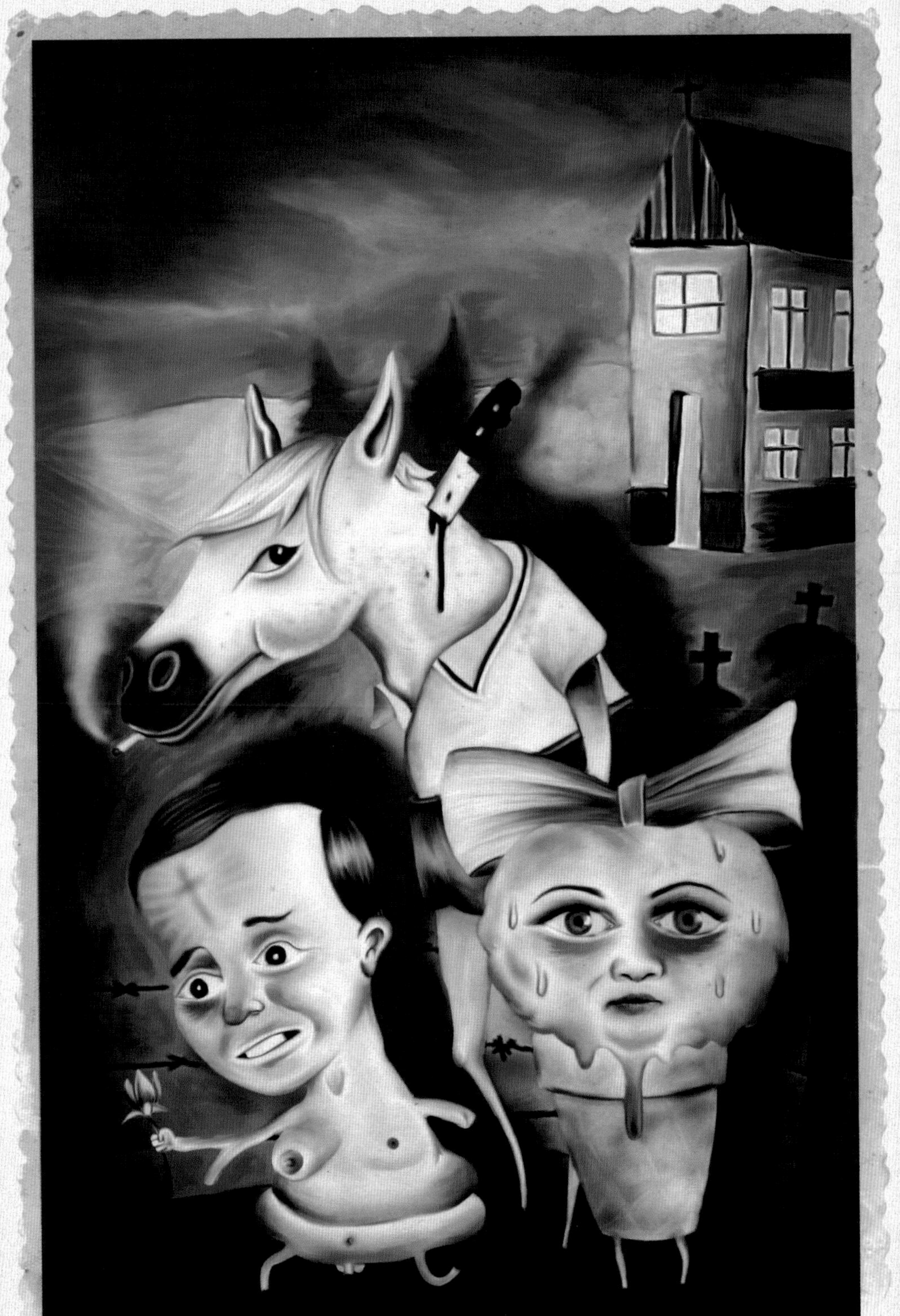

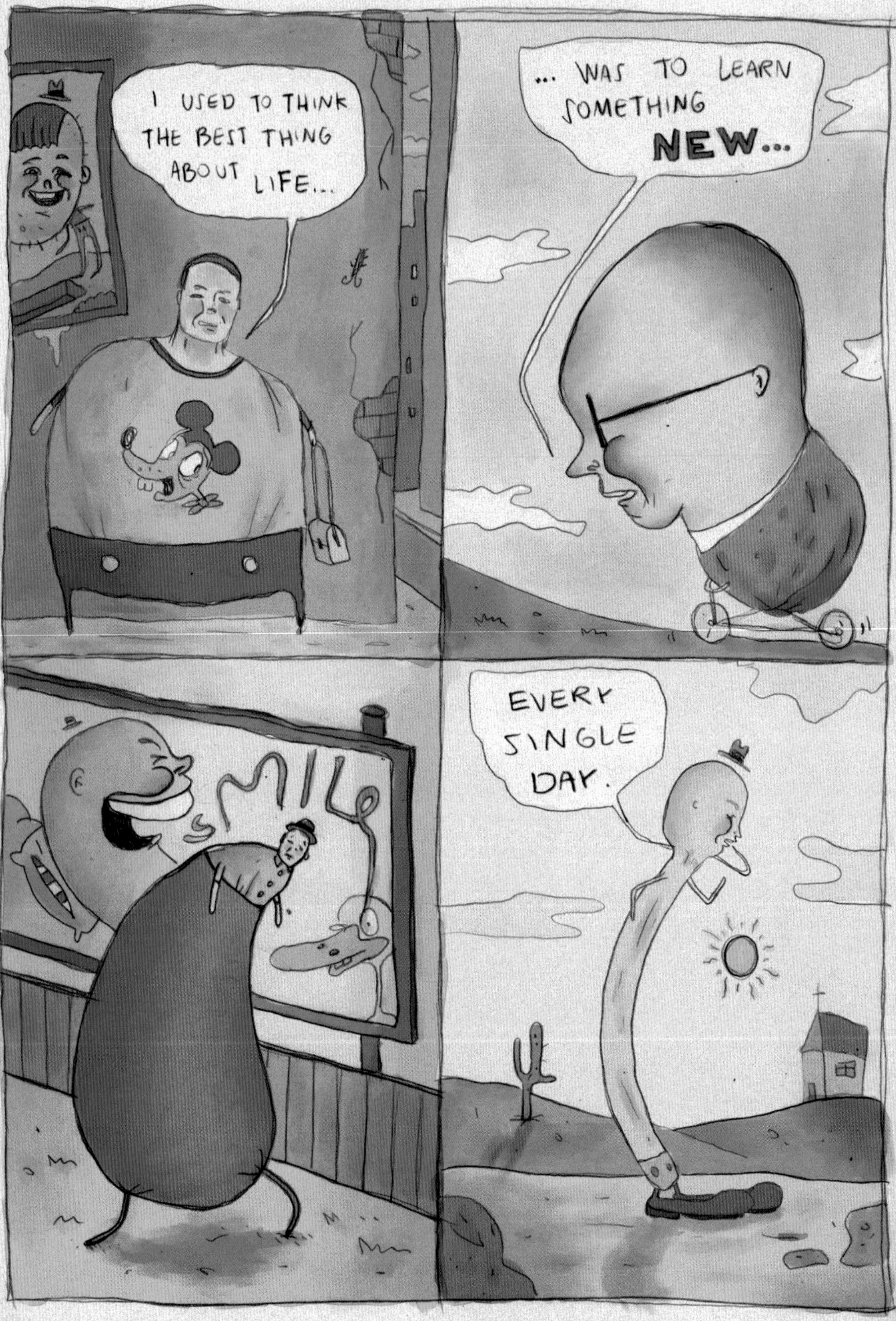
I USED TO THINK THE BEST THING ABOUT LIFE...
... WAS TO LEARN SOMETHING NEW...
EVERY SINGLE DAY.

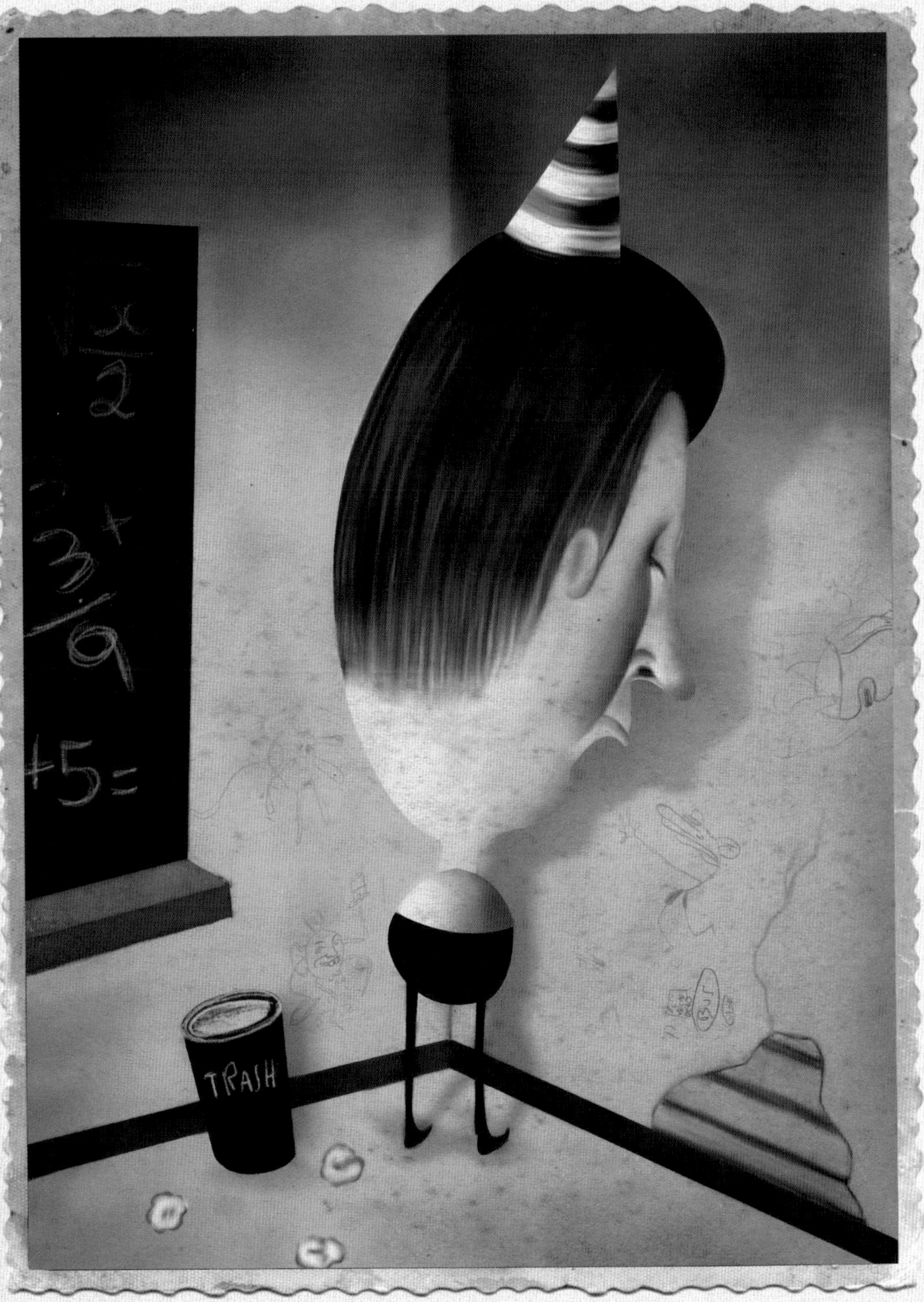
TRASH

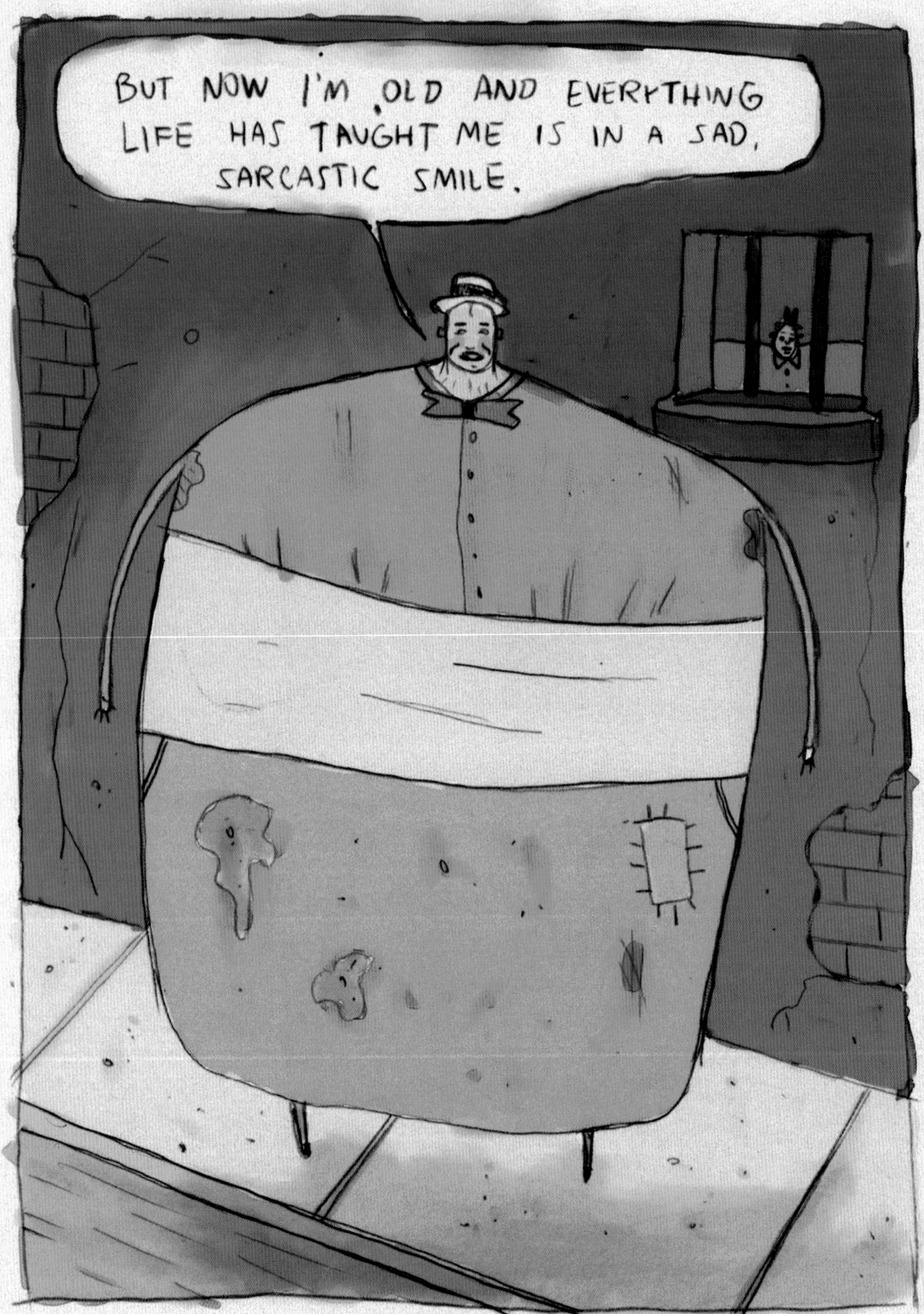
BUT NOW I'M OLD AND EVERYTHING LIFE HAS TAUGHT ME IS IN A SAD, SARCASTIC SMILE.

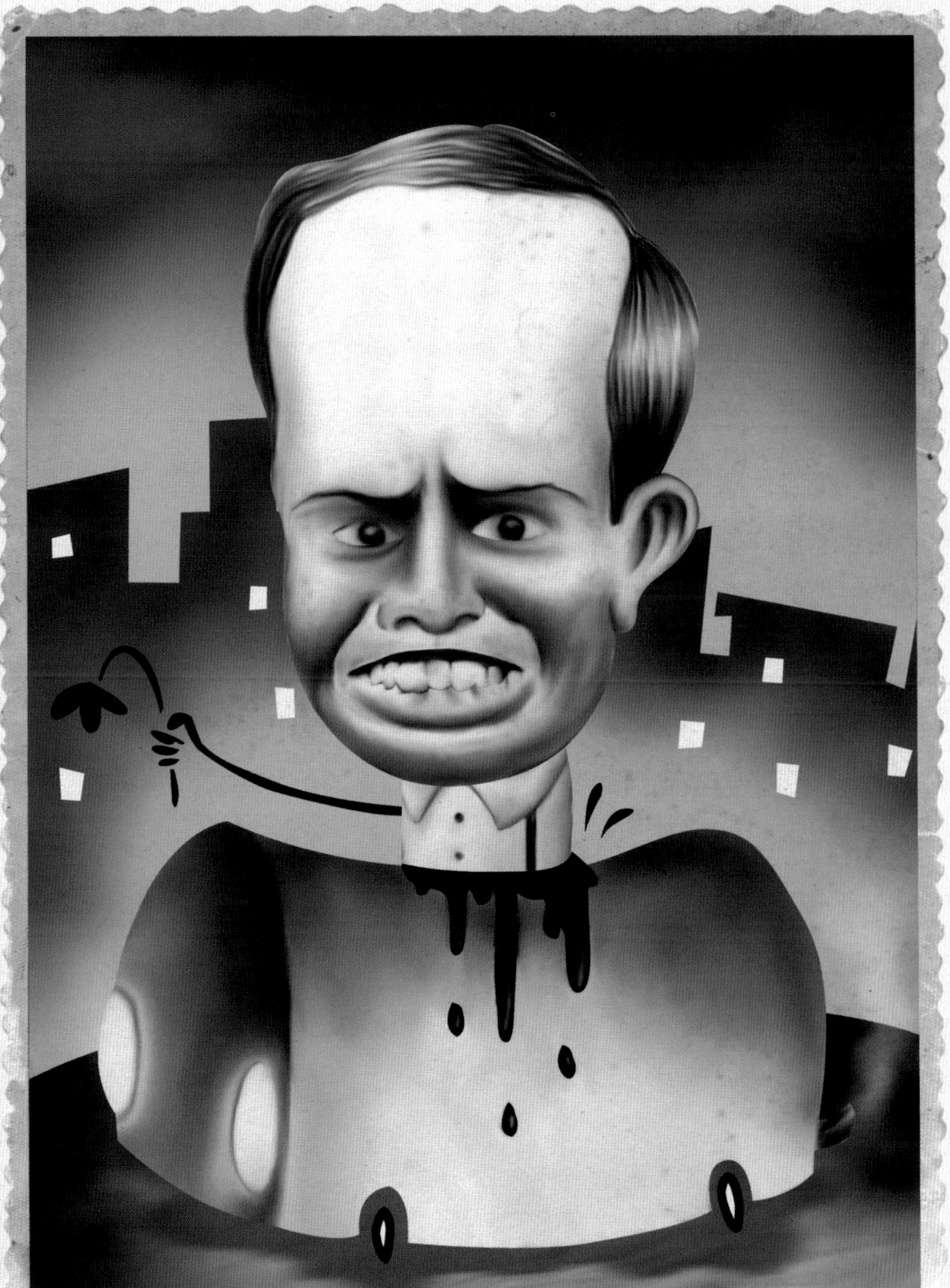

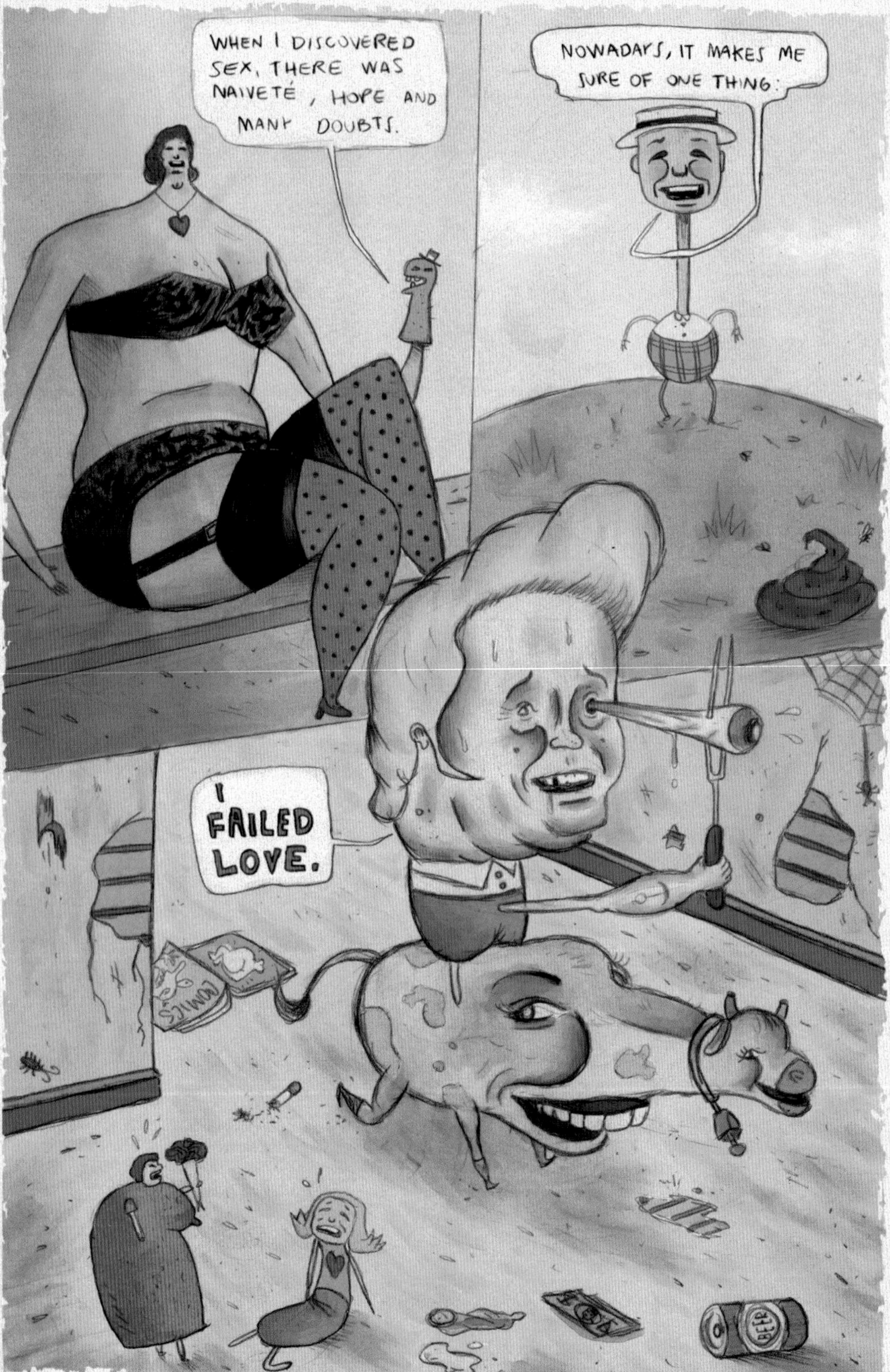
WHEN I DISCOVERED SEX, THERE WAS NAIVETÉ, HOPE AND MANY DOUBTS.
NOWADAYS, IT MAKES ME SURE OF ONE THING:
I FAILED LOVE.
COMICS
BEER

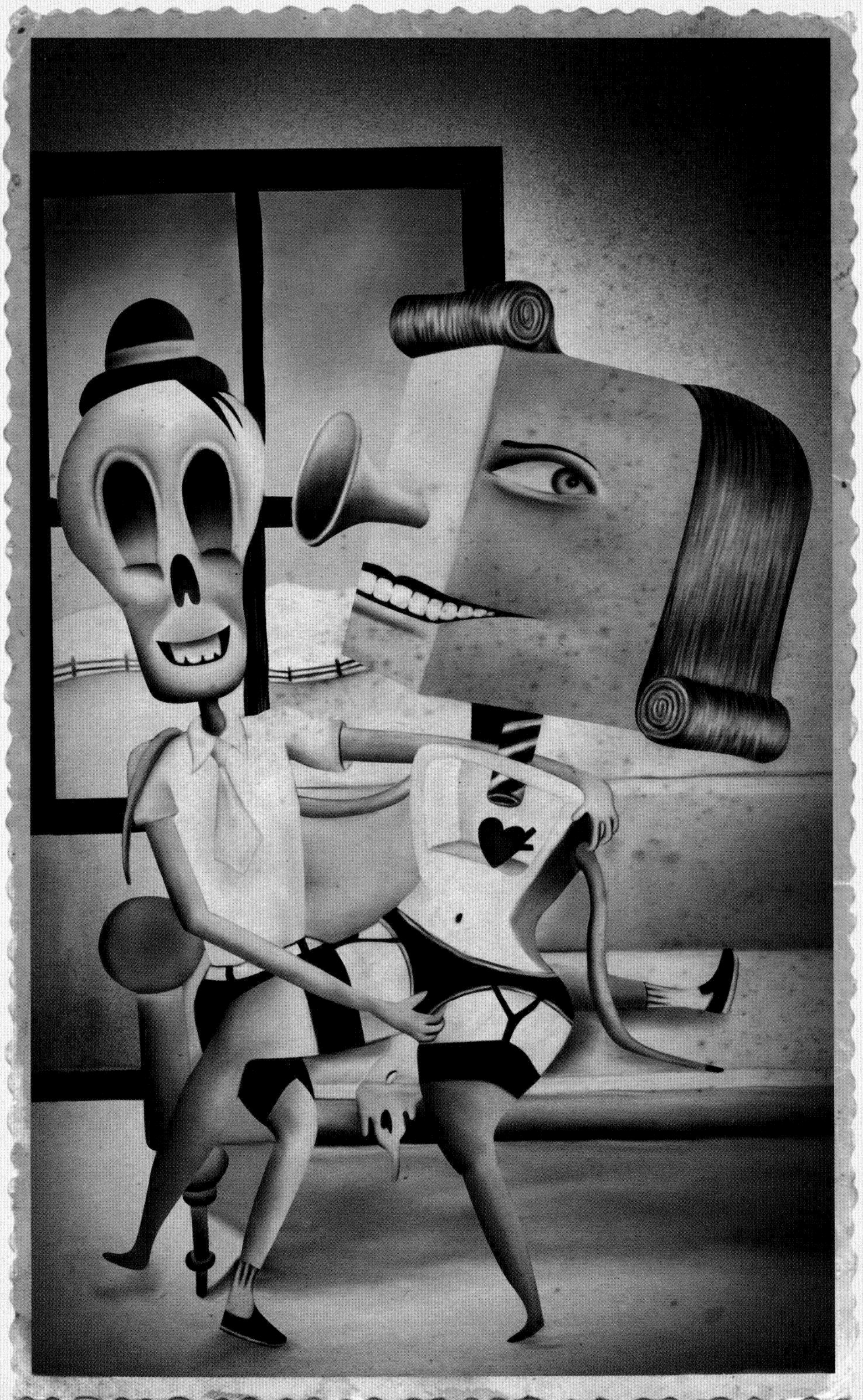

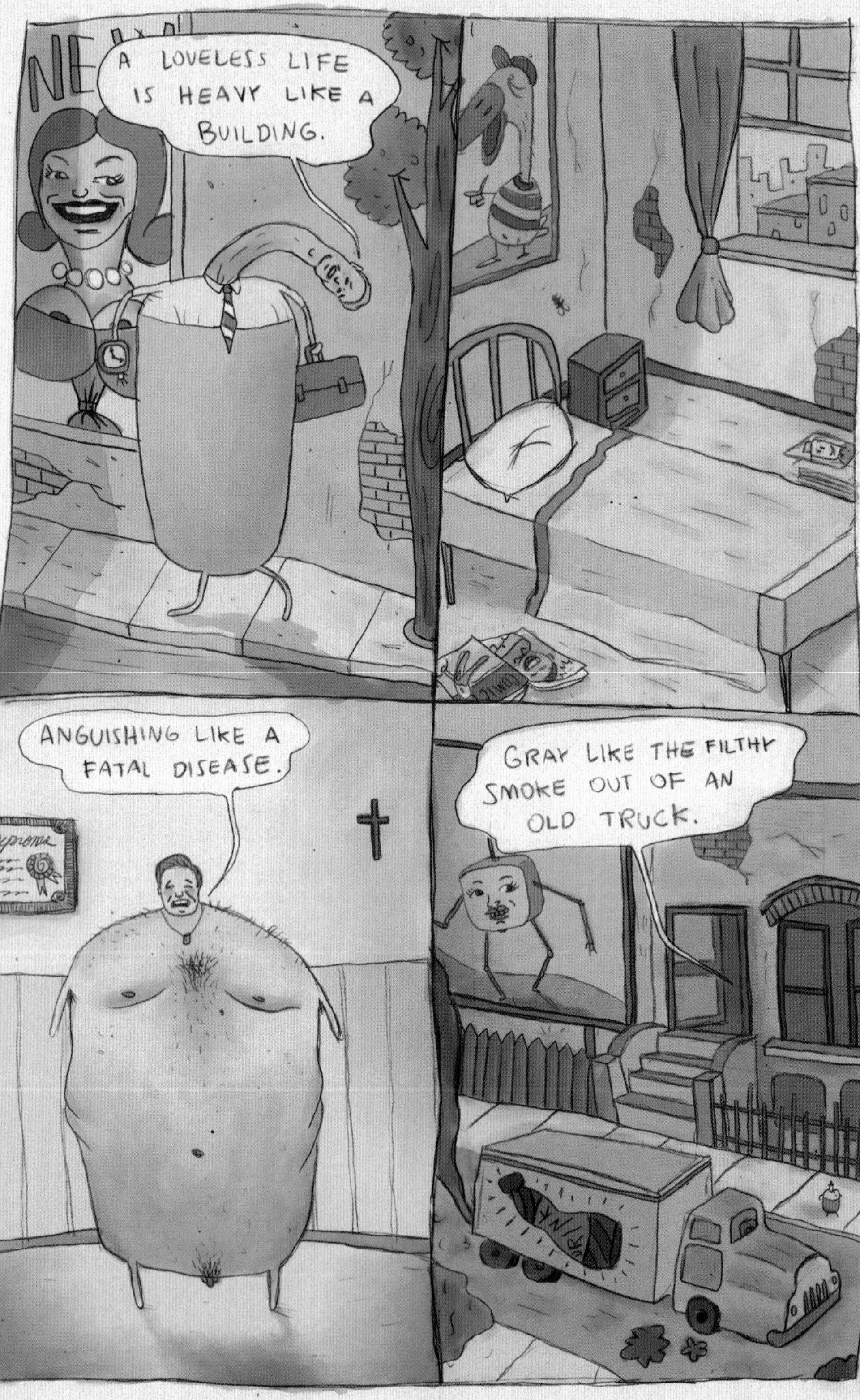
A LOVELESS LIFE IS HEAVY LIKE A BUILDING.
ANGUISHING LIKE A FATAL DISEASE.
GRAY LIKE THE FILTHY SMOKE OUT OF AN OLD TRUCK.

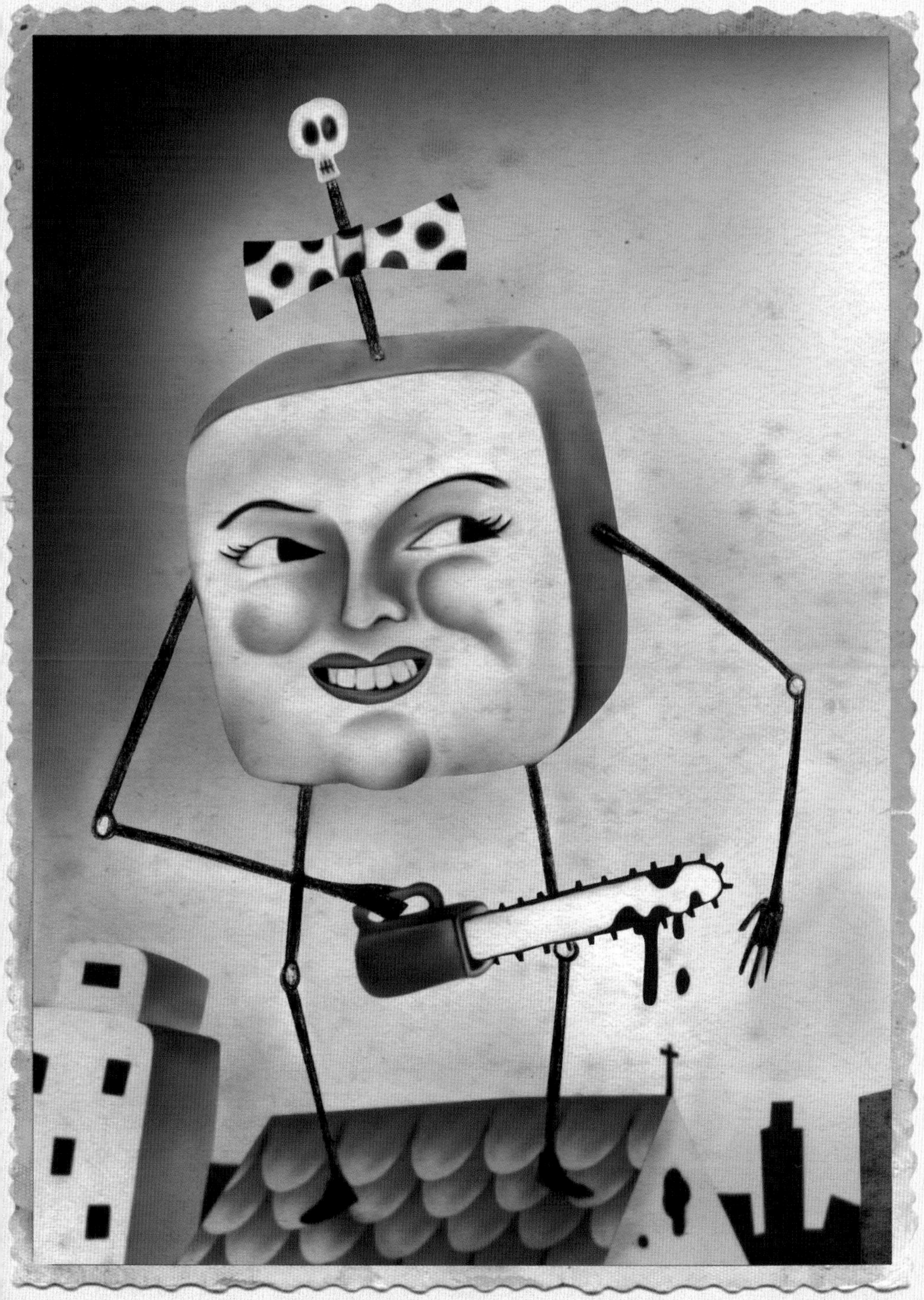

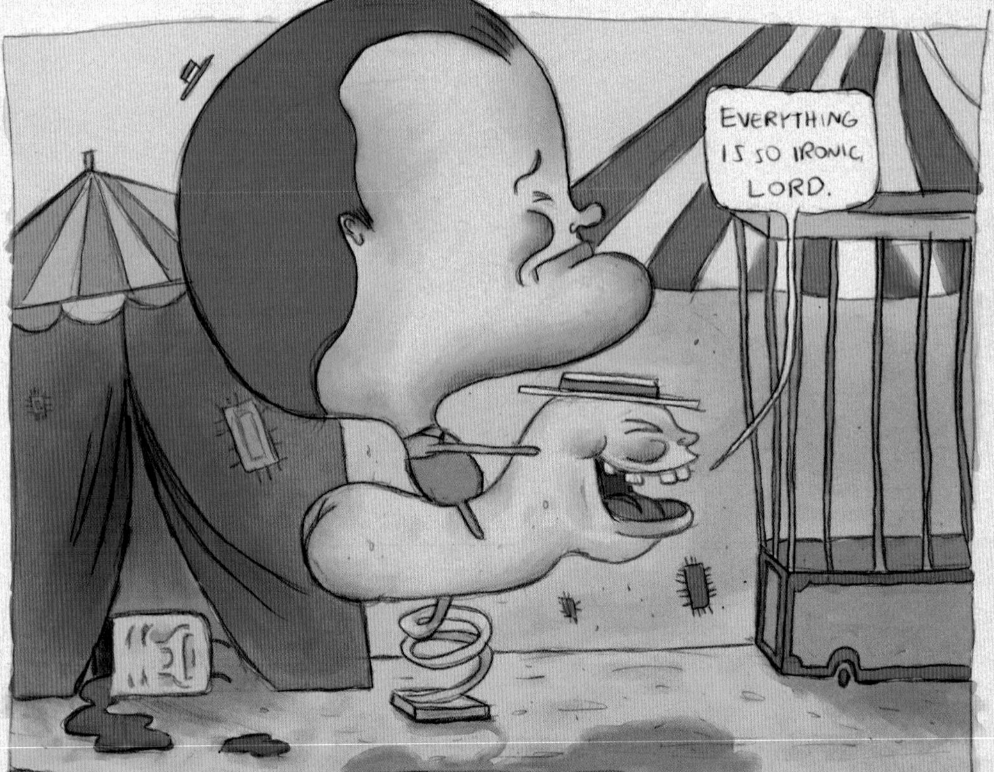
EVERYTHING IS SO IRONIC LORD.

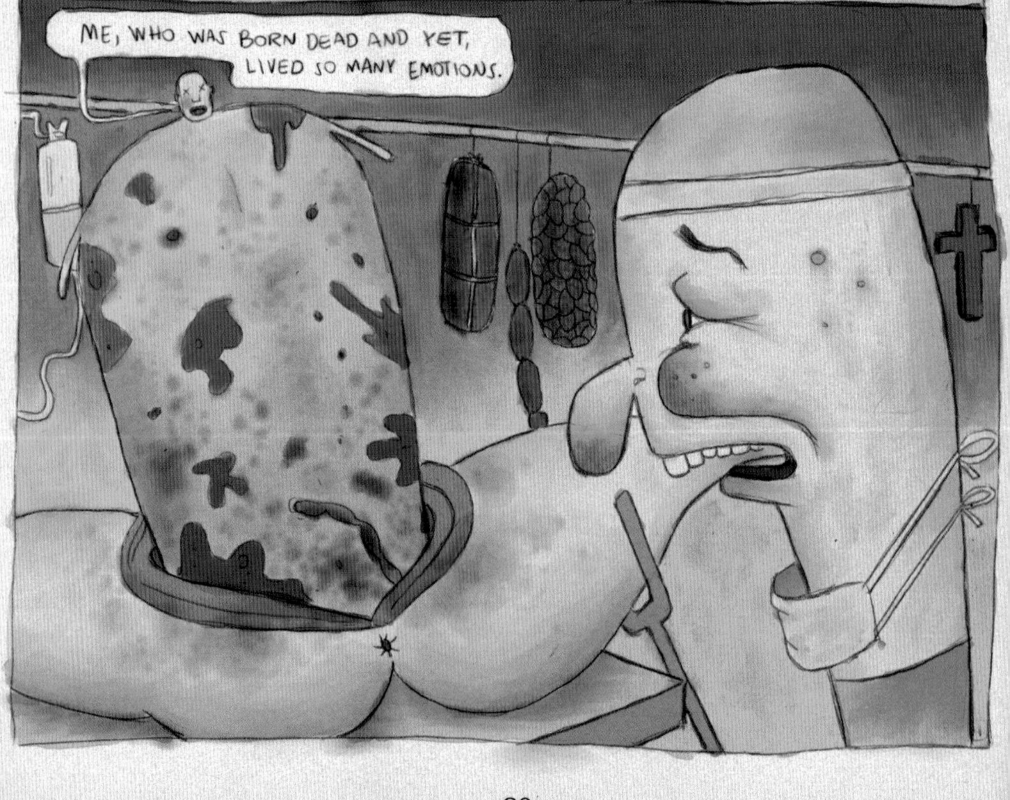
ME, WHO WAS BORN DEAD AND YET, LIVED SO MANY EMOTIONS.

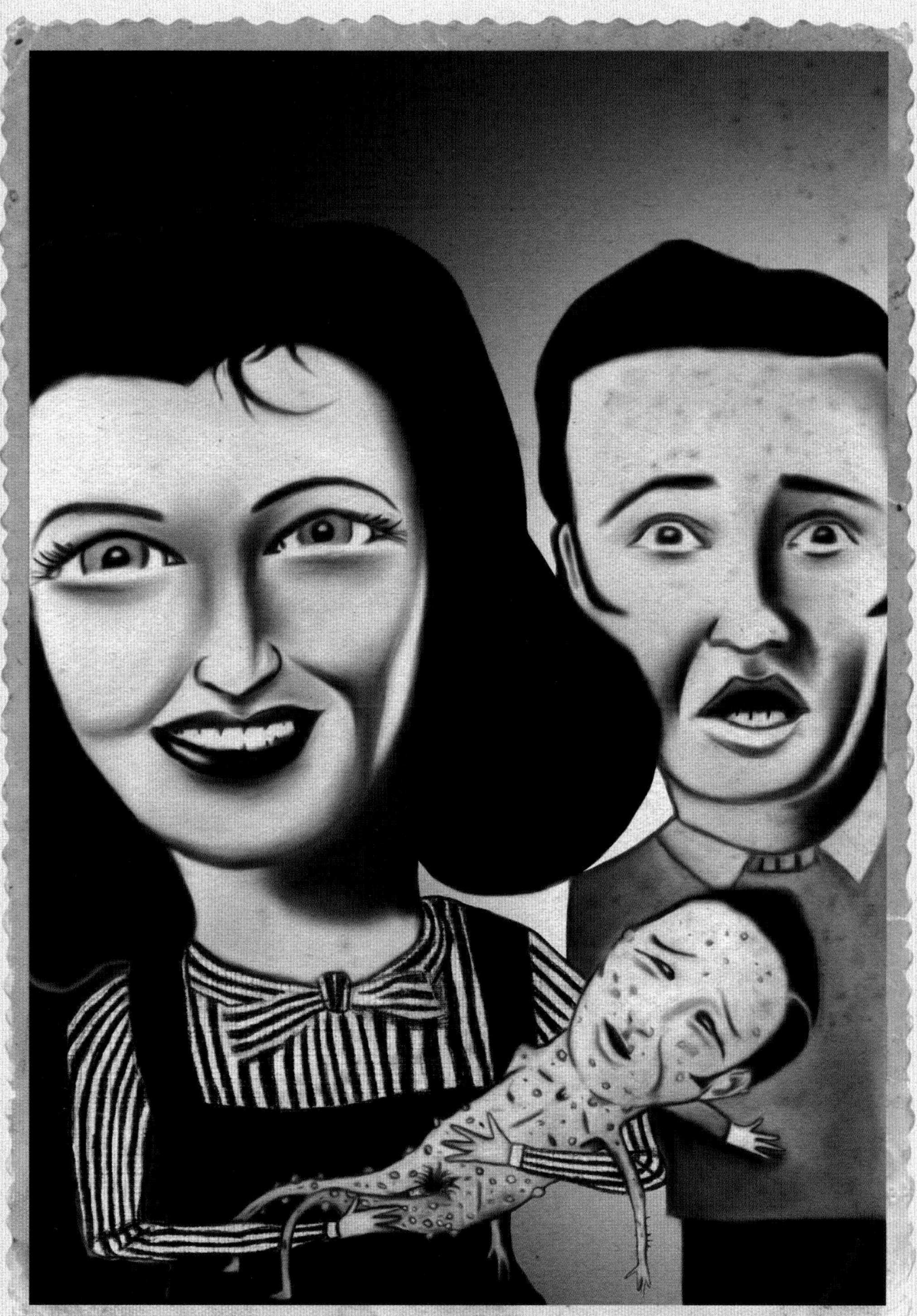

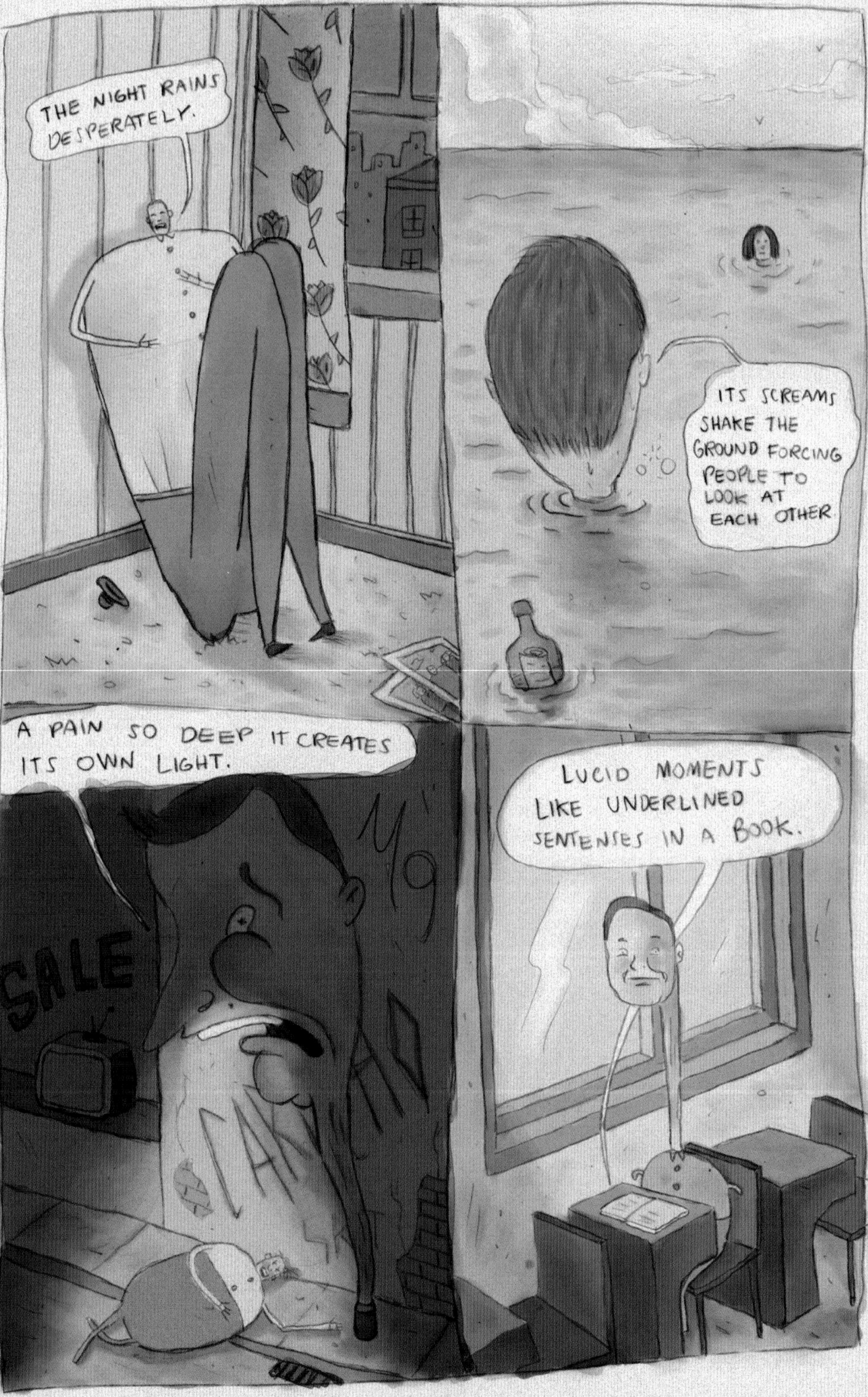
THE NIGHT RAINS DESPERATELY.
ITS SCREAMS SHAKE THE GROUND FORCING PEOPLE TO LOOK AT EACH OTHER
A PAIN SO DEEP IT CREATES ITS OWN LIGHT.
SALE
LUCID MOMENTS LIKE UNDERLINED SENTENSES IN A BOOK.

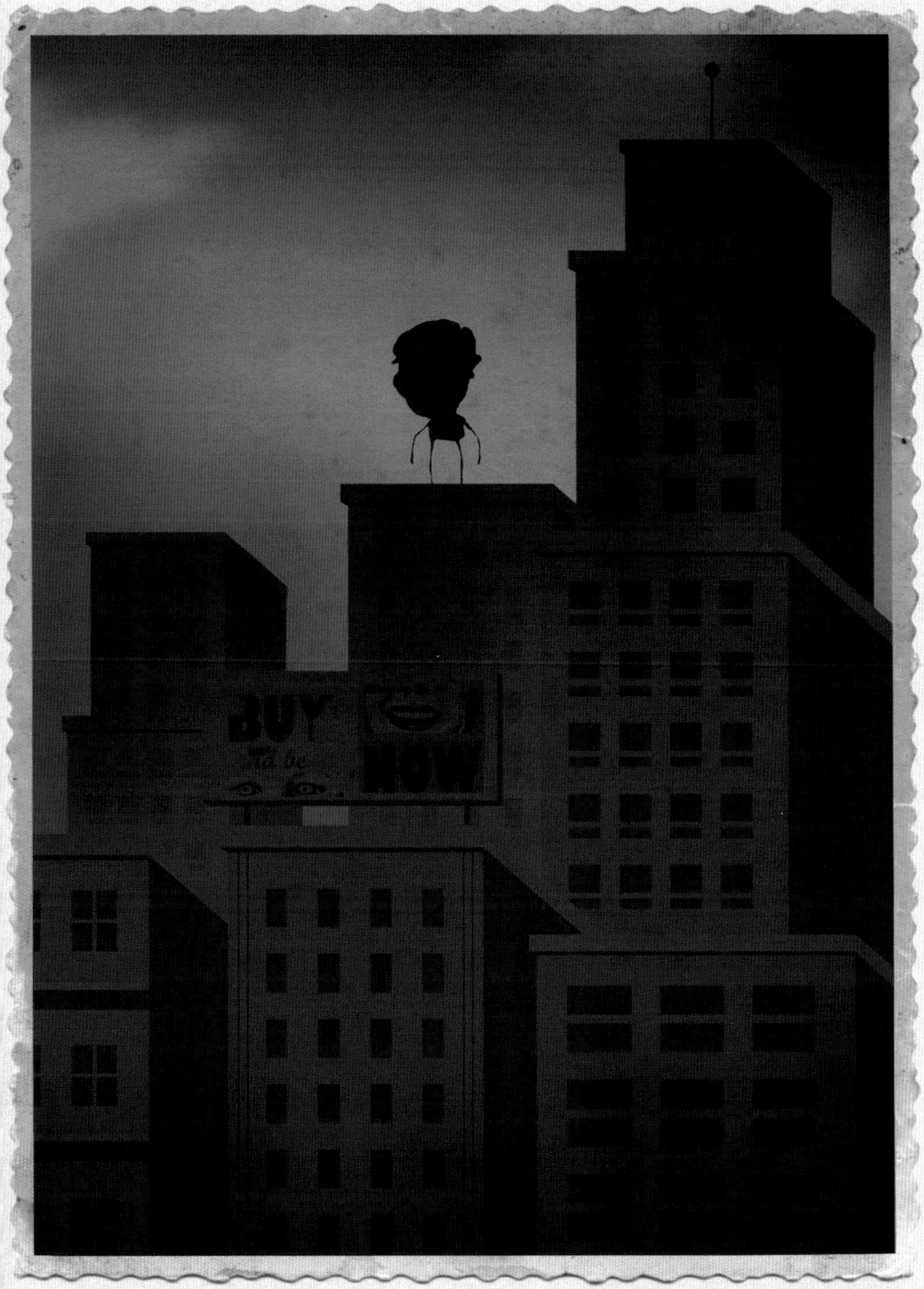
BUY
NOW

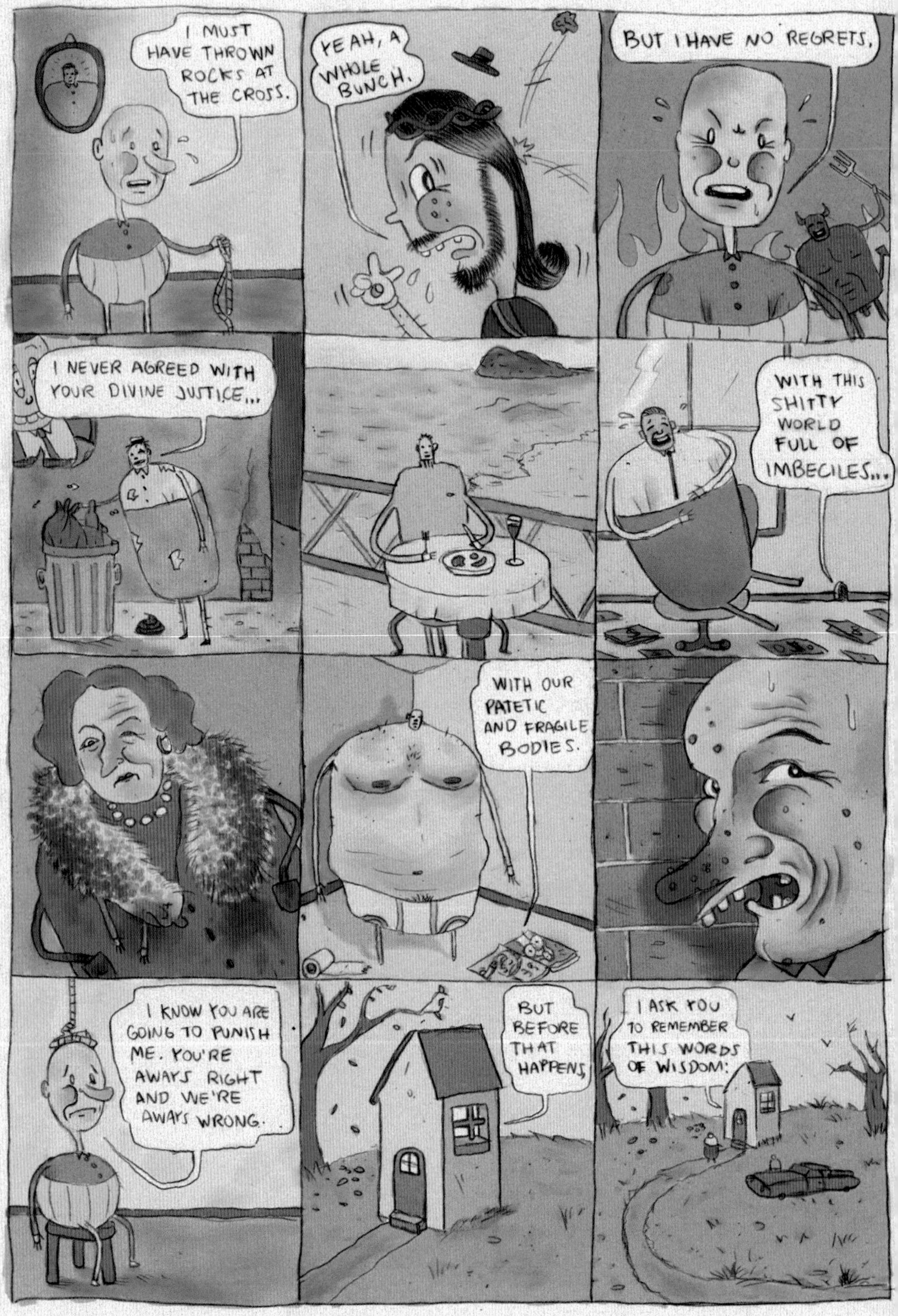
I MUST HAVE THROWN ROCKS AT THE CROSS.
YEAH, A WHOLE BUNCH.
BUT I HAVE NO REGRETS.
I NEVER AGREED WITH YOUR DIVINE JUSTICE...
WITH THIS SHITTY WORLD FULL OF IMBECILES...
WITH OUR PATETIC AND FRAGILE BODIES.
I KNOW YOU ARE GOING TO PUNISH ME. YOU'RE AWAYS RIGHT AND WE'RE AWAYS WRONG.
BUT BEFORE THAT HAPPENS,
I ASK YOU TO REMEMBER THIS WORDS OF WISDOM:

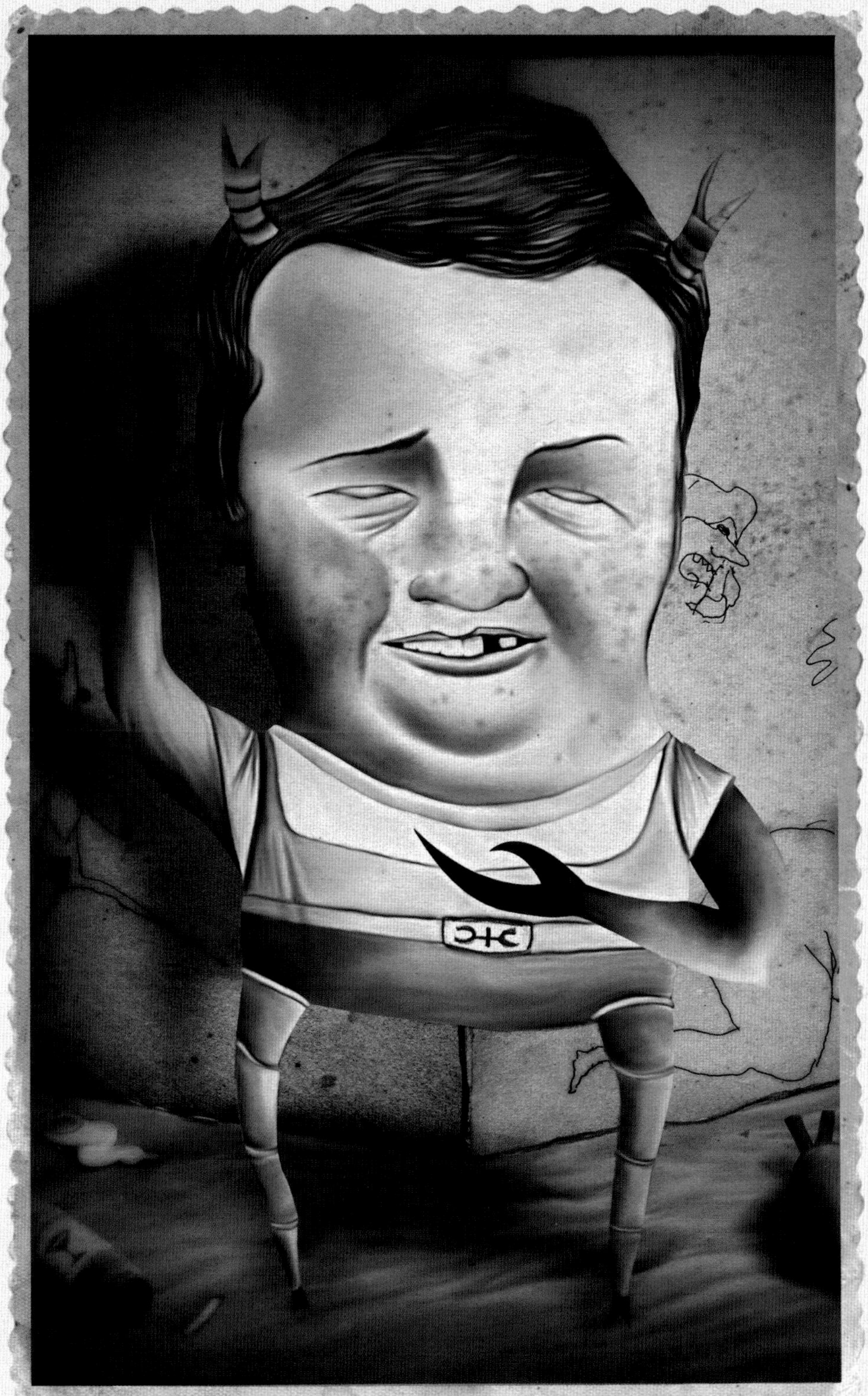

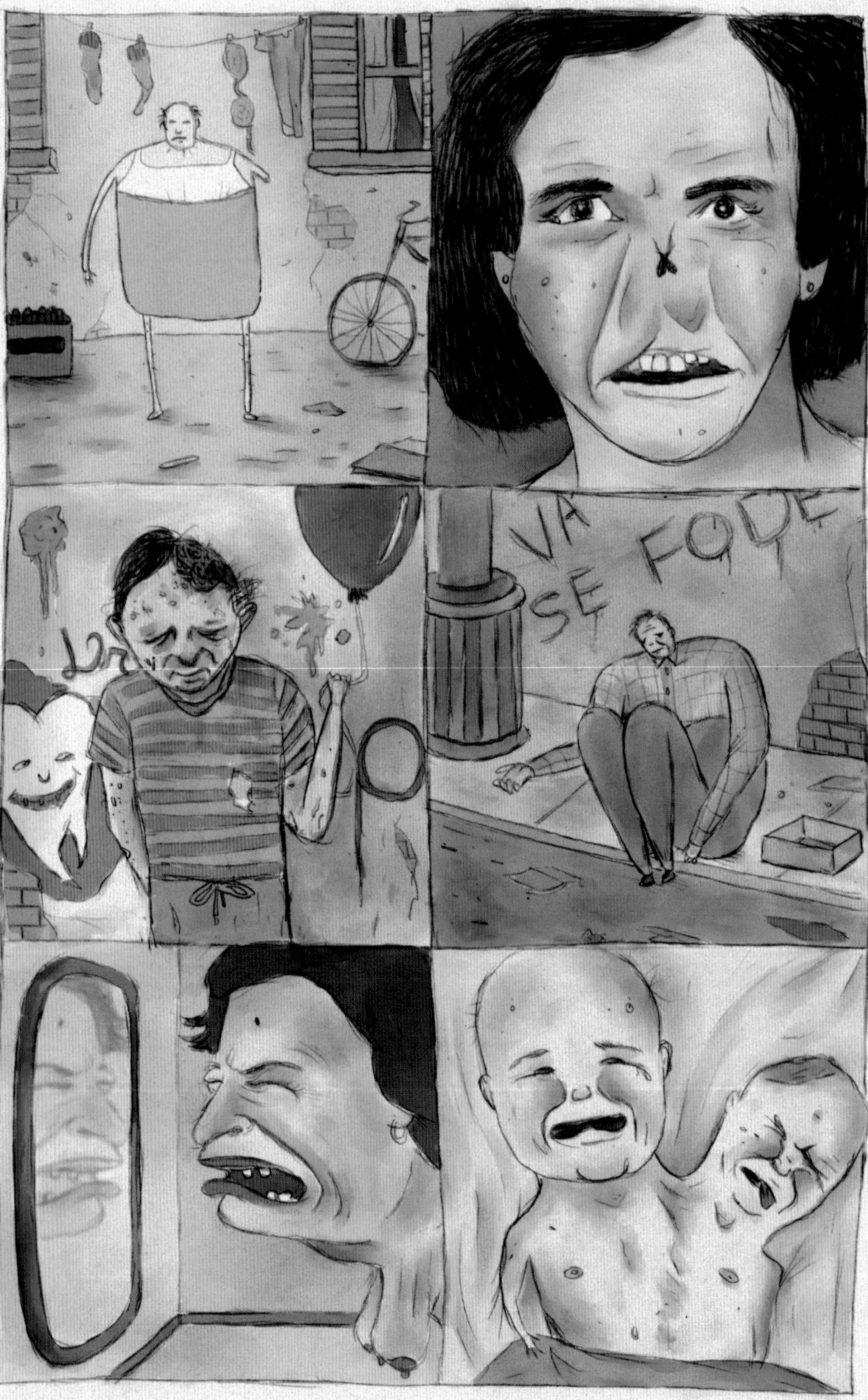
VÁ
SE FODE

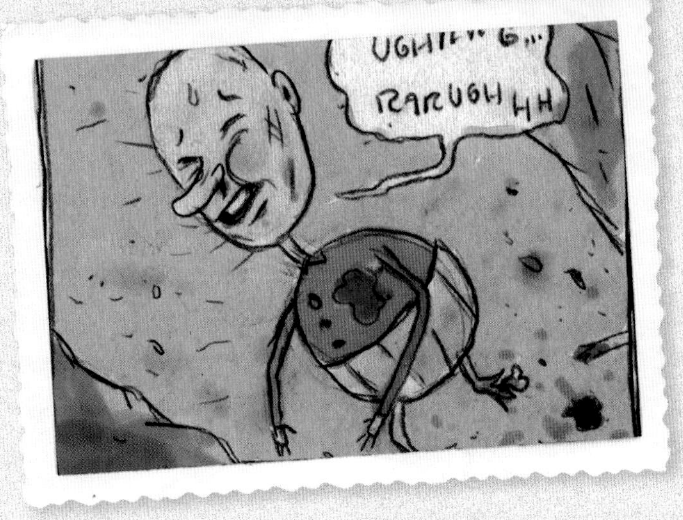
RARUGH HH

JUST BECOUSE YOU'RE RIGHT DOESEN'T GIVE YOU THE RIGHT TO BE STUPID.

MAHATMA GANDHI

Andrew Krahnke's interest in drawing started at a very young age and his life was forever changed after being introduced to his older brother's comic book collection. Since that day he has spent his time trying to improve his artistic abilities. He enrolled in every art course offered while in high school and in 2002 he received a diploma from the Joe Kubert School Of Cartoon and Graphic Art. Since graduating he has also taken an interest in writing and hopes to one day complete his own graphic novel.

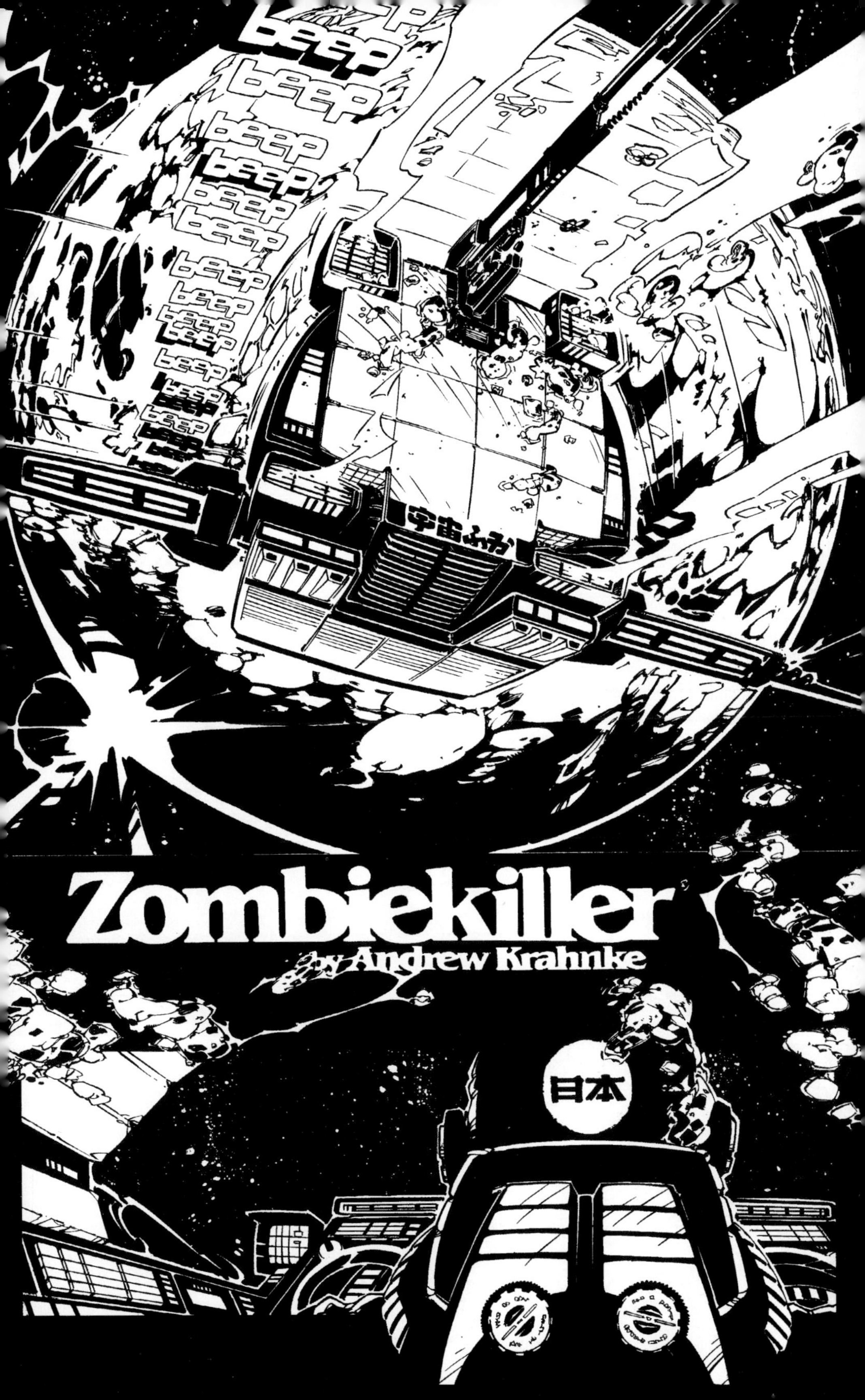

beep beep beep beep beep beep beep beep beep beep beep beep beep beep beep beep
宇宙ふか
Zombiekiller
by Andrew Krahnke
日本

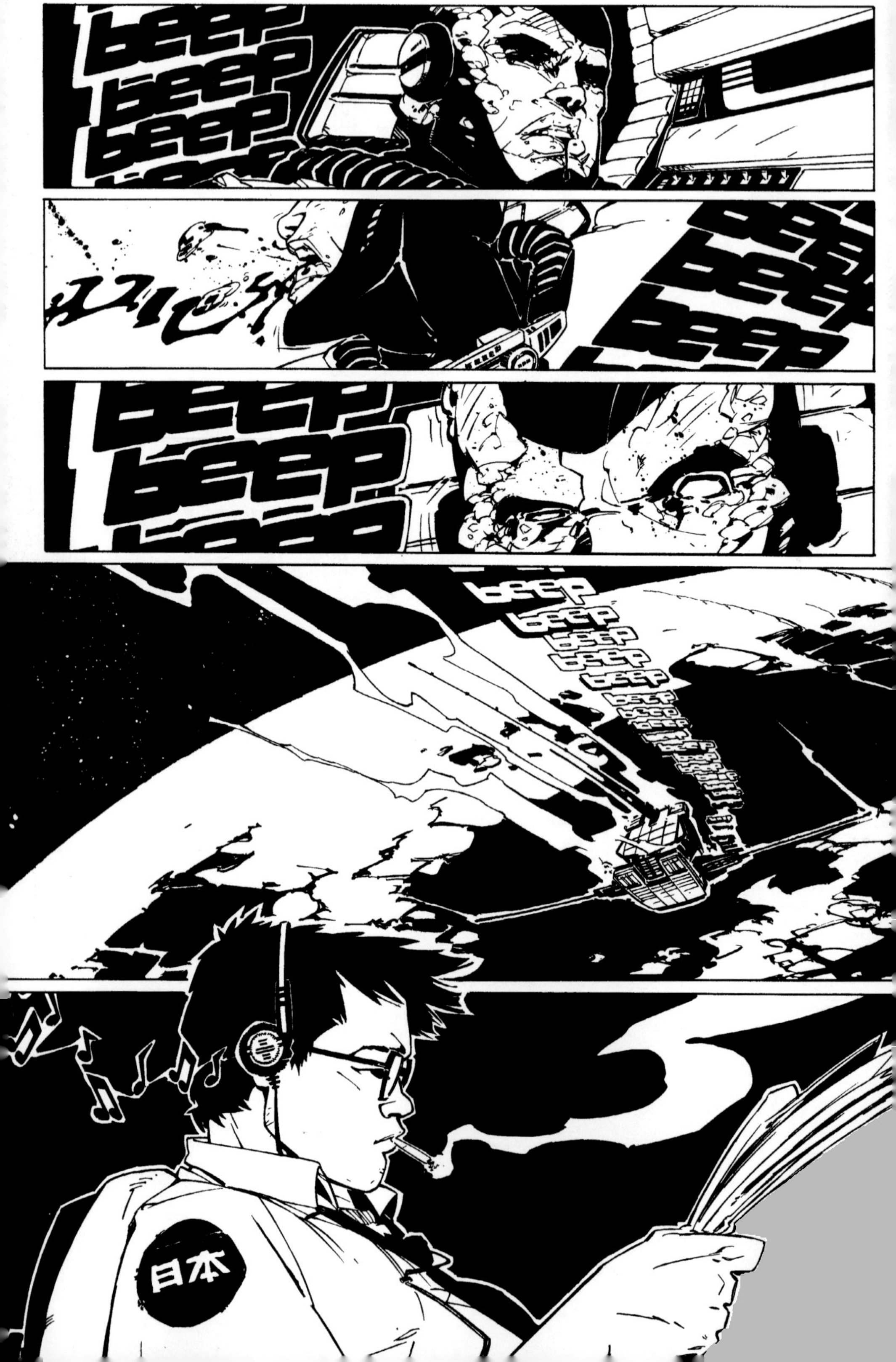
beep
beep
beep
beep
beep
beep
beep
beep
beep
beep
beep
beep
日本

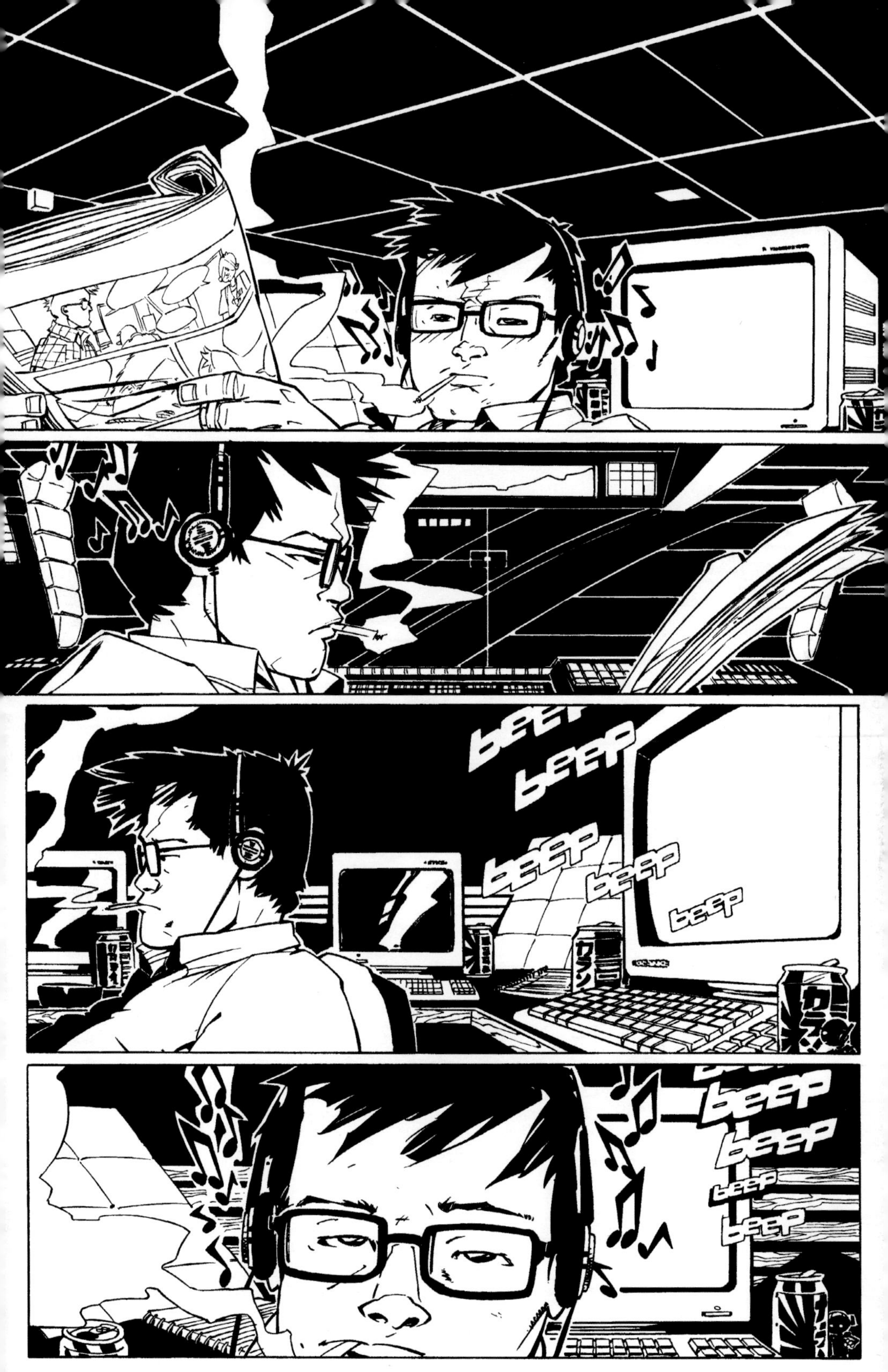
beep
beep
beep
beep
beep
beep
beep
beep
beep

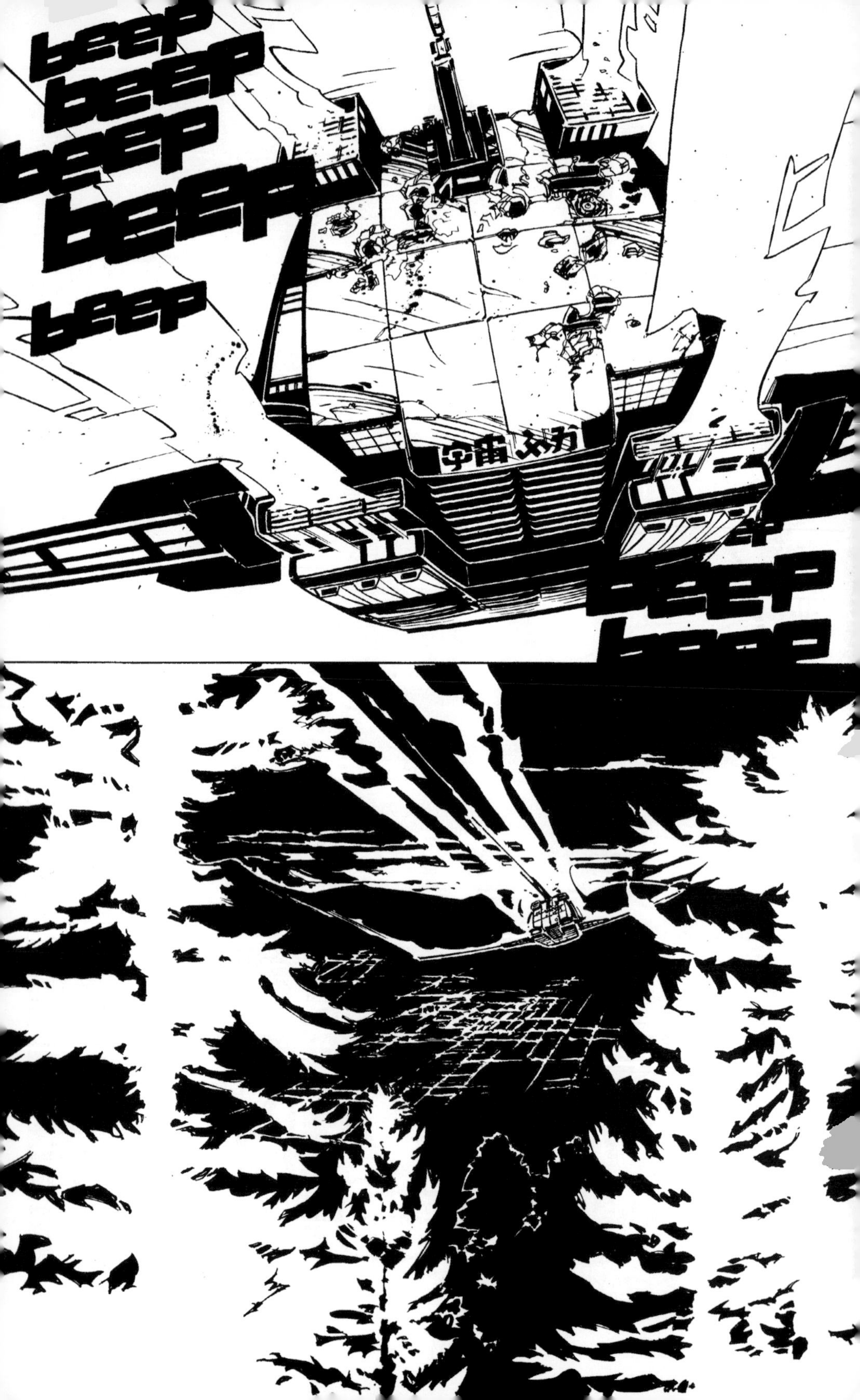
beep
beep
beep
beep
beep
beep
beep
beep

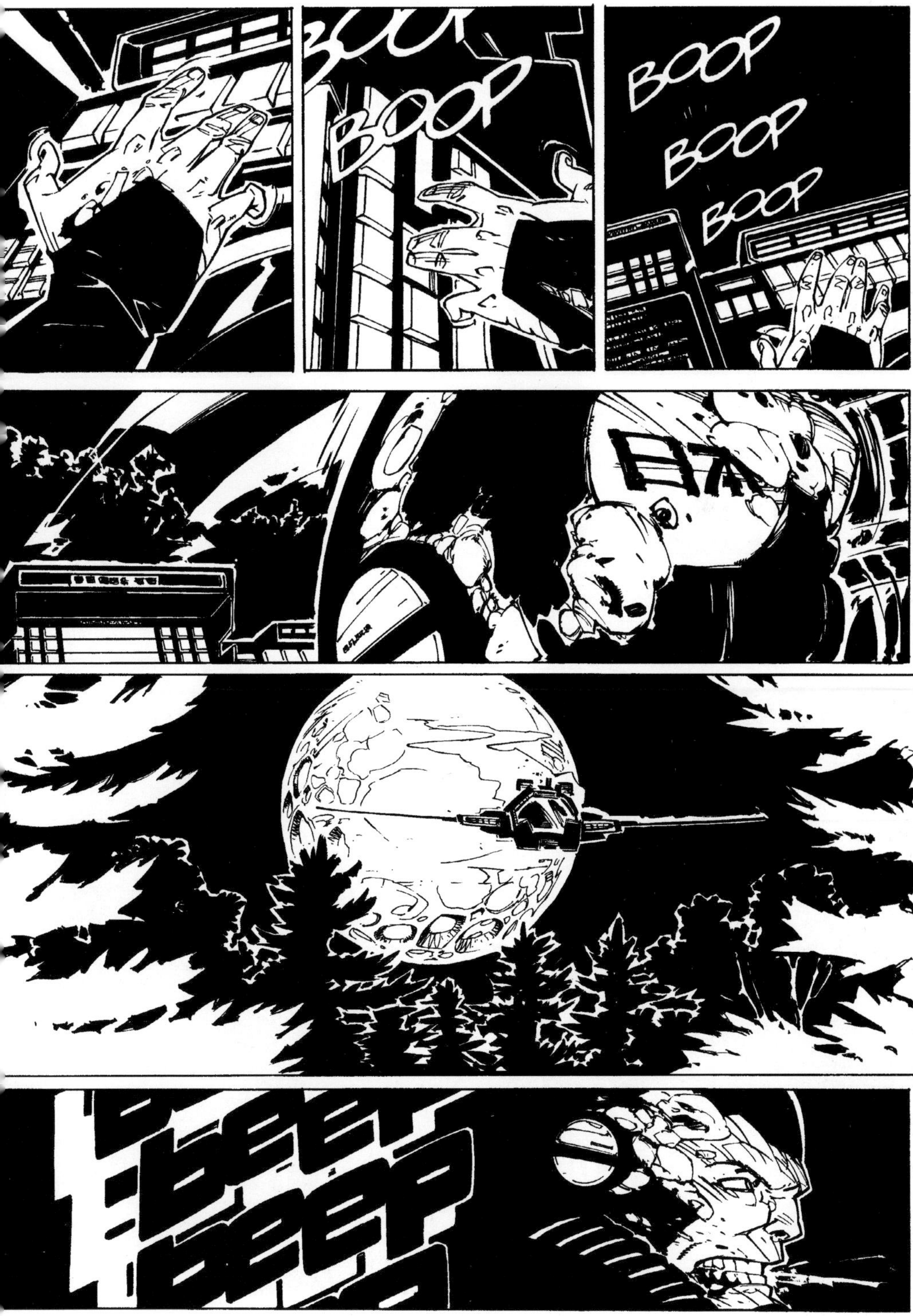
BOOP
BOOP
BOOP
BOOP
BEEP
BEEP

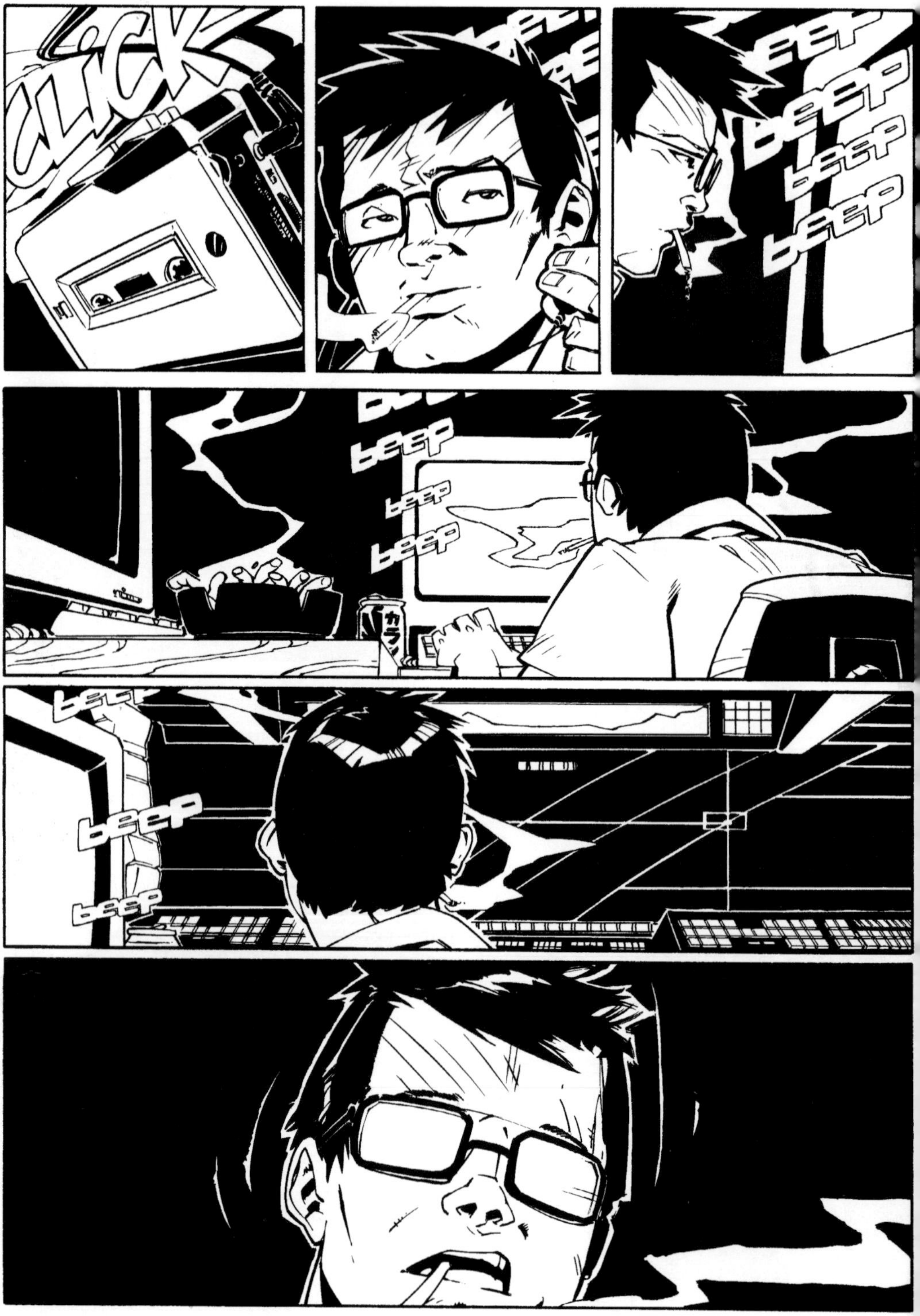
CLICK
beep
beep
beep
beep
beep
beep
beep
beep

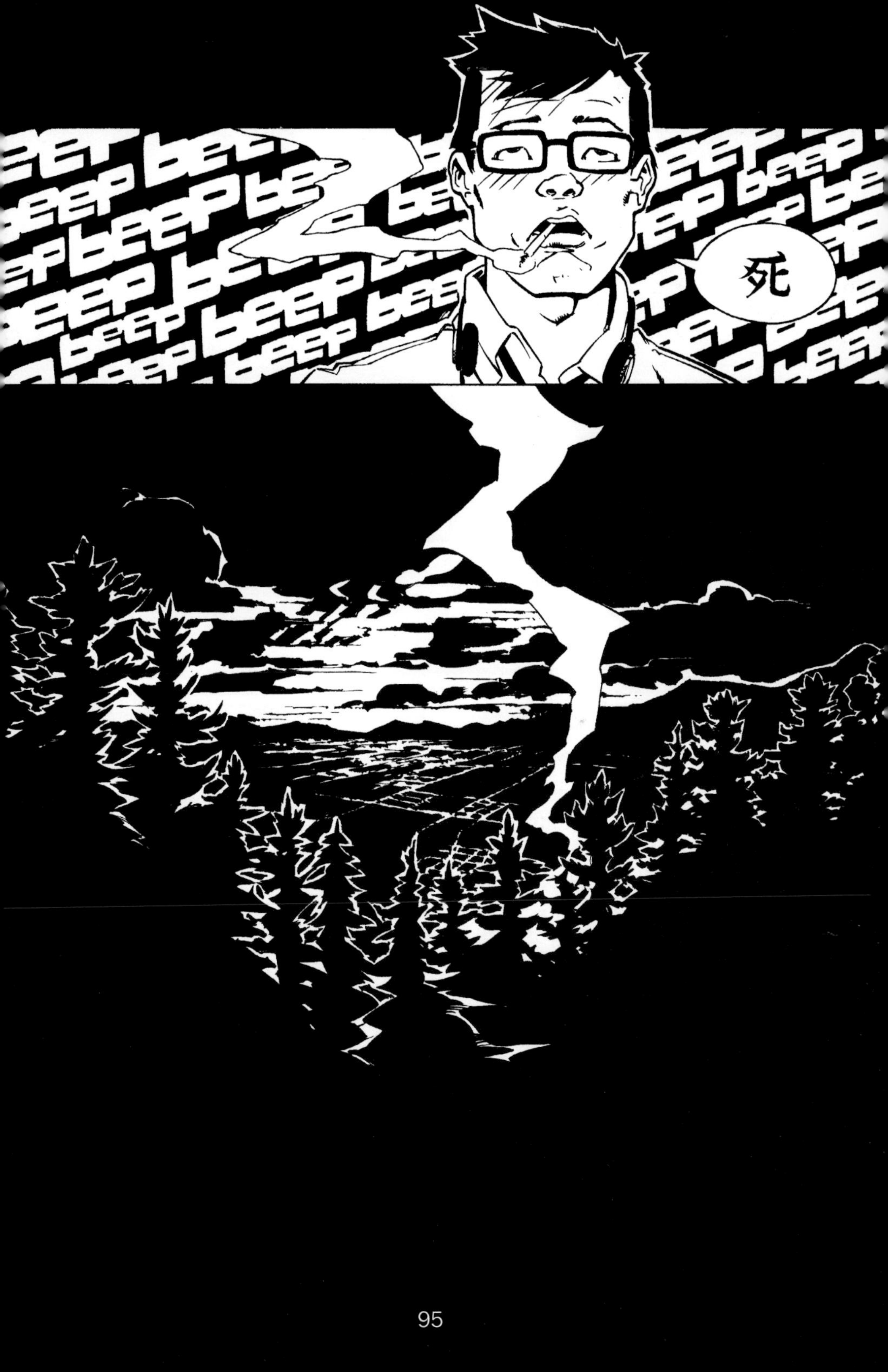
beep beep beep
死

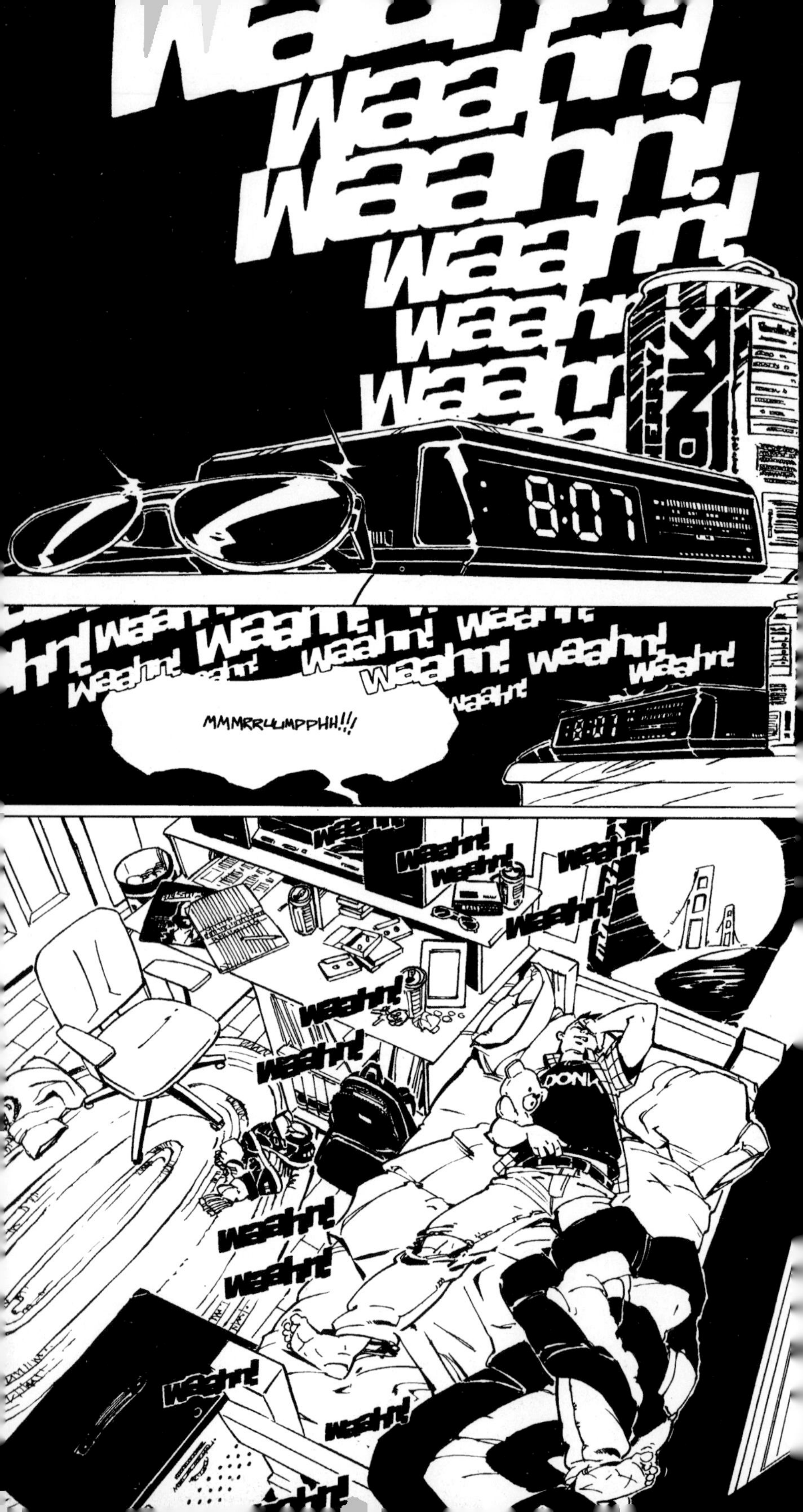
waahn!
waahn!
waahn!
waahn!
waahn!
waahn!
8:07
waahn! waahn! waahn! waahn! waahn! waahn! waahn! waahn!
MMMRRUUMPPHH!!!
8:07
waahn!
waahn!
waahn!
waahn!
waahn!
waahn!
waahn!
waahn!
waahn!
waahn!

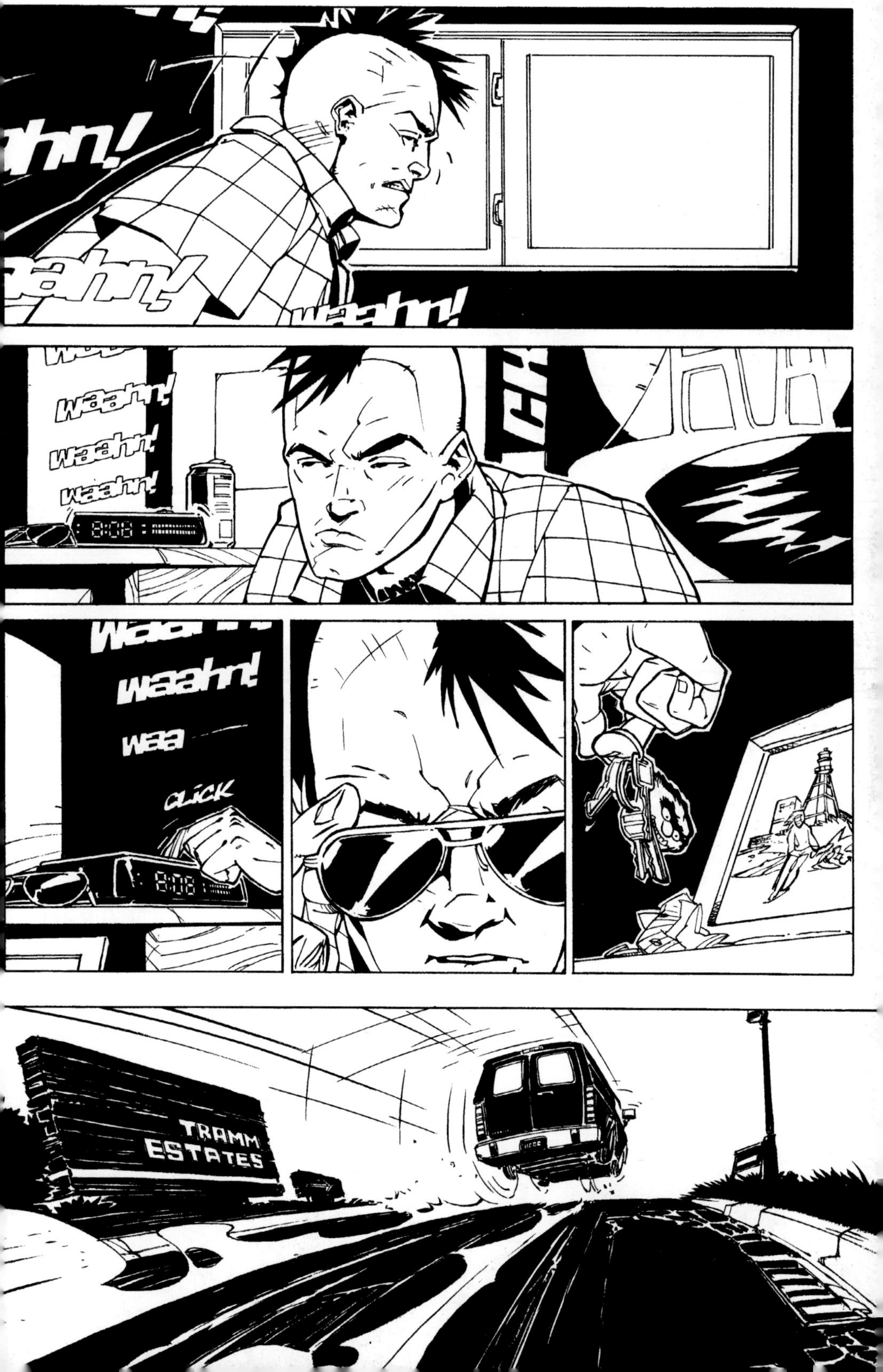

ahn!
waahn!
waahn!
waahn!
waahn!
waahn!
8:08
waahn!
waa
CLICK
8:08
TRAMM
ESTATES

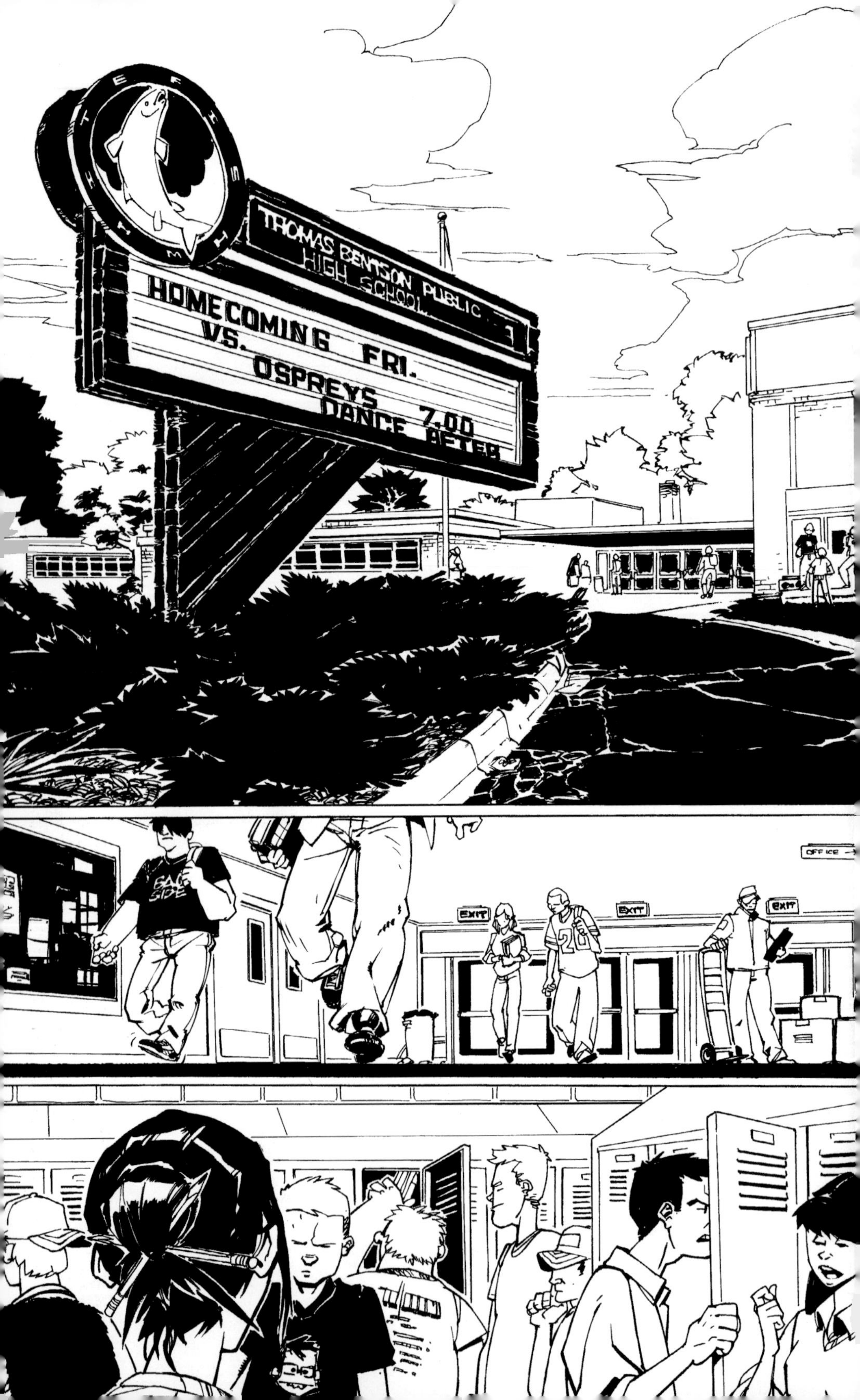

THOMAS BENTSON PUBLIC HIGH SCHOOL
HOMECOMING FRI.
VS.
OSPREYS 7.00
DANCE AFTER
OFFICE →
EXIT
EXIT
EXIT

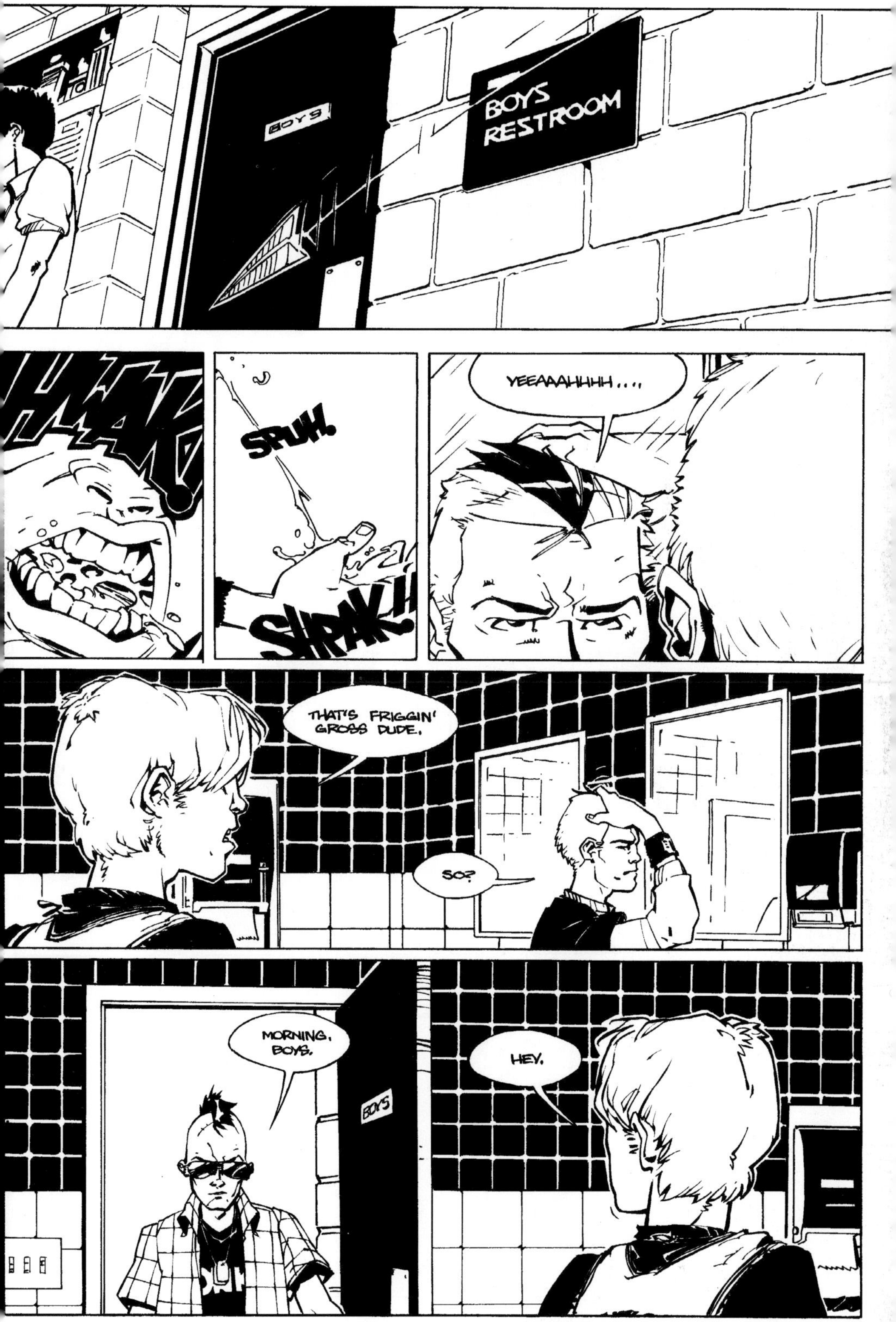
BOYS
BOYS RESTROOM
WHAK
SPUH!
SHPAK!!
YEEAAAHHHH....
THAT'S FRIGGIN' GROSS DUDE.
SO?
MORNING, BOYS.
HEY.
BOYS

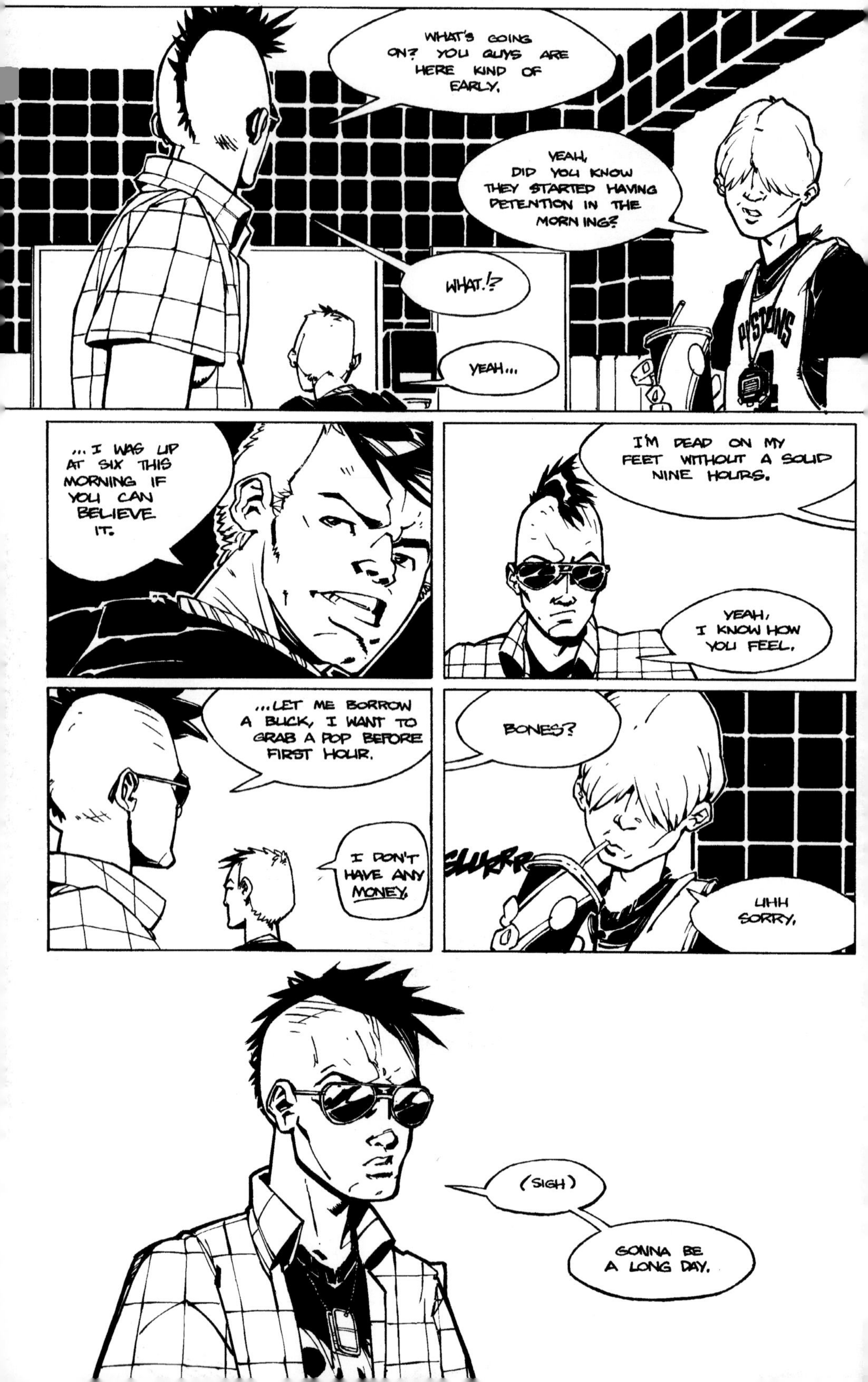
WHAT'S GOING ON? YOU GUYS ARE HERE KIND OF EARLY.
YEAH, DID YOU KNOW THEY STARTED HAVING DETENTION IN THE MORN ING?
WHAT.!?
YEAH...
PISTONS
...I WAS UP AT SIX THIS MORNING IF YOU CAN BELIEVE IT.
I'M DEAD ON MY FEET WITHOUT A SOLID NINE HOURS.
YEAH, I KNOW HOW YOU FEEL.
...LET ME BORROW A BUCK, I WANT TO GRAB A POP BEFORE FIRST HOUR.
I DON'T HAVE ANY MONEY.
BONES?
SLURRR
UHH SORRY.
(SIGH)
GONNA BE A LONG DAY.

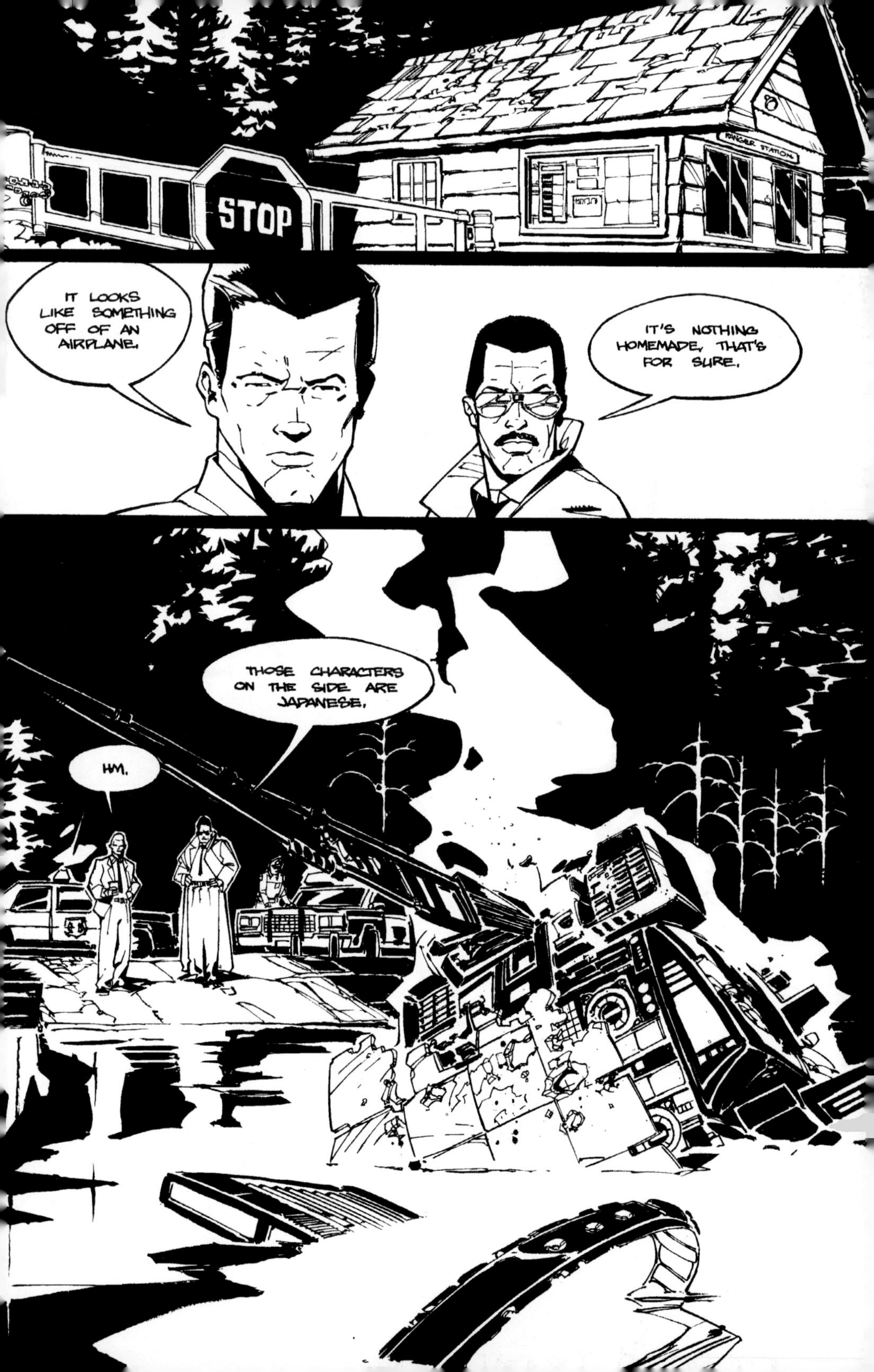
STOP
RANGER STATION
IT LOOKS LIKE SOMETHING OFF OF AN AIRPLANE.
IT'S NOTHING HOMEMADE, THAT'S FOR SURE.
HM.
THOSE CHARACTERS ON THE SIDE ARE JAPANESE.

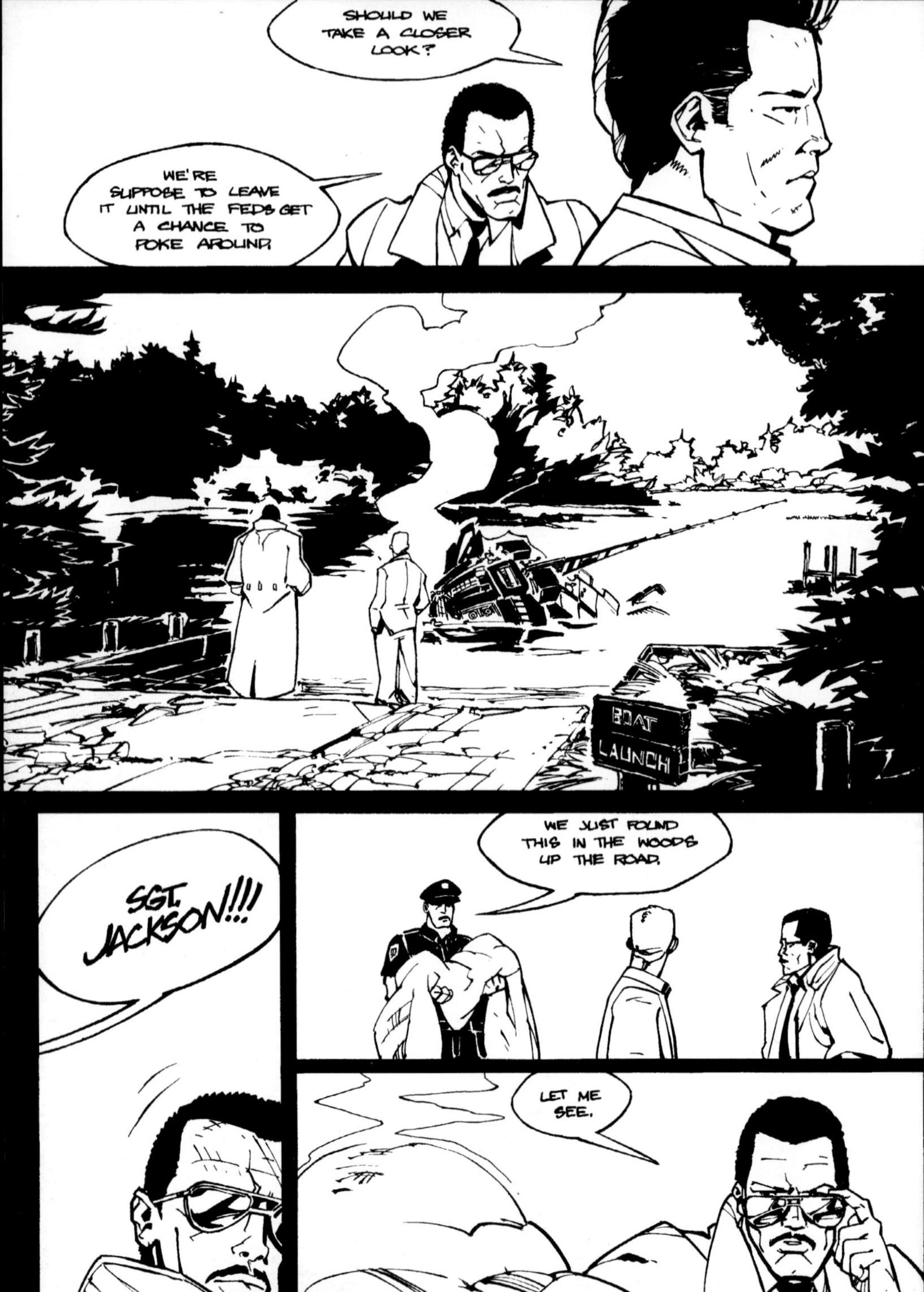
SHOULD WE TAKE A CLOSER LOOK?
WE'RE SUPPOSE TO LEAVE IT UNTIL THE FEDS GET A CHANCE TO POKE AROUND.
BOAT LAUNCH
SGT. JACKSON!!!!
WE JUST FOUND THIS IN THE WOODS UP THE ROAD.
LET ME SEE.

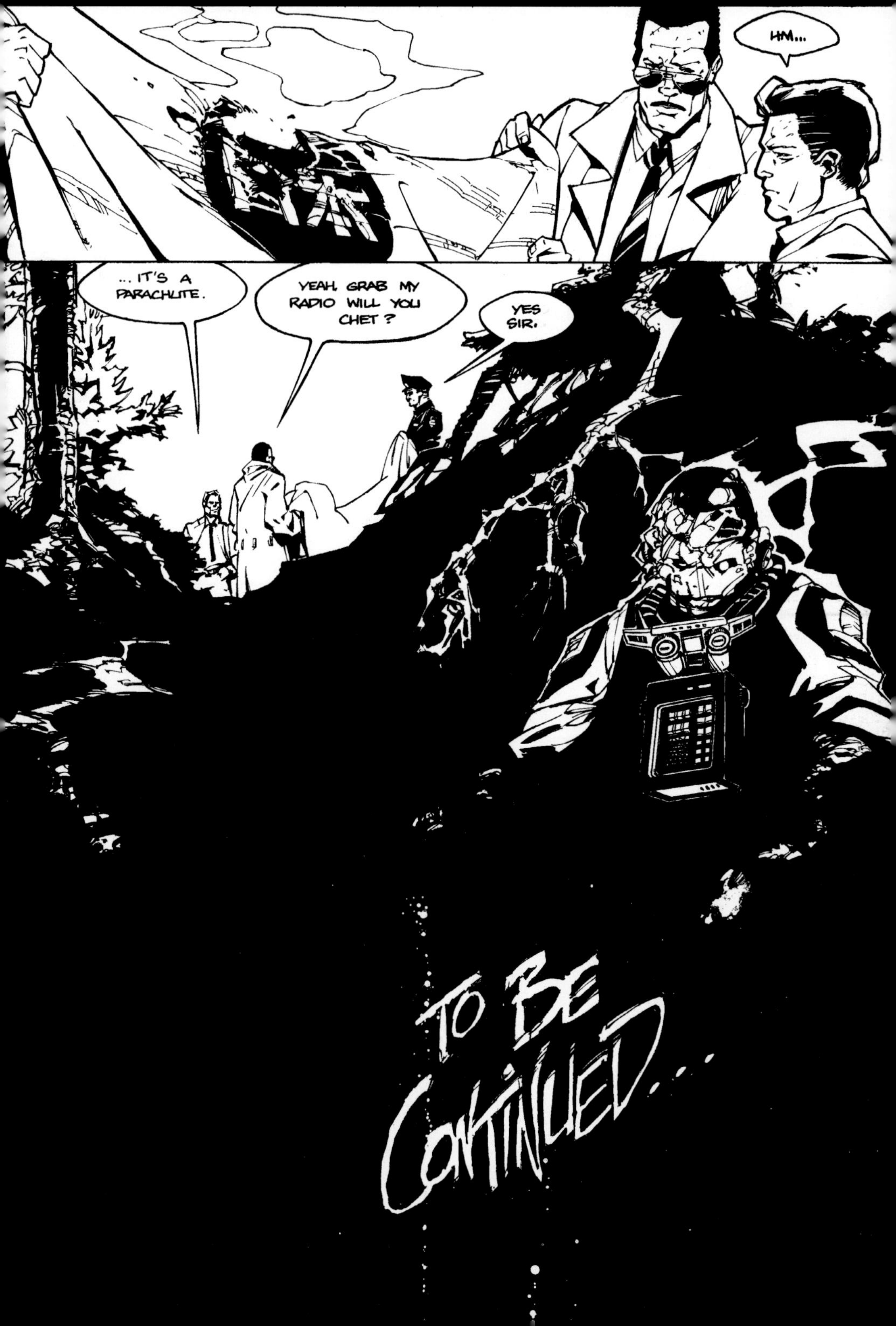
HM...
... IT'S A PARACHUTE.
YEAH, GRAB MY RADIO WILL YOU CHET ?
YES SIR.
TO BE CONTINUED...

Jacob Chabot is the creator of the generally non-despised comic "The Mighty Skullboy Army" which can be found in certain issues of *Savage Dragon*, *Marmalade* magazine, and your local The Internet. He's also done some work for those darn kids today in *Nickelodeon Magazine*'s "When Chins Collide!" special. In the future ... look for flying cars, robot housekeepers, more *Skullboy* comics, and the coming of *Space Chicken*!

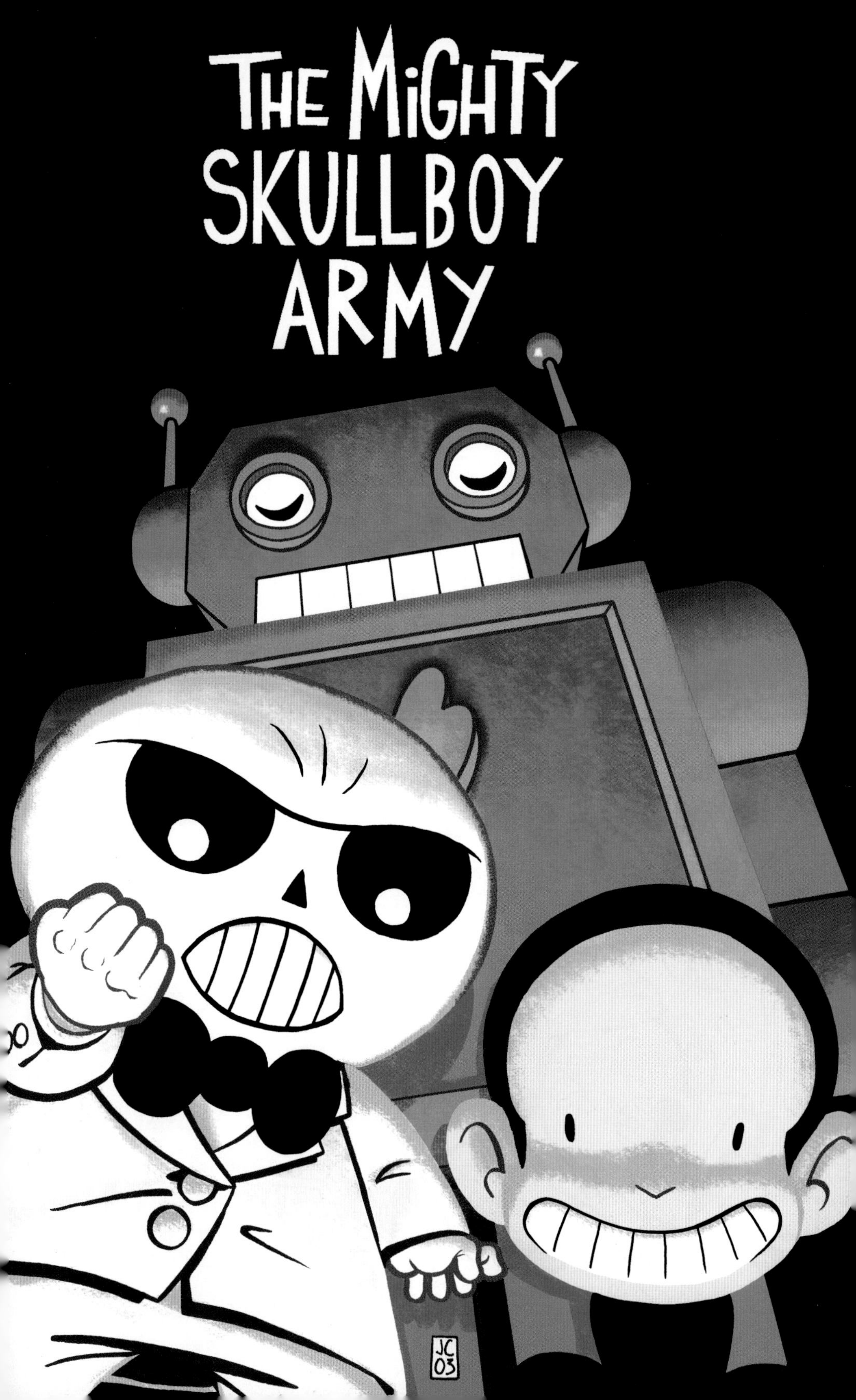
THE MIGHTY SKULLBOY ARMY
JC 03

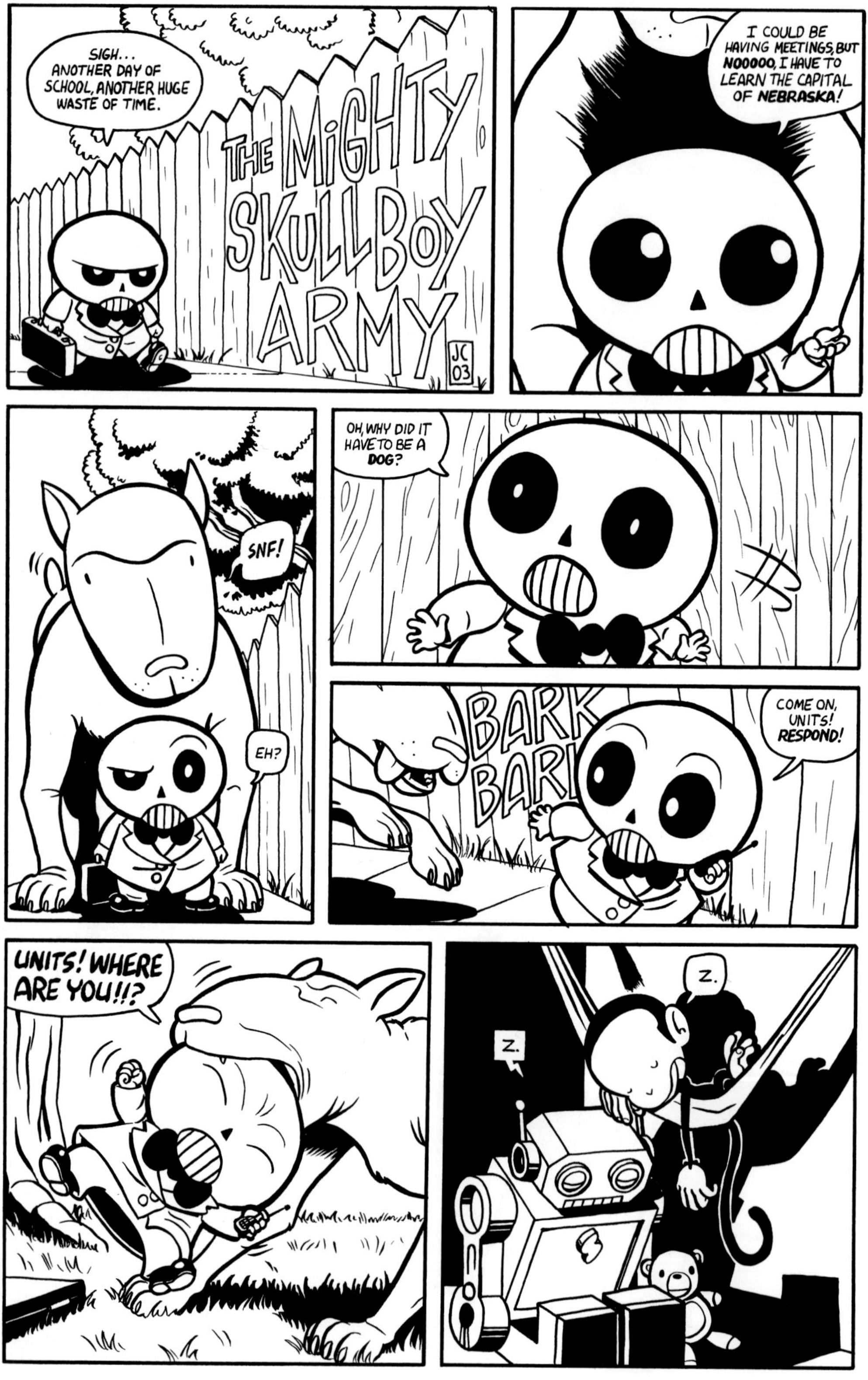
SIGH... ANOTHER DAY OF SCHOOL, ANOTHER HUGE WASTE OF TIME.
THE MIGHTY SKULLBOY ARMY
JC 03
I COULD BE HAVING MEETINGS, BUT NOOOOO, I HAVE TO LEARN THE CAPITAL OF NEBRASKA!
SNF!
EH?
OH, WHY DID IT HAVE TO BE A DOG?
BARK BARK
COME ON, UNITS! RESPOND!
UNITS! WHERE ARE YOU!!?
Z.
Z.

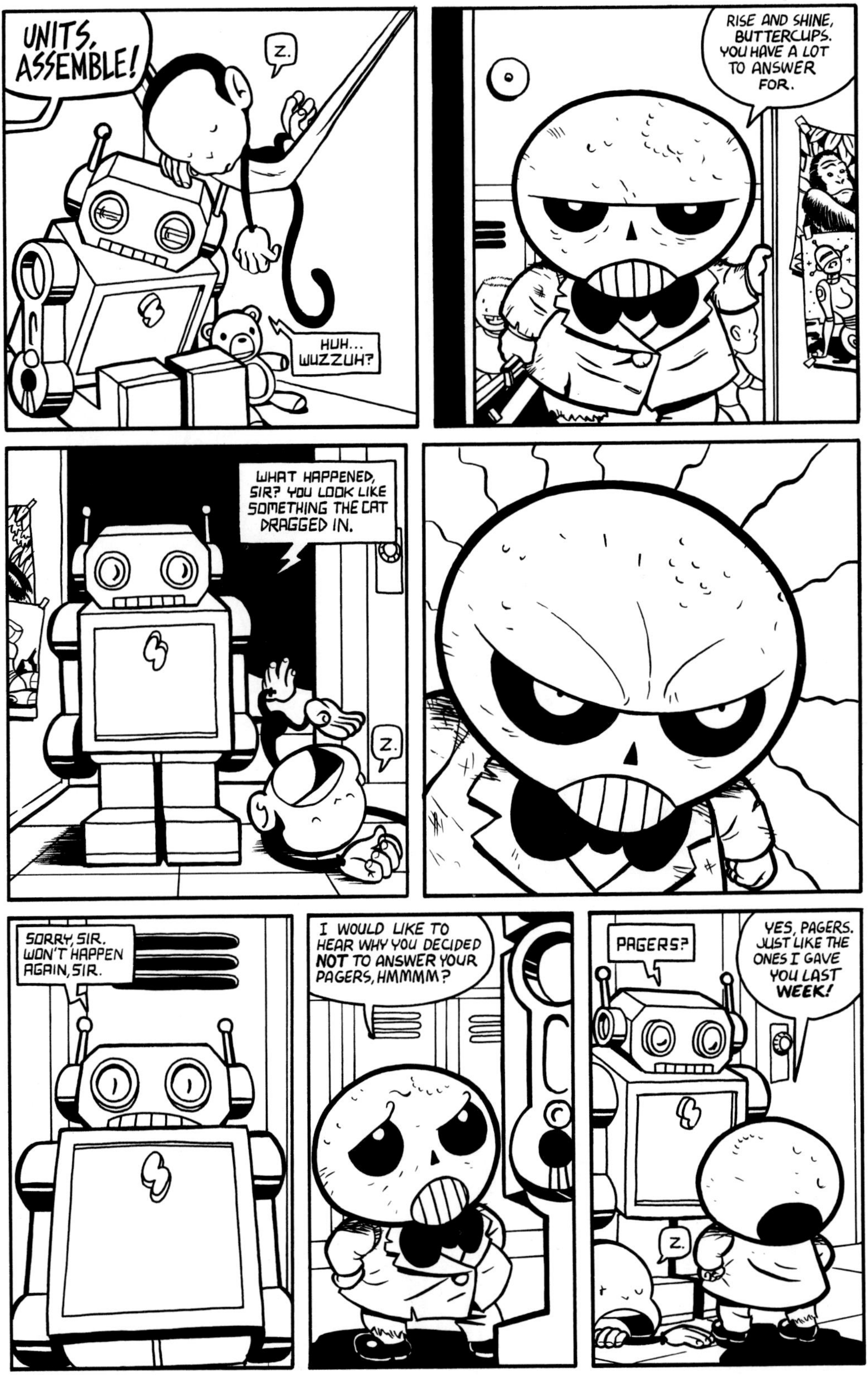
UNITS, ASSEMBLE!
Z.
HUH... WUZZUH?
RISE AND SHINE, BUTTERCUPS. YOU HAVE A LOT TO ANSWER FOR.
WHAT HAPPENED, SIR? YOU LOOK LIKE SOMETHING THE CAT DRAGGED IN.
Z.
SORRY, SIR. WON'T HAPPEN AGAIN, SIR.
I WOULD LIKE TO HEAR WHY YOU DECIDED **NOT** TO ANSWER YOUR PAGERS, HMMMM?
PAGERS?
YES, PAGERS. JUST LIKE THE ONES I GAVE YOU LAST **WEEK!**
Z.

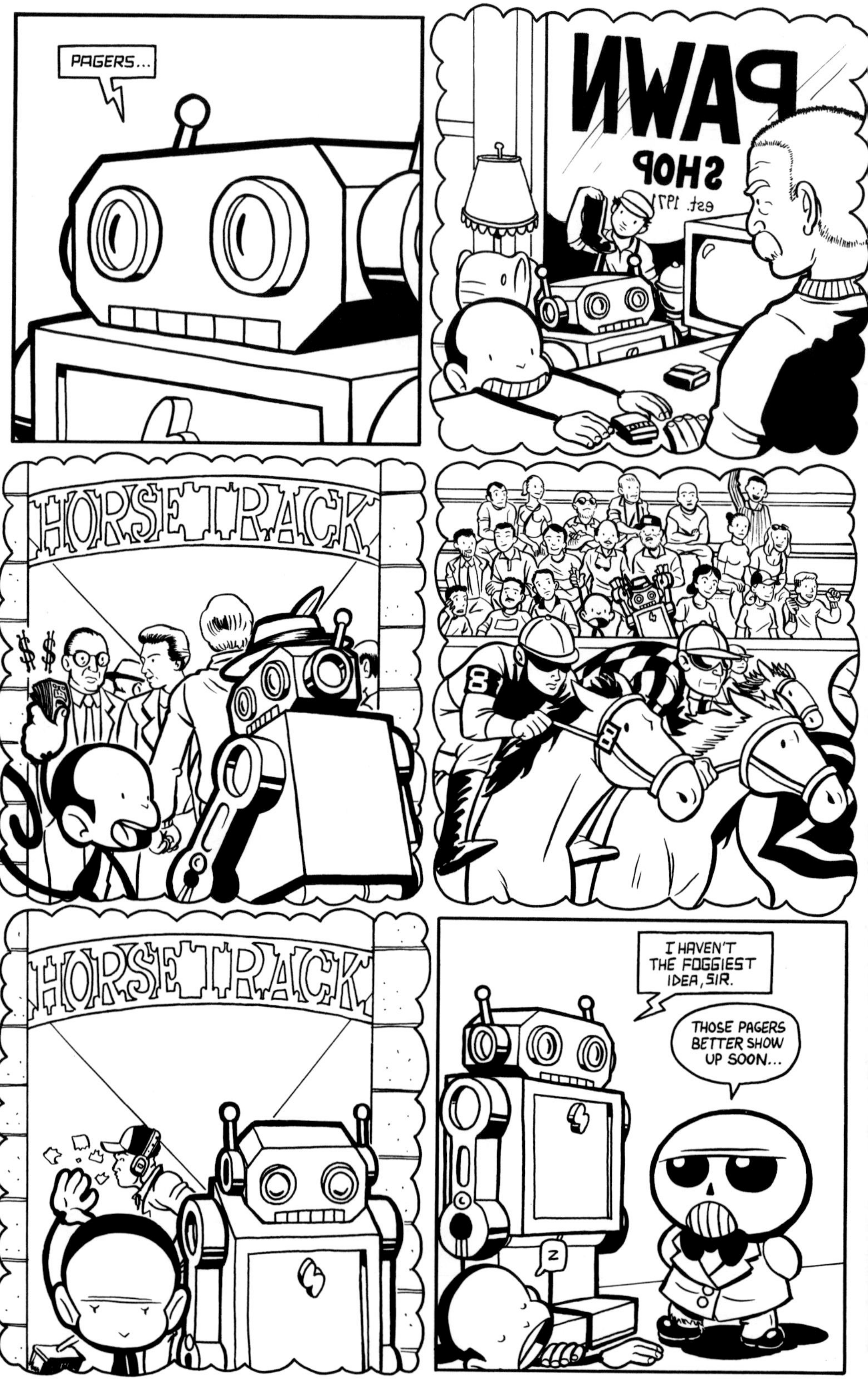
PAGERS...
PAWN SHOP
est. 1971
HORSE TRACK
HORSE TRACK
I HAVEN'T THE FOGGIEST IDEA, SIR.
THOSE PAGERS BETTER SHOW UP SOON...

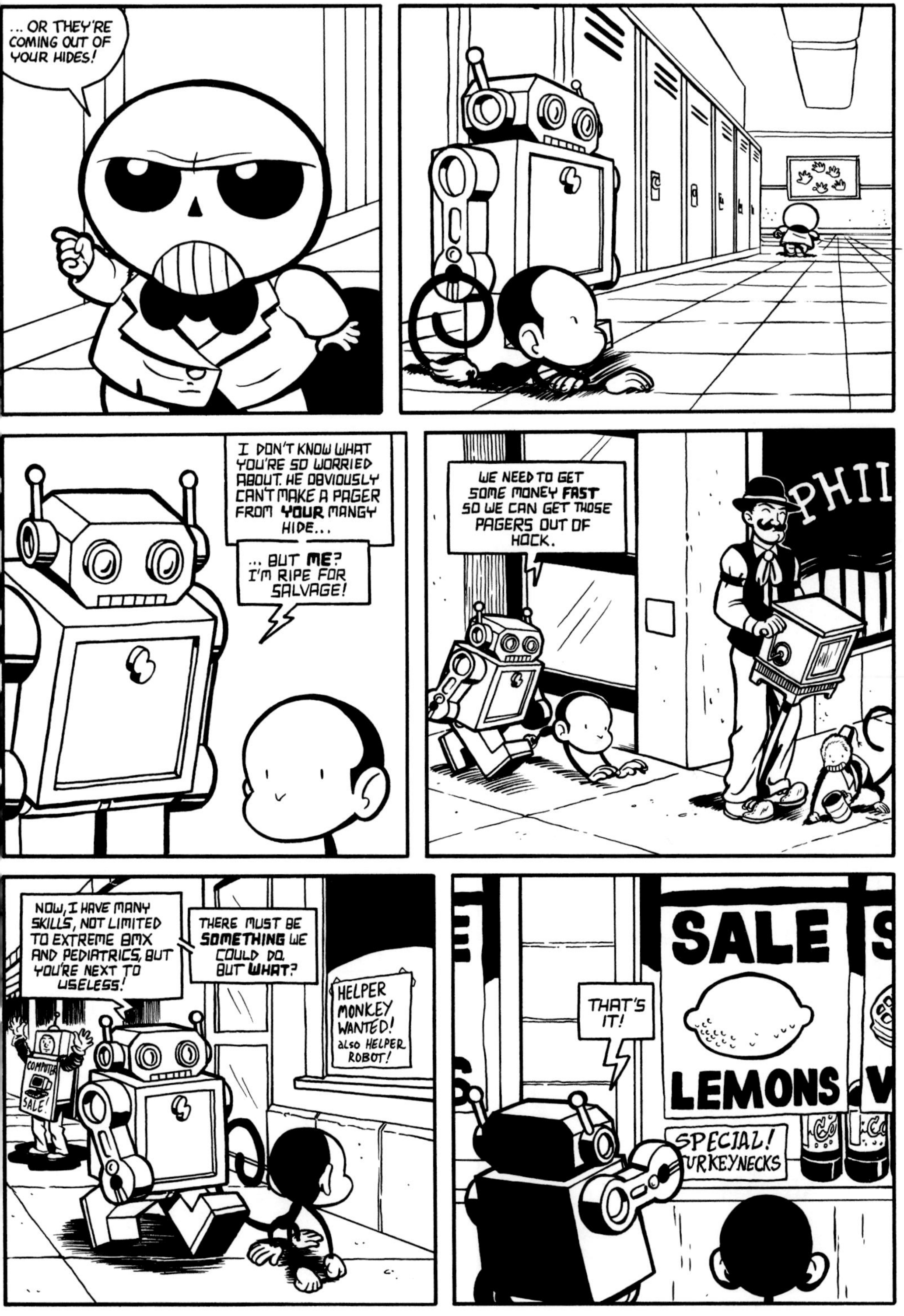
...OR THEY'RE COMING OUT OF YOUR HIDES!
I DON'T KNOW WHAT YOU'RE SO WORRIED ABOUT. HE OBVIOUSLY CAN'T MAKE A PAGER FROM YOUR MANGY HIDE...
...BUT ME? I'M RIPE FOR SALVAGE!
WE NEED TO GET SOME MONEY FAST SO WE CAN GET THOSE PAGERS OUT OF HOCK.
PHII
NOW, I HAVE MANY SKILLS, NOT LIMITED TO EXTREME BMX AND PEDIATRICS, BUT YOU'RE NEXT TO USELESS!
THERE MUST BE SOMETHING WE COULD DO. BUT WHAT?
HELPER MONKEY WANTED! also HELPER ROBOT!
COMPUTER SALE!
SALE
LEMONS
SPECIAL! TURKEYNECKS
THAT'S IT!

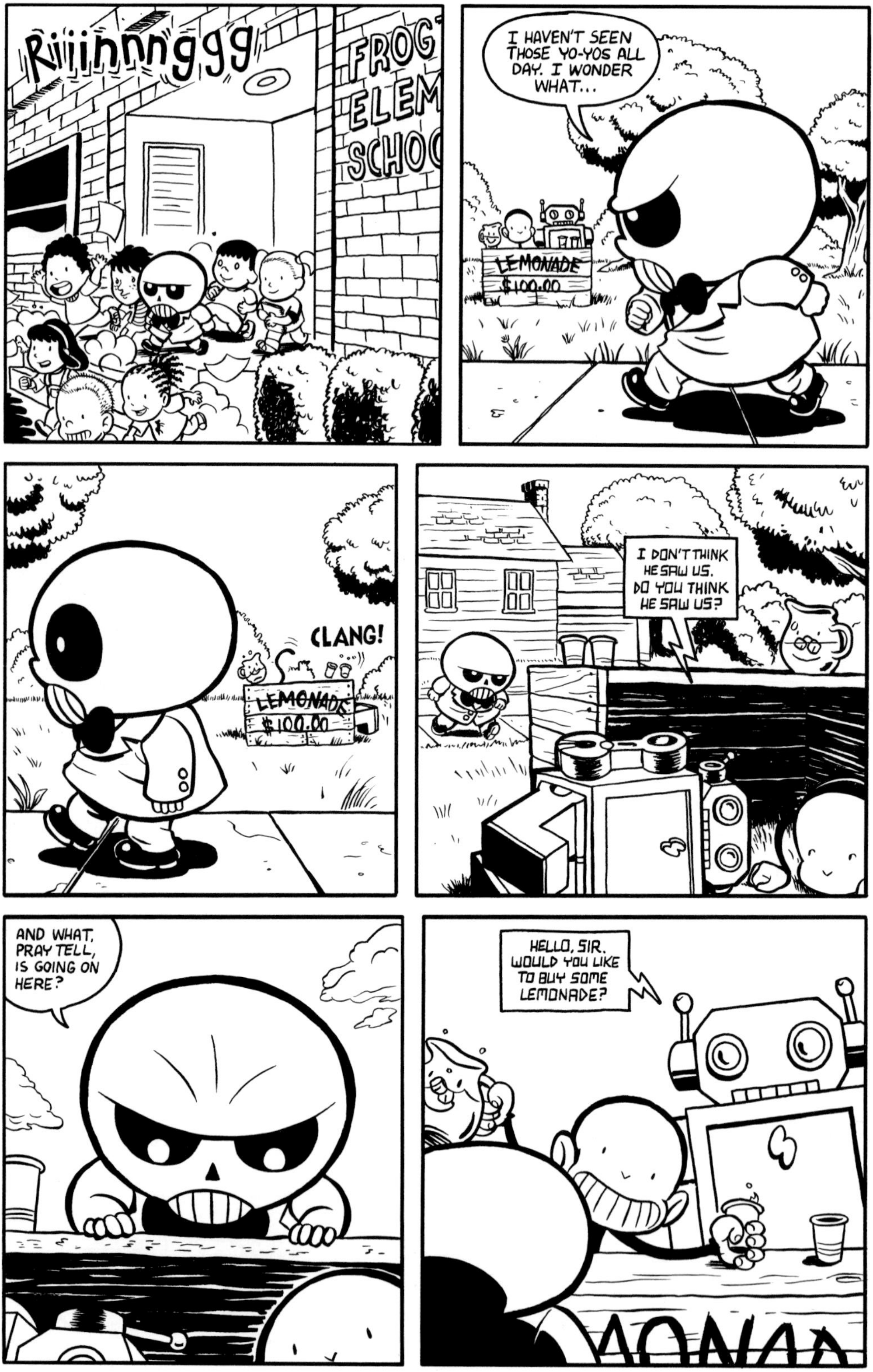
Riiinnnggg
FROG
ELEM
SCHOO
I HAVEN'T SEEN THOSE YO-YOS ALL DAY. I WONDER WHAT...
LEMONADE $100.00
CLANG!
LEMONADE $100.00
I DON'T THINK HE SAW US. DO YOU THINK HE SAW US?
AND WHAT, PRAY TELL, IS GOING ON HERE?
HELLO, SIR. WOULD YOU LIKE TO BUY SOME LEMONADE?

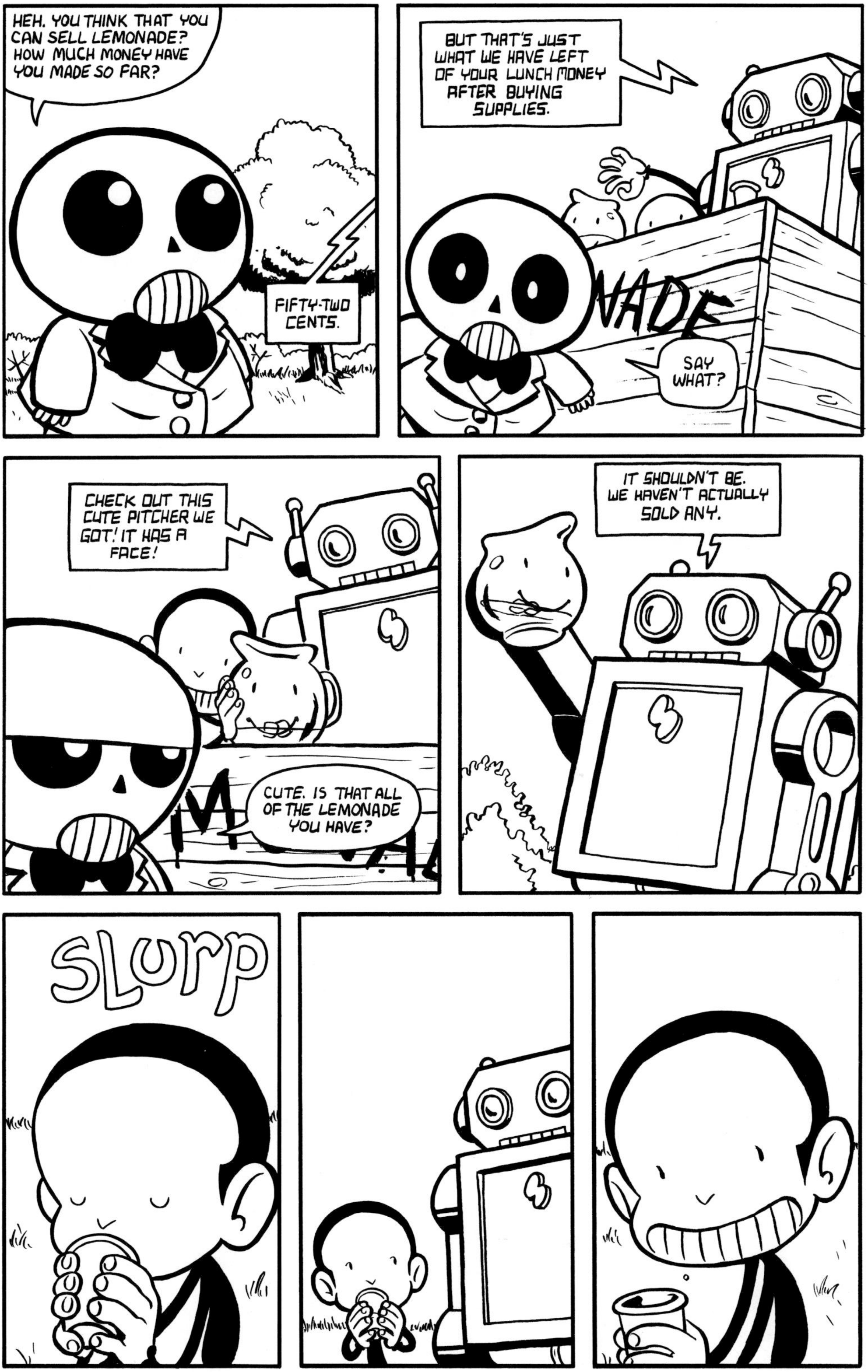
HEH. YOU THINK THAT YOU CAN SELL LEMONADE? HOW MUCH MONEY HAVE YOU MADE SO FAR?
FIFTY-TWO CENTS.
BUT THAT'S JUST WHAT WE HAVE LEFT OF YOUR LUNCH MONEY AFTER BUYING SUPPLIES.
NADE
SAY WHAT?
CHECK OUT THIS CUTE PITCHER WE GOT! IT HAS A FACE!
CUTE. IS THAT ALL OF THE LEMONADE YOU HAVE?
IT SHOULDN'T BE. WE HAVEN'T ACTUALLY SOLD ANY.
SLURP

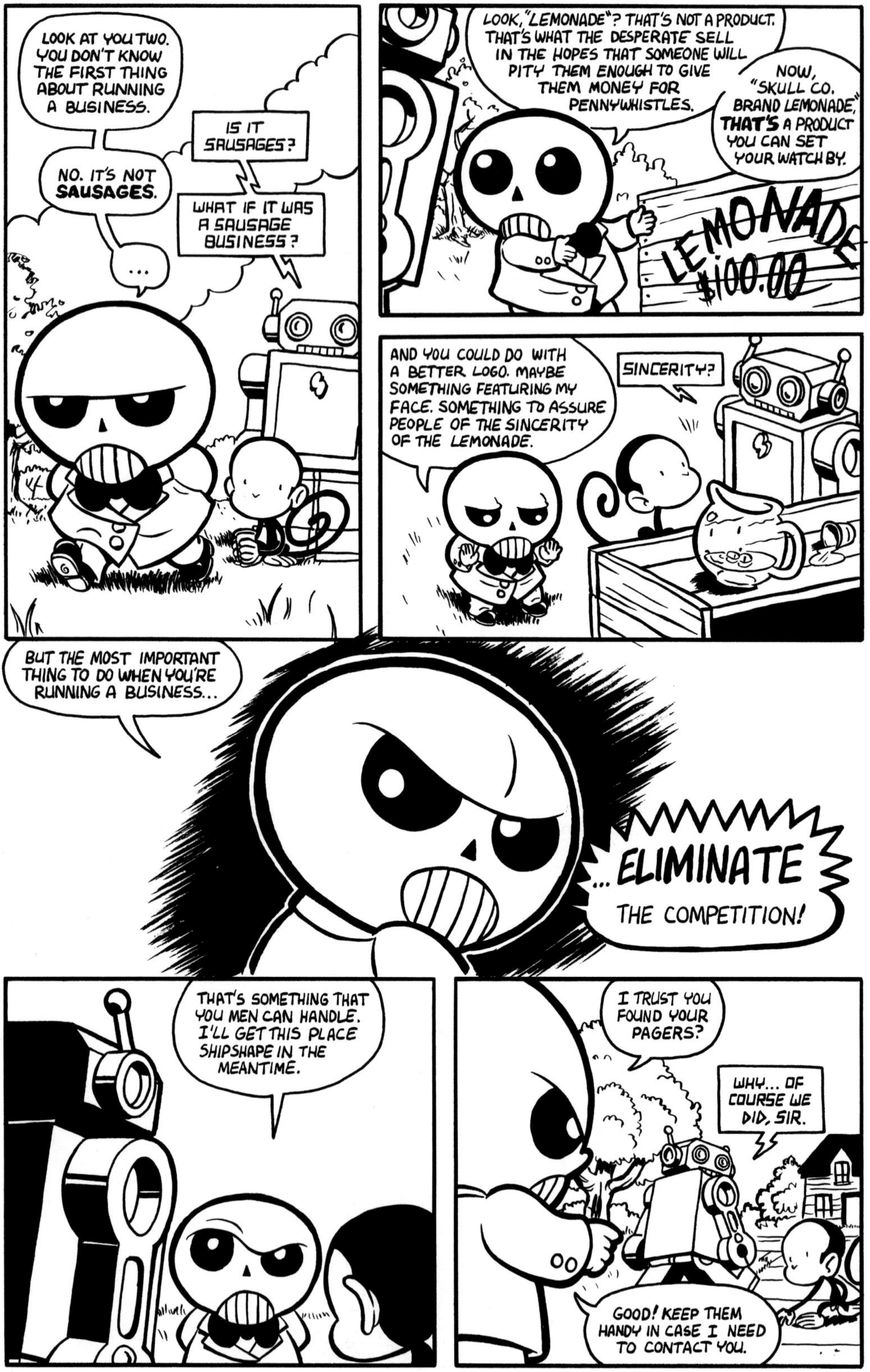
LOOK AT YOU TWO. YOU DON'T KNOW THE FIRST THING ABOUT RUNNING A BUSINESS.
IS IT SAUSAGES?
NO. IT'S NOT **SAUSAGES**.
WHAT IF IT WAS A SAUSAGE BUSINESS?
...
LOOK, "LEMONADE"? THAT'S NOT A PRODUCT. THAT'S WHAT THE DESPERATE SELL IN THE HOPES THAT SOMEONE WILL PITY THEM ENOUGH TO GIVE THEM MONEY FOR PENNYWHISTLES.
NOW, "SKULL CO. BRAND LEMONADE," **THAT'S** A PRODUCT YOU CAN SET YOUR WATCH BY.
LEMONADE
$100.00
AND YOU COULD DO WITH A BETTER LOGO. MAYBE SOMETHING FEATURING MY FACE. SOMETHING TO ASSURE PEOPLE OF THE SINCERITY OF THE LEMONADE.
SINCERITY?
BUT THE MOST IMPORTANT THING TO DO WHEN YOU'RE RUNNING A BUSINESS...
...ELIMINATE THE COMPETITION!
THAT'S SOMETHING THAT YOU MEN CAN HANDLE. I'LL GET THIS PLACE SHIPSHAPE IN THE MEANTIME.
I TRUST YOU FOUND YOUR PAGERS?
WHY... OF COURSE WE DID, SIR.
GOOD! KEEP THEM HANDY IN CASE I NEED TO CONTACT YOU.

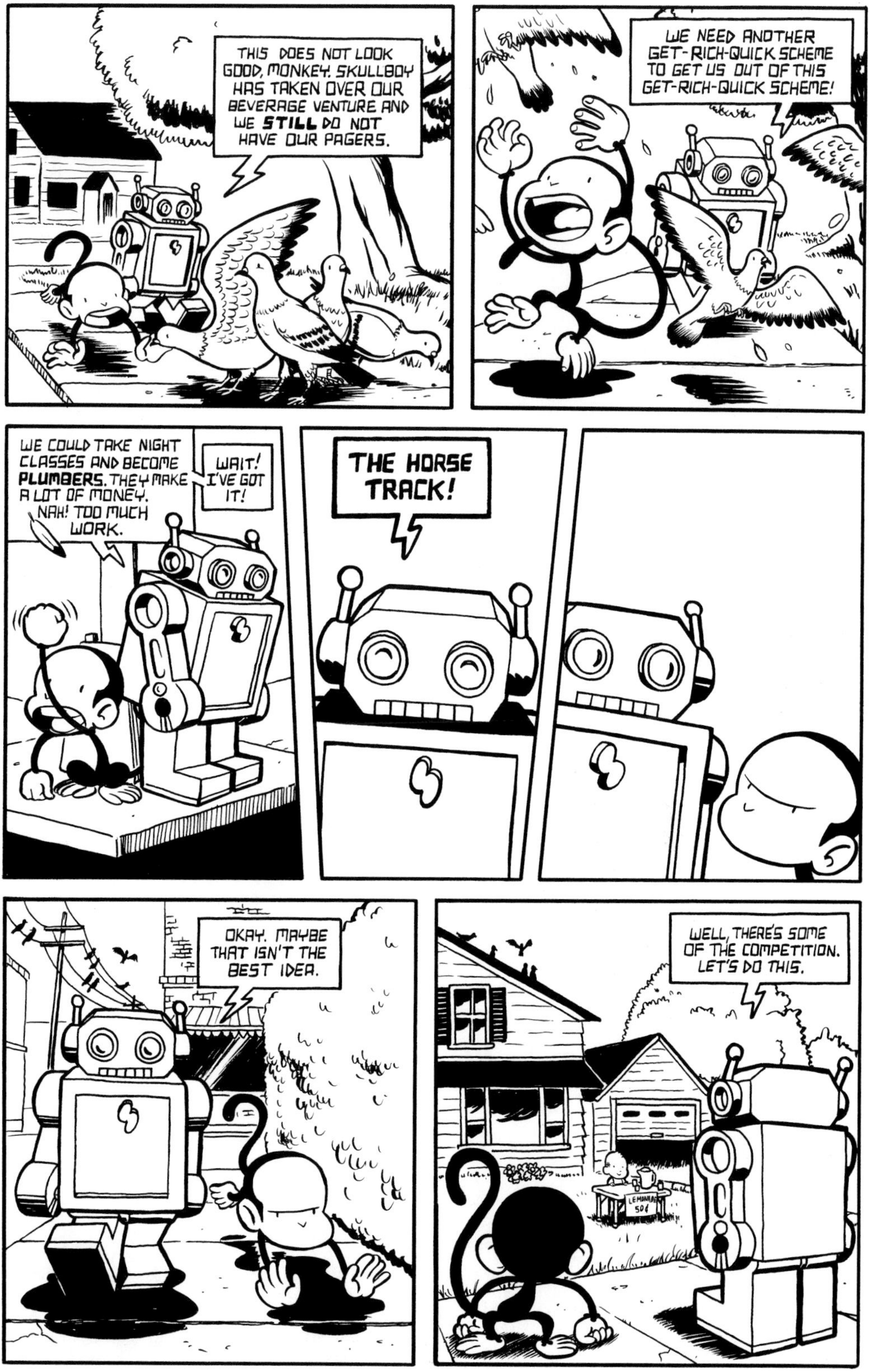
THIS DOES NOT LOOK GOOD, MONKEY. SKULLBOY HAS TAKEN OVER OUR BEVERAGE VENTURE AND WE STILL DO NOT HAVE OUR PAGERS.
WE NEED ANOTHER GET-RICH-QUICK SCHEME TO GET US OUT OF THIS GET-RICH-QUICK SCHEME!
WE COULD TAKE NIGHT CLASSES AND BECOME PLUMBERS. THEY MAKE A LOT OF MONEY. NAH! TOO MUCH WORK.
WAIT! I'VE GOT IT!
THE HORSE TRACK!
OKAY. MAYBE THAT ISN'T THE BEST IDEA.
WELL, THERE'S SOME OF THE COMPETITION. LET'S DO THIS.

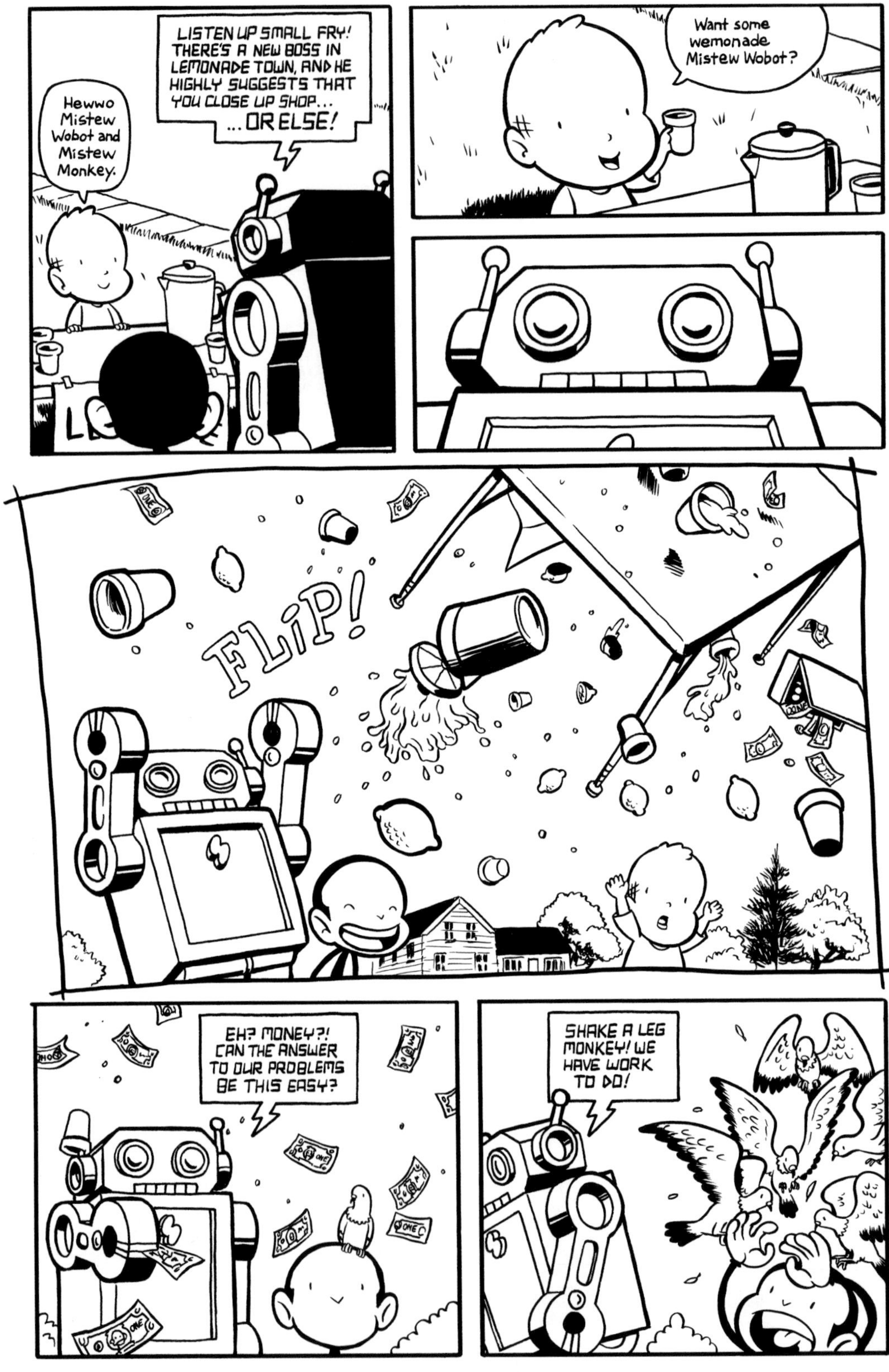
Hewwo Mistew Wobot and Mistew Monkey.
LISTEN UP SMALL FRY! THERE'S A NEW BOSS IN LEMONADE TOWN, AND HE HIGHLY SUGGESTS THAT YOU CLOSE UP SHOP... ...OR ELSE!
Want some wemonade Mistew Wobot?
FLIP!
EH? MONEY?! CAN THE ANSWER TO OUR PROBLEMS BE THIS EASY?
SHAKE A LEG MONKEY! WE HAVE WORK TO DO!

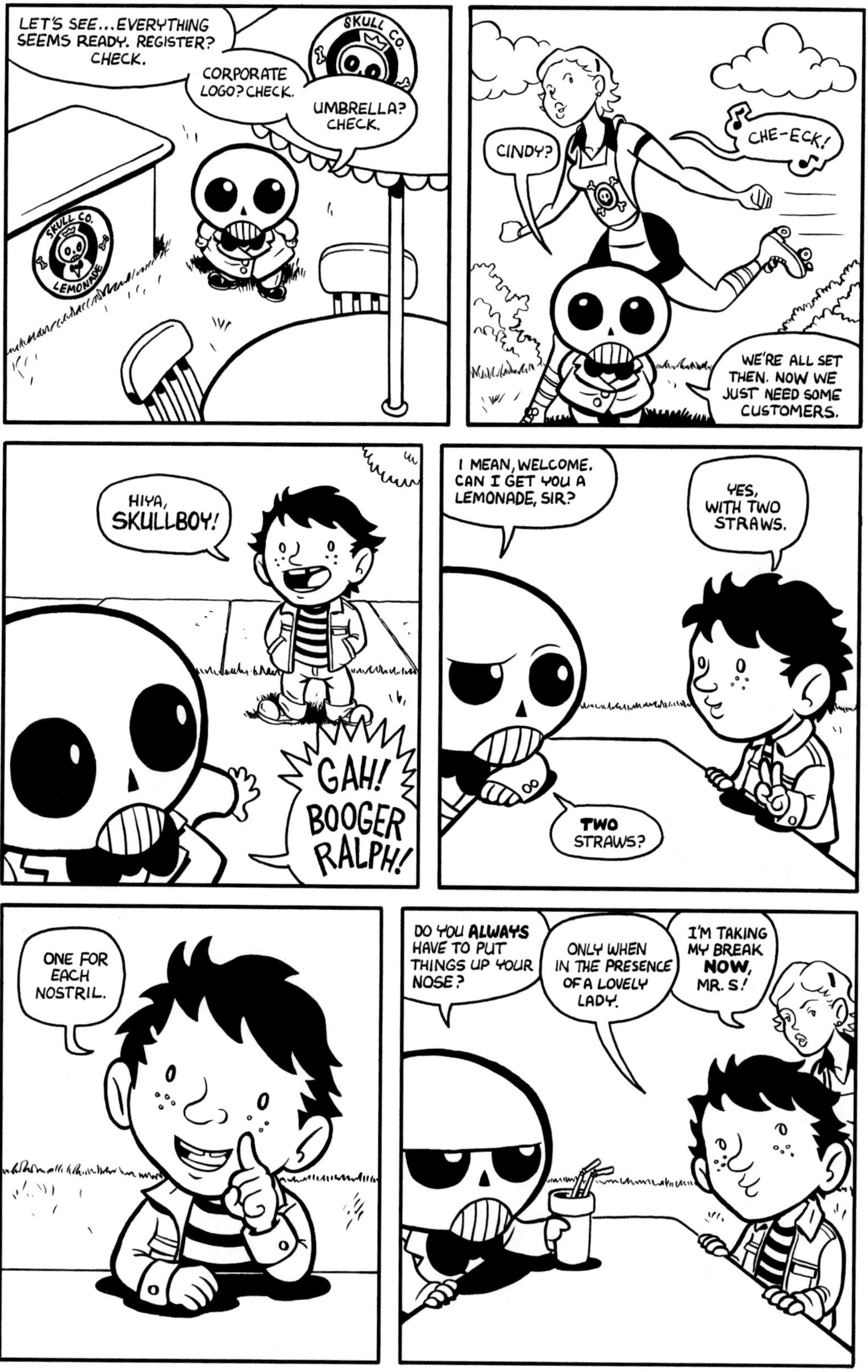

LET'S SEE...EVERYTHING SEEMS READY. REGISTER? CHECK.
SKULL CO.
CORPORATE LOGO? CHECK.
UMBRELLA? CHECK.
SKULL CO. LEMONADE
CINDY?
CHE-ECK!
WE'RE ALL SET THEN. NOW WE JUST NEED SOME CUSTOMERS.
HIYA, SKULLBOY!
GAH! BOOGER RALPH!
I MEAN, WELCOME. CAN I GET YOU A LEMONADE, SIR?
YES, WITH TWO STRAWS.
TWO STRAWS?
ONE FOR EACH NOSTRIL.
DO YOU ALWAYS HAVE TO PUT THINGS UP YOUR NOSE?
ONLY WHEN IN THE PRESENCE OF A LOVELY LADY.
I'M TAKING MY BREAK NOW, MR. S!

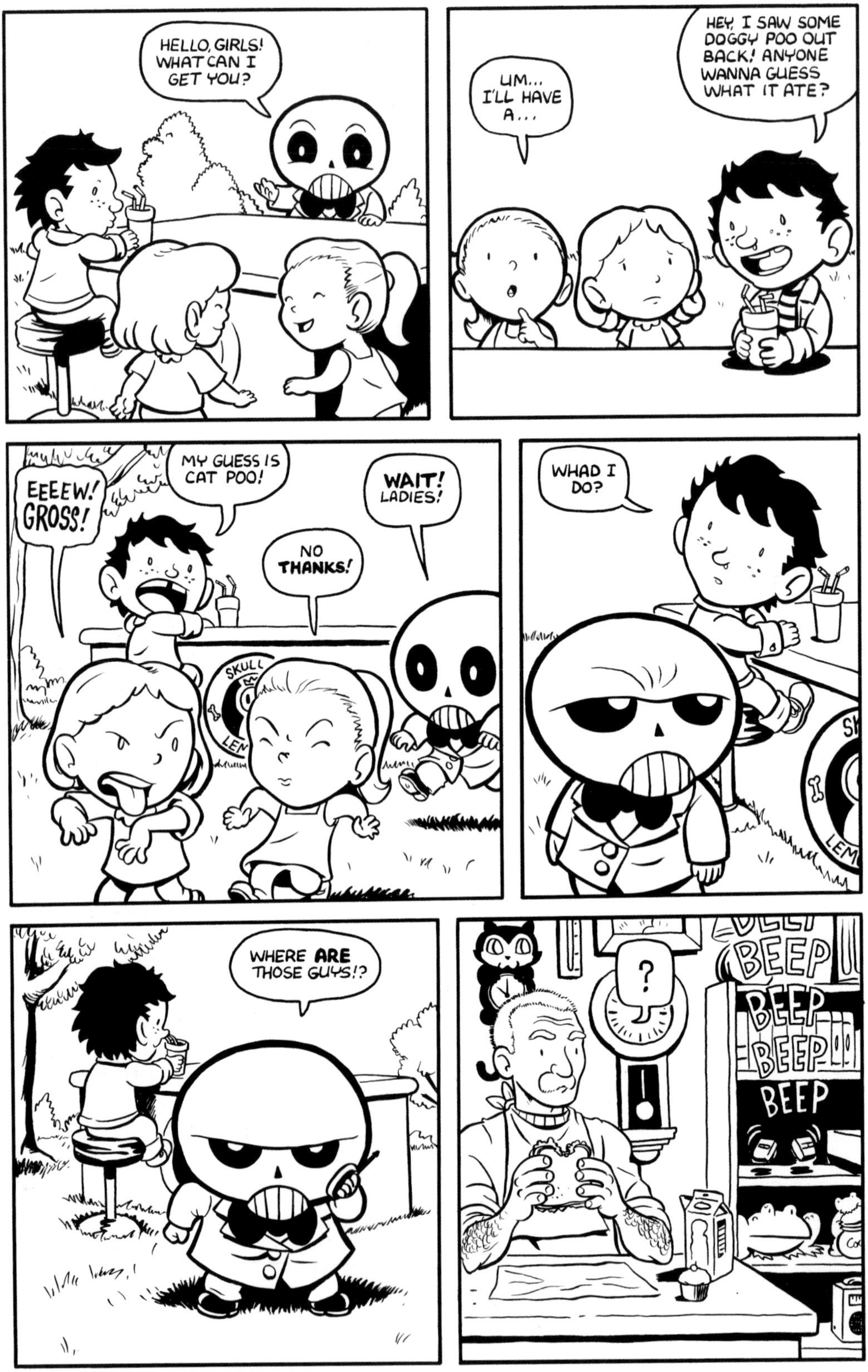
HELLO, GIRLS! WHAT CAN I GET YOU?
UM... I'LL HAVE A...
HEY, I SAW SOME DOGGY POO OUT BACK! ANYONE WANNA GUESS WHAT IT ATE?
EEEEW! GROSS!
MY GUESS IS CAT POO!
NO THANKS!
WAIT! LADIES!
SKULL
LEM
WHAD I DO?
WHERE ARE THOSE GUYS!?
?
BEEP
BEEP
BEEP
BEEP

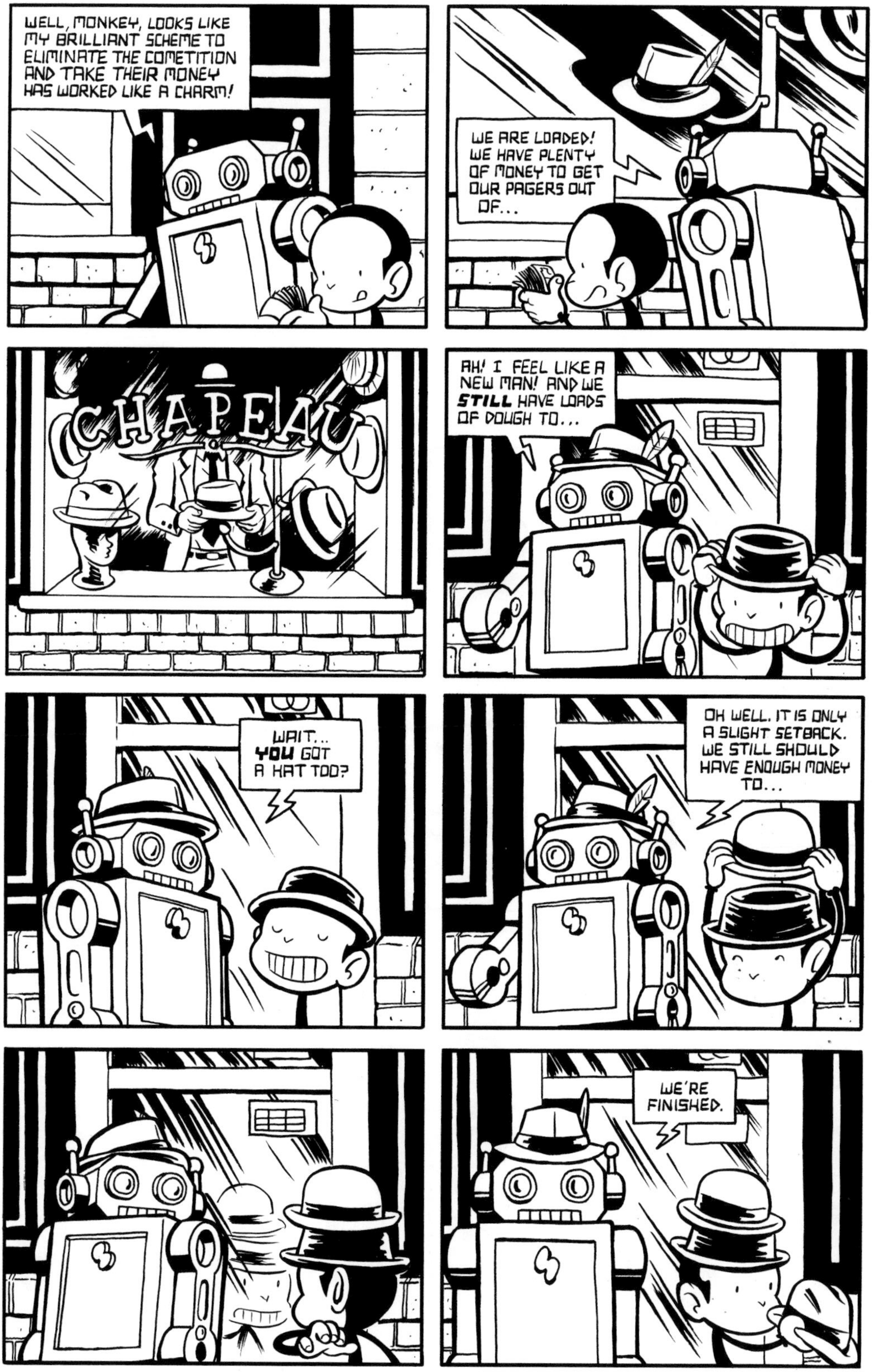
WELL, MONKEY, LOOKS LIKE MY BRILLIANT SCHEME TO ELIMINATE THE COMETITION AND TAKE THEIR MONEY HAS WORKED LIKE A CHARM!
WE ARE LOADED! WE HAVE PLENTY OF MONEY TO GET OUR PAGERS OUT OF...
CHAPEAU
AH! I FEEL LIKE A NEW MAN! AND WE STILL HAVE LOADS OF DOUGH TO...
WAIT... YOU GOT A HAT TOO?
OH WELL. IT IS ONLY A SLIGHT SETBACK. WE STILL SHOULD HAVE ENOUGH MONEY TO...
WE'RE FINISHED.

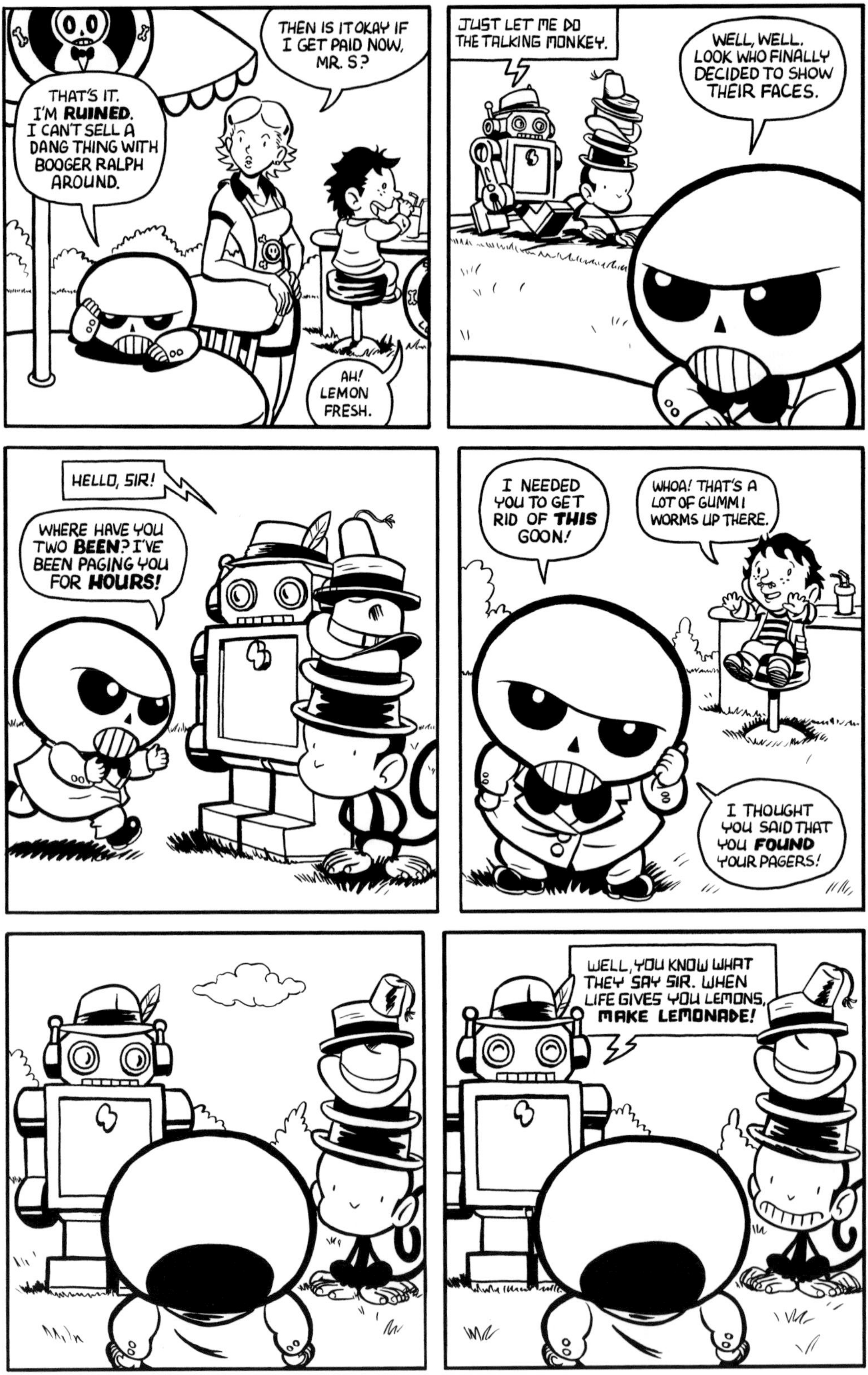
THAT'S IT. I'M RUINED. I CAN'T SELL A DANG THING WITH BOOGER RALPH AROUND.
THEN IS IT OKAY IF I GET PAID NOW, MR. S?
AH! LEMON FRESH.
JUST LET ME DO THE TALKING MONKEY.
WELL, WELL. LOOK WHO FINALLY DECIDED TO SHOW THEIR FACES.
HELLO, SIR!
WHERE HAVE YOU TWO BEEN? I'VE BEEN PAGING YOU FOR HOURS!
I NEEDED YOU TO GET RID OF THIS GOON!
WHOA! THAT'S A LOT OF GUMMI WORMS UP THERE.
I THOUGHT YOU SAID THAT YOU FOUND YOUR PAGERS!
WELL, YOU KNOW WHAT THEY SAY SIR. WHEN LIFE GIVES YOU LEMONS, MAKE LEMONADE!

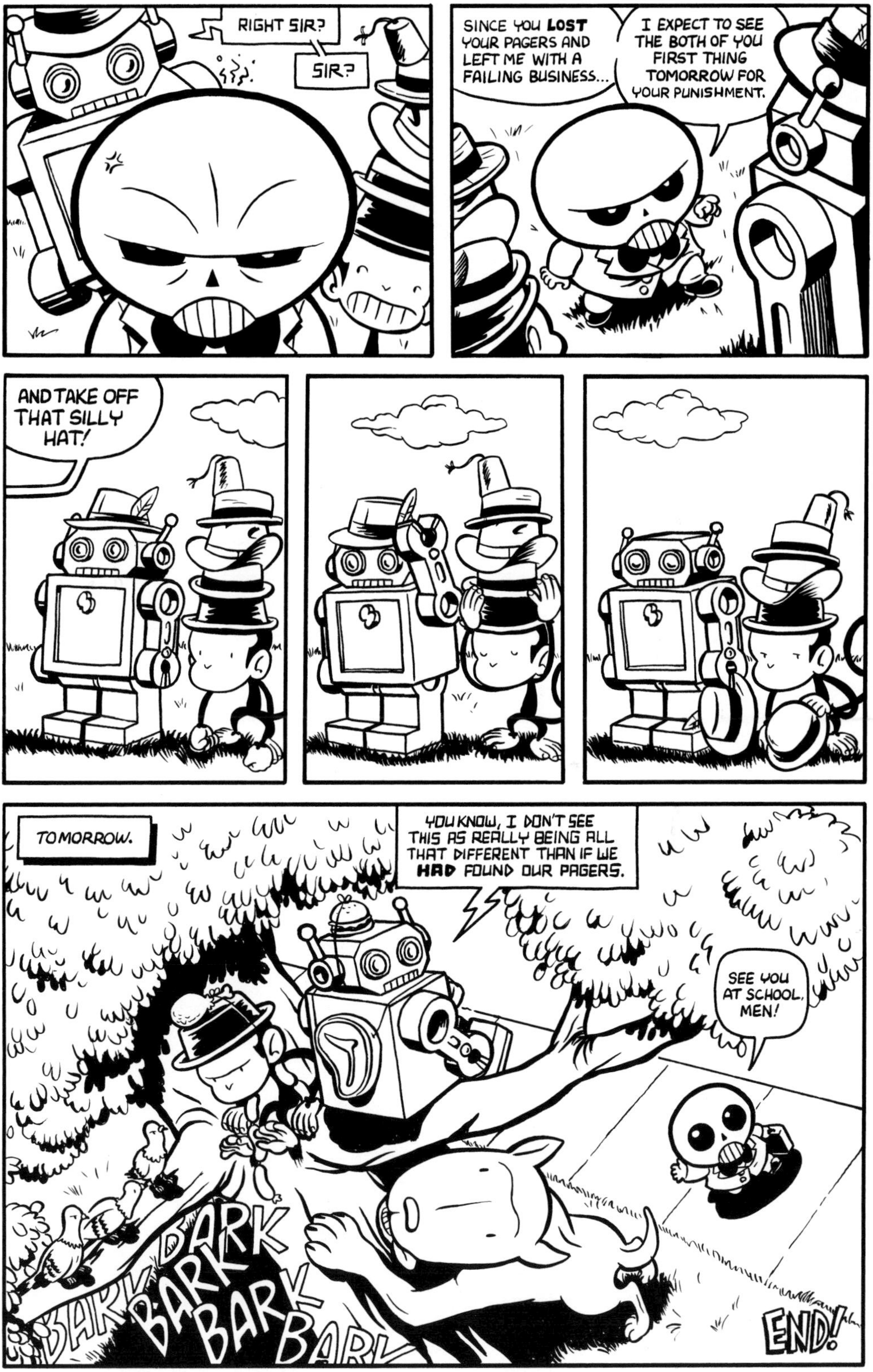
RIGHT SIR?
SIR?
SINCE YOU LOST YOUR PAGERS AND LEFT ME WITH A FAILING BUSINESS...
I EXPECT TO SEE THE BOTH OF YOU FIRST THING TOMORROW FOR YOUR PUNISHMENT.
AND TAKE OFF THAT SILLY HAT!
TOMORROW.
YOU KNOW, I DON'T SEE THIS AS REALLY BEING ALL THAT DIFFERENT THAN IF WE HAD FOUND OUR PAGERS.
SEE YOU AT SCHOOL, MEN!
BARK BARK BARK BARK BARK
END!

In the early stages of the development of this anthology, **I. N. J. Culbard** and the editor of this book found they had something in common: a love of zombies.

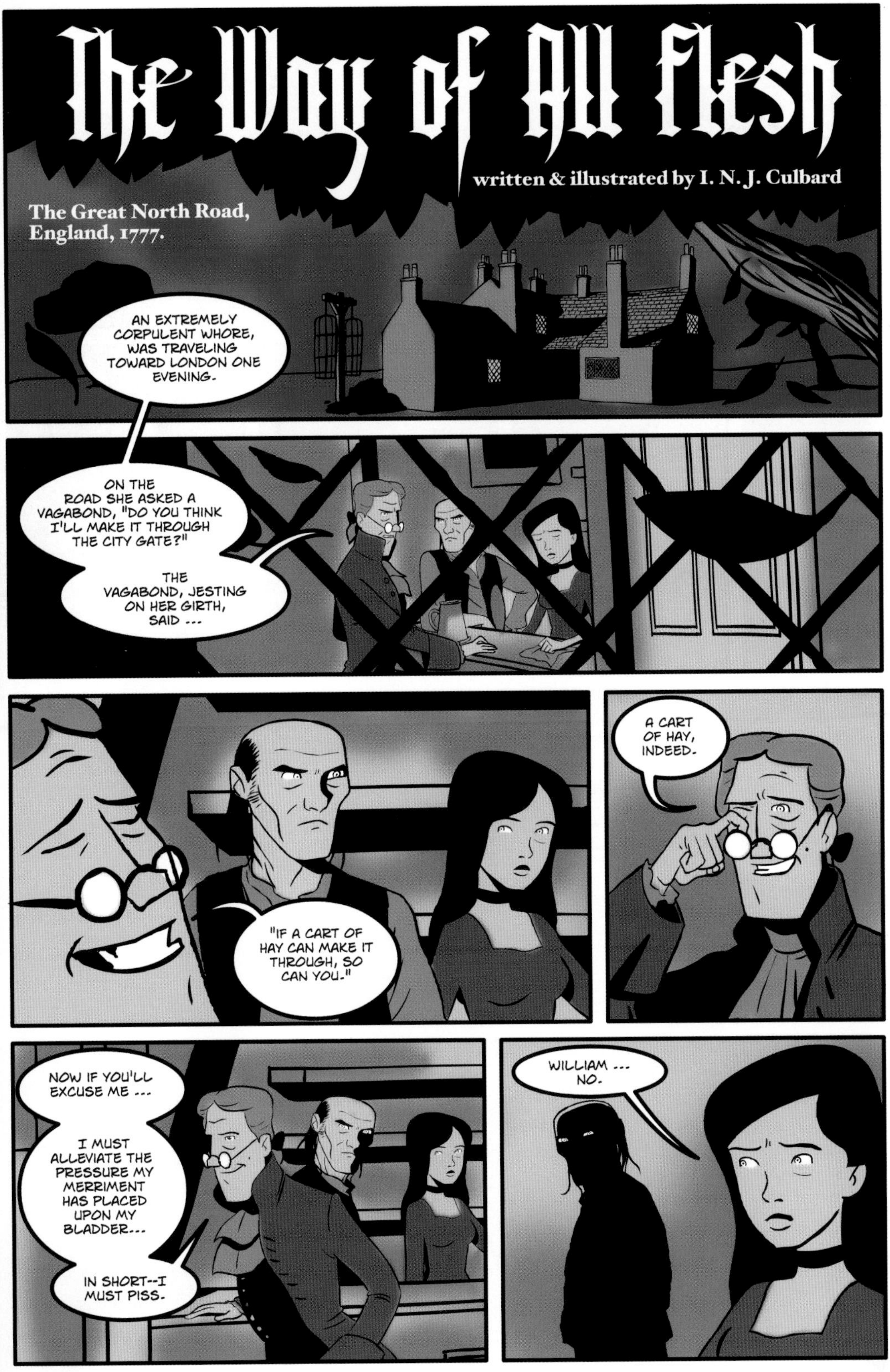
The Way of All Flesh
written & illustrated by I. N. J. Culbard
The Great North Road, England, 1777.
AN EXTREMELY CORPULENT WHORE, WAS TRAVELING TOWARD LONDON ONE EVENING.
ON THE ROAD SHE ASKED A VAGABOND, "DO YOU THINK I'LL MAKE IT THROUGH THE CITY GATE?"
THE VAGABOND, JESTING ON HER GIRTH, SAID ...
"IF A CART OF HAY CAN MAKE IT THROUGH, SO CAN YOU."
A CART OF HAY, INDEED.
NOW IF YOU'LL EXCUSE ME ...
I MUST ALLEVIATE THE PRESSURE MY MERRIMENT HAS PLACED UPON MY BLADDER...
IN SHORT--I MUST PISS.
WILLIAM ... NO.

PLEASE ...
THE BOYS,
THEY'LL HEAR
LIKE THEY DID
LAST TIME ...
PLEASE.

HARLOT!

HELLO?

YOU
TRAVELERS
ARE ALL THE
SAME. THINK
YOU CAN LOOK
AT MY WIFE,
DO YOU?

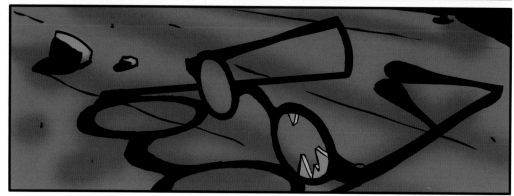

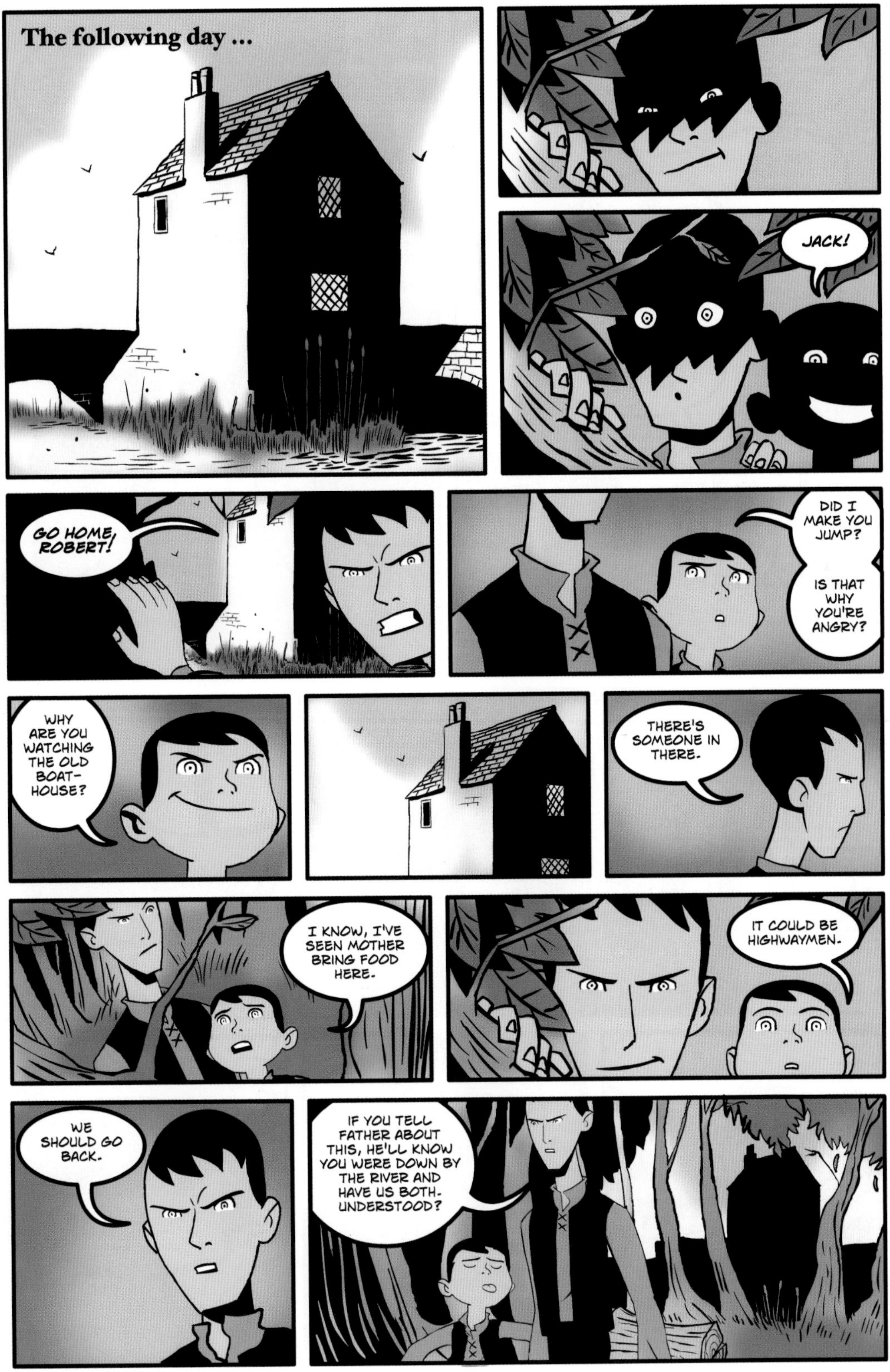
The following day ...
JACK!
GO HOME, ROBERT!
DID I MAKE YOU JUMP?
IS THAT WHY YOU'RE ANGRY?
WHY ARE YOU WATCHING THE OLD BOAT-HOUSE?
THERE'S SOMEONE IN THERE.
I KNOW, I'VE SEEN MOTHER BRING FOOD HERE.
IT COULD BE HIGHWAYMEN.
WE SHOULD GO BACK.
IF YOU TELL FATHER ABOUT THIS, HE'LL KNOW YOU WERE DOWN BY THE RIVER AND HAVE US BOTH. UNDERSTOOD?

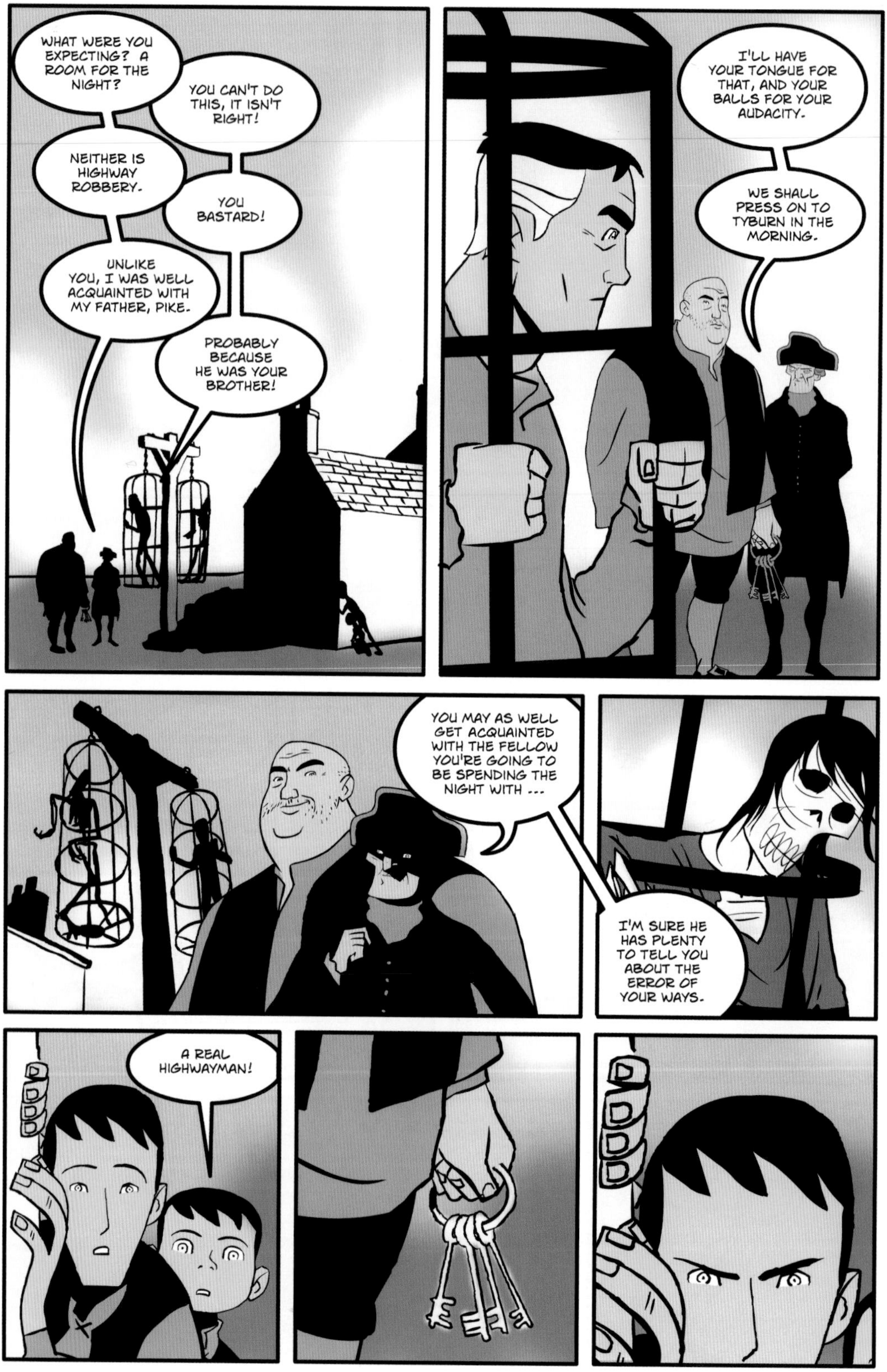
WHAT WERE YOU EXPECTING? A ROOM FOR THE NIGHT?
YOU CAN'T DO THIS, IT ISN'T RIGHT!
NEITHER IS HIGHWAY ROBBERY.
YOU BASTARD!
UNLIKE YOU, I WAS WELL ACQUAINTED WITH MY FATHER, PIKE.
PROBABLY BECAUSE HE WAS YOUR BROTHER!
I'LL HAVE YOUR TONGUE FOR THAT, AND YOUR BALLS FOR YOUR AUDACITY.
WE SHALL PRESS ON TO TYBURN IN THE MORNING.
YOU MAY AS WELL GET ACQUAINTED WITH THE FELLOW YOU'RE GOING TO BE SPENDING THE NIGHT WITH ...
I'M SURE HE HAS PLENTY TO TELL YOU ABOUT THE ERROR OF YOUR WAYS.
A REAL HIGHWAYMAN!

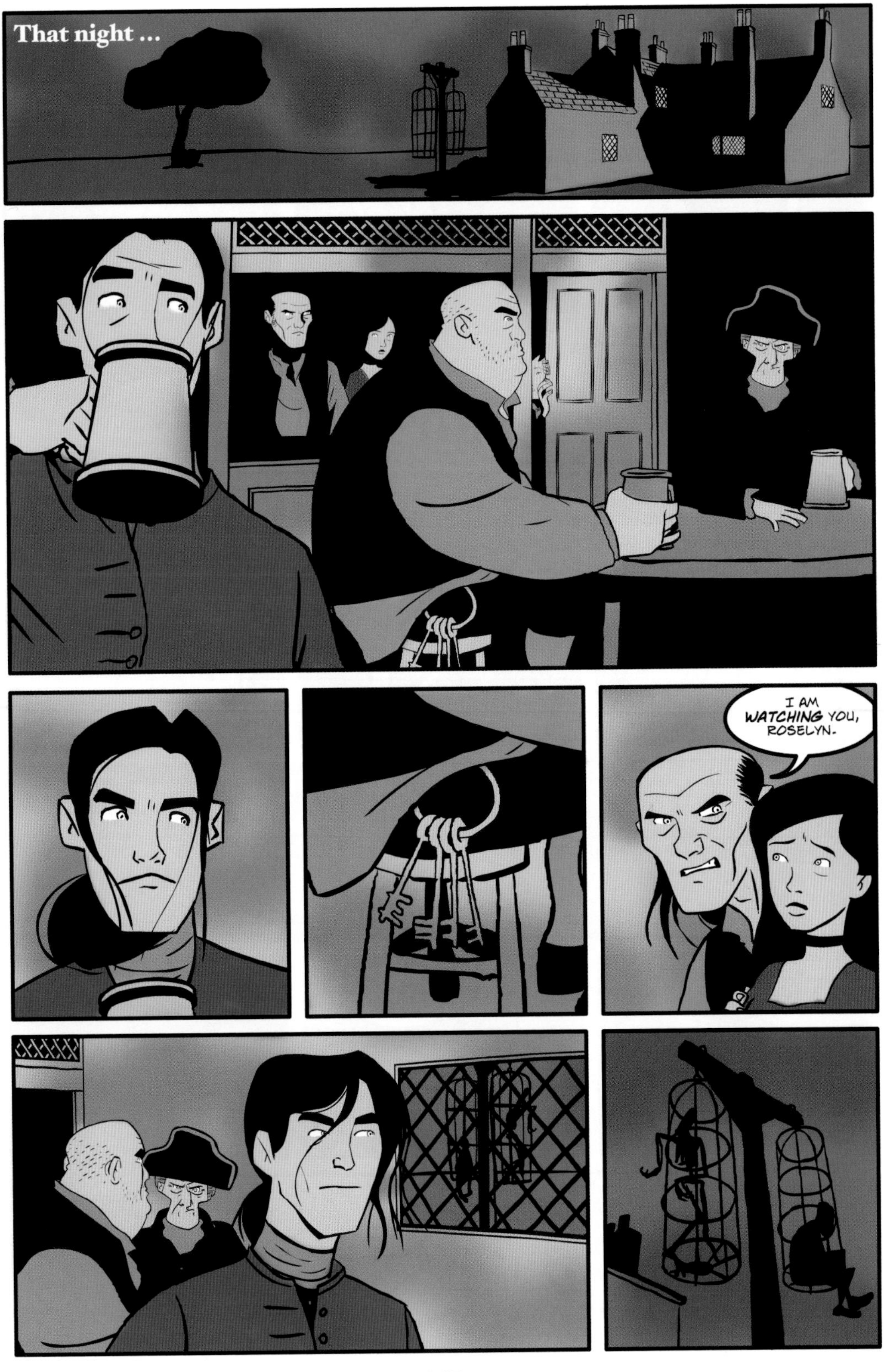
That night ...
I AM WATCHING YOU, ROSELYN.

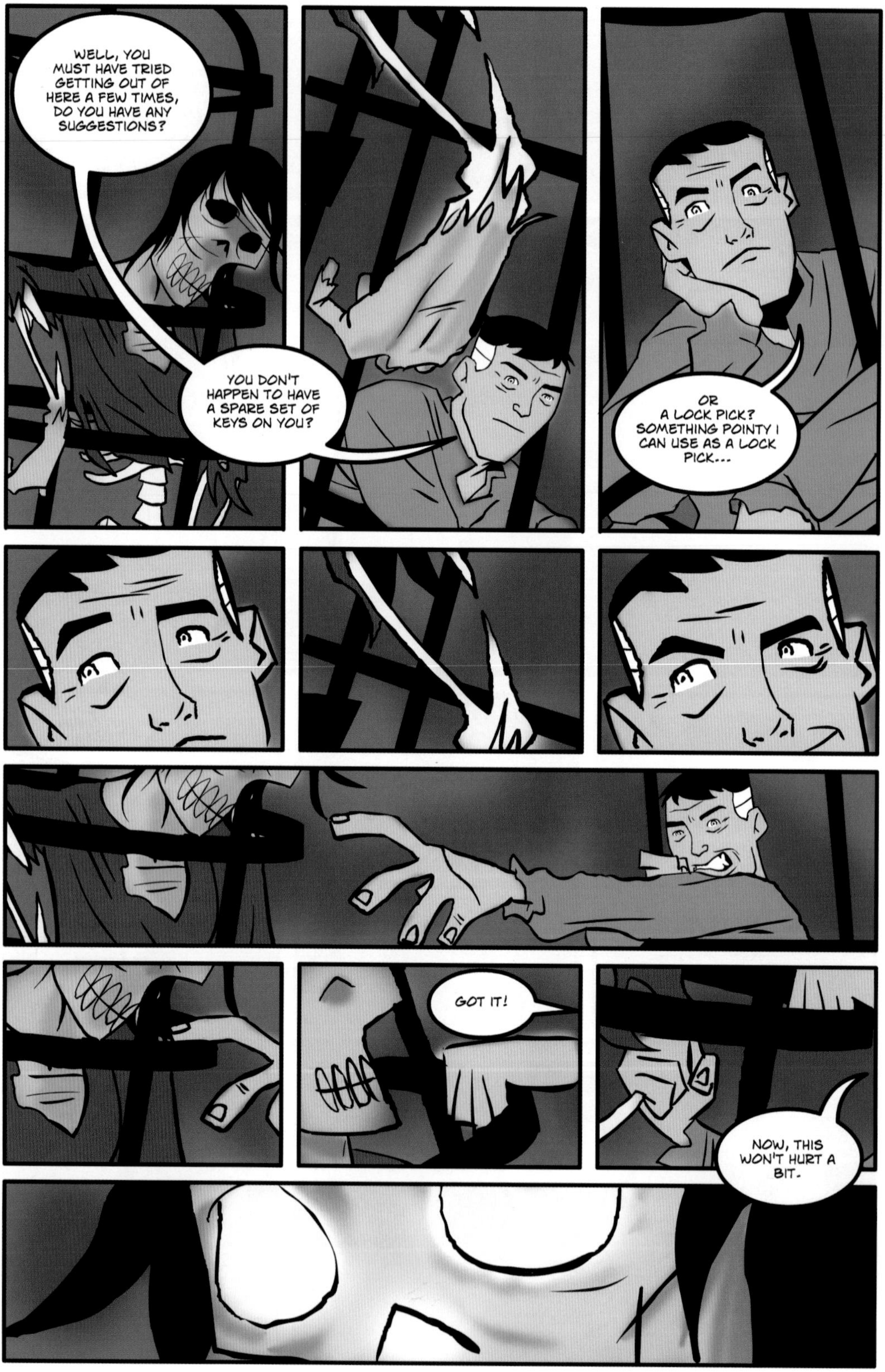
WELL, YOU MUST HAVE TRIED GETTING OUT OF HERE A FEW TIMES, DO YOU HAVE ANY SUGGESTIONS?
YOU DON'T HAPPEN TO HAVE A SPARE SET OF KEYS ON YOU?
OR A LOCK PICK? SOMETHING POINTY I CAN USE AS A LOCK PICK...
GOT IT!
NOW, THIS WON'T HURT A BIT.

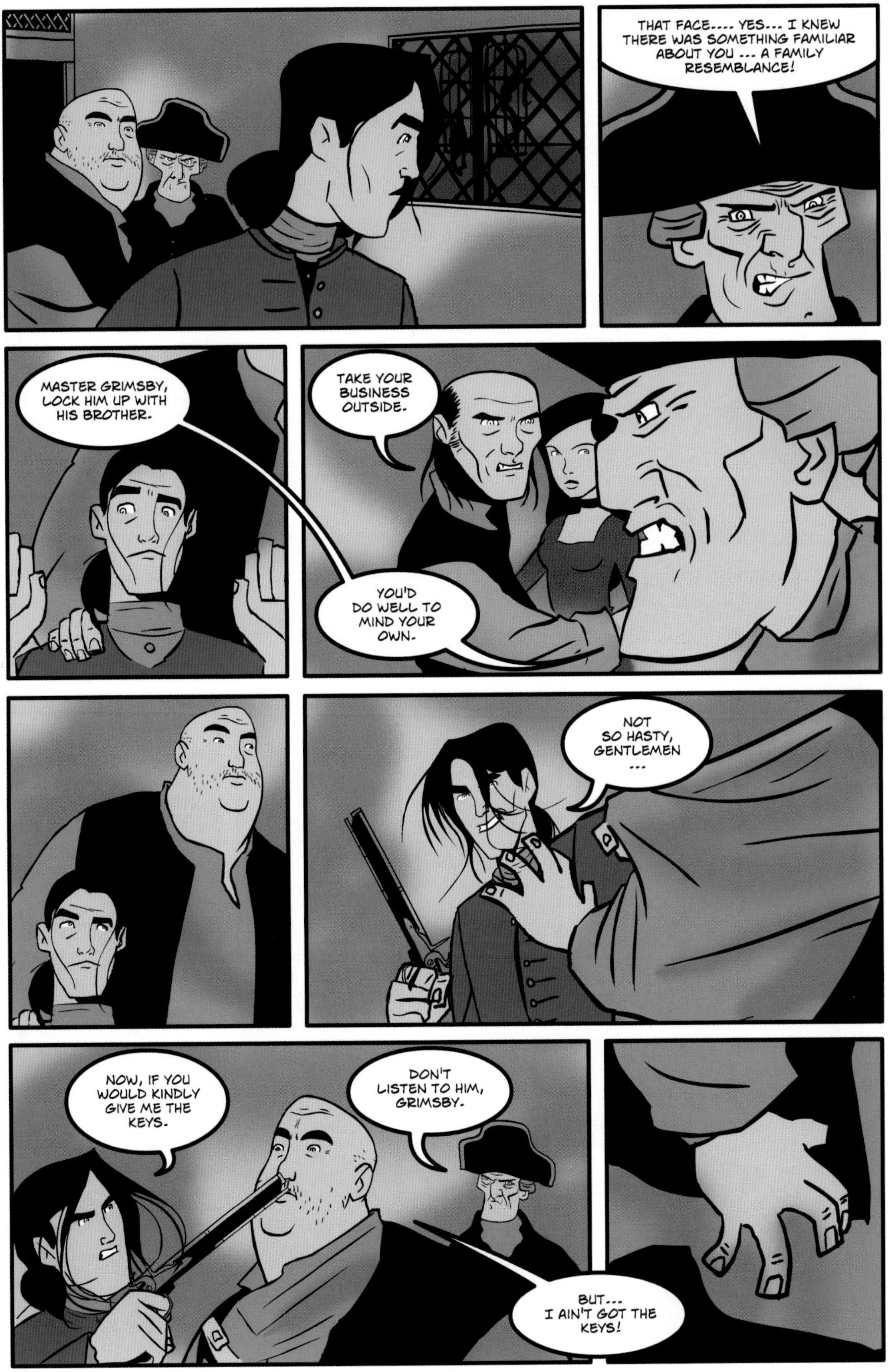
THAT FACE.... YES... I KNEW THERE WAS SOMETHING FAMILIAR ABOUT YOU ... A FAMILY RESEMBLANCE!
MASTER GRIMSBY, LOCK HIM UP WITH HIS BROTHER.
TAKE YOUR BUSINESS OUTSIDE.
YOU'D DO WELL TO MIND YOUR OWN.
NOT SO HASTY, GENTLEMEN ...
NOW, IF YOU WOULD KINDLY GIVE ME THE KEYS.
DON'T LISTEN TO HIM, GRIMSBY.
BUT... I AIN'T GOT THE KEYS!

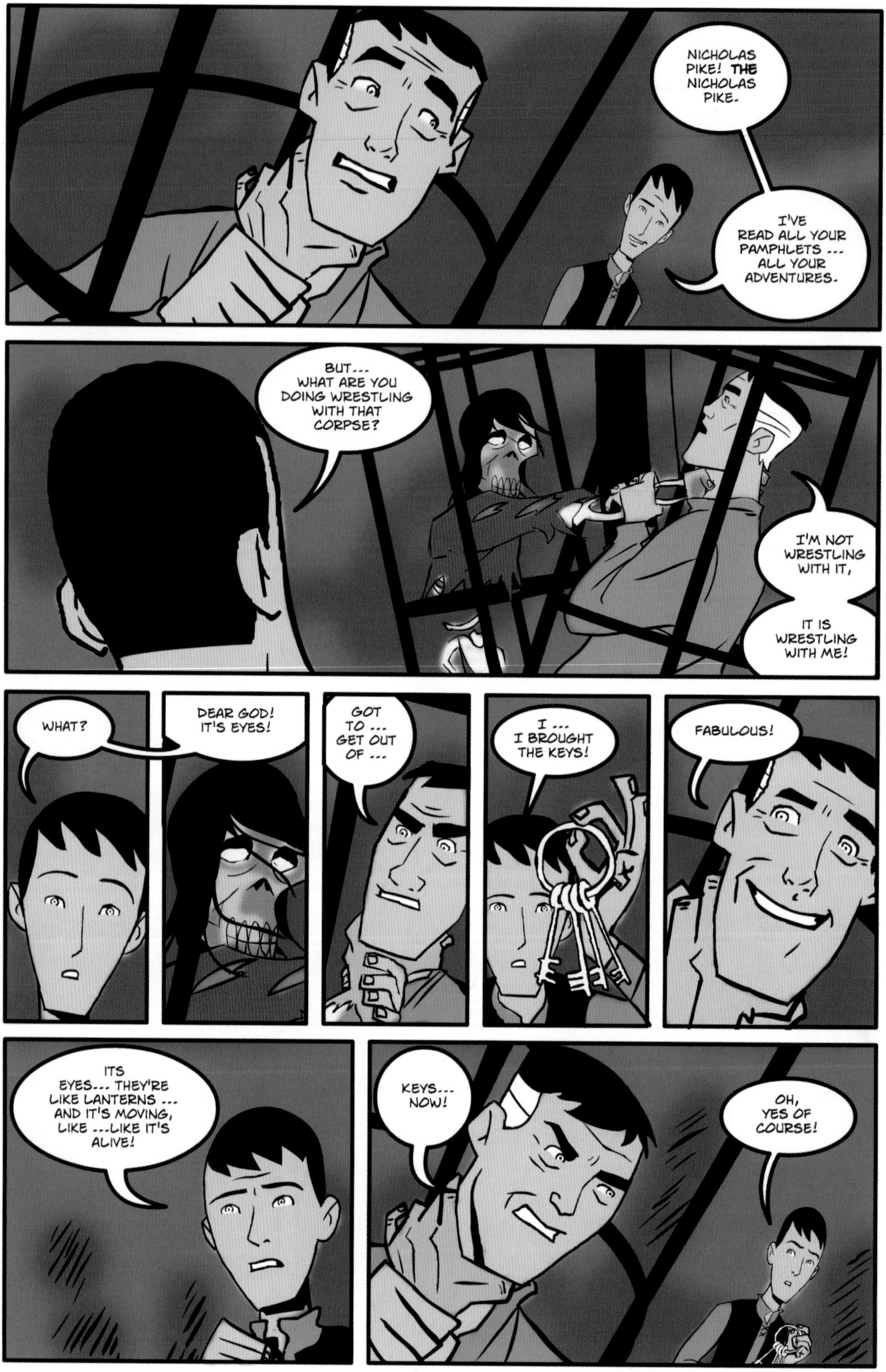
NICHOLAS PIKE! THE NICHOLAS PIKE.
I'VE READ ALL YOUR PAMPHLETS --- ALL YOUR ADVENTURES.
BUT--- WHAT ARE YOU DOING WRESTLING WITH THAT CORPSE?
I'M NOT WRESTLING WITH IT,
IT IS WRESTLING WITH ME!
WHAT?
DEAR GOD! IT'S EYES!
GOT TO --- GET OUT OF ---
I --- I BROUGHT THE KEYS!
FABULOUS!
ITS EYES--- THEY'RE LIKE LANTERNS --- AND IT'S MOVING, LIKE ---LIKE IT'S ALIVE!
KEYS--- NOW!
OH, YES OF COURSE!

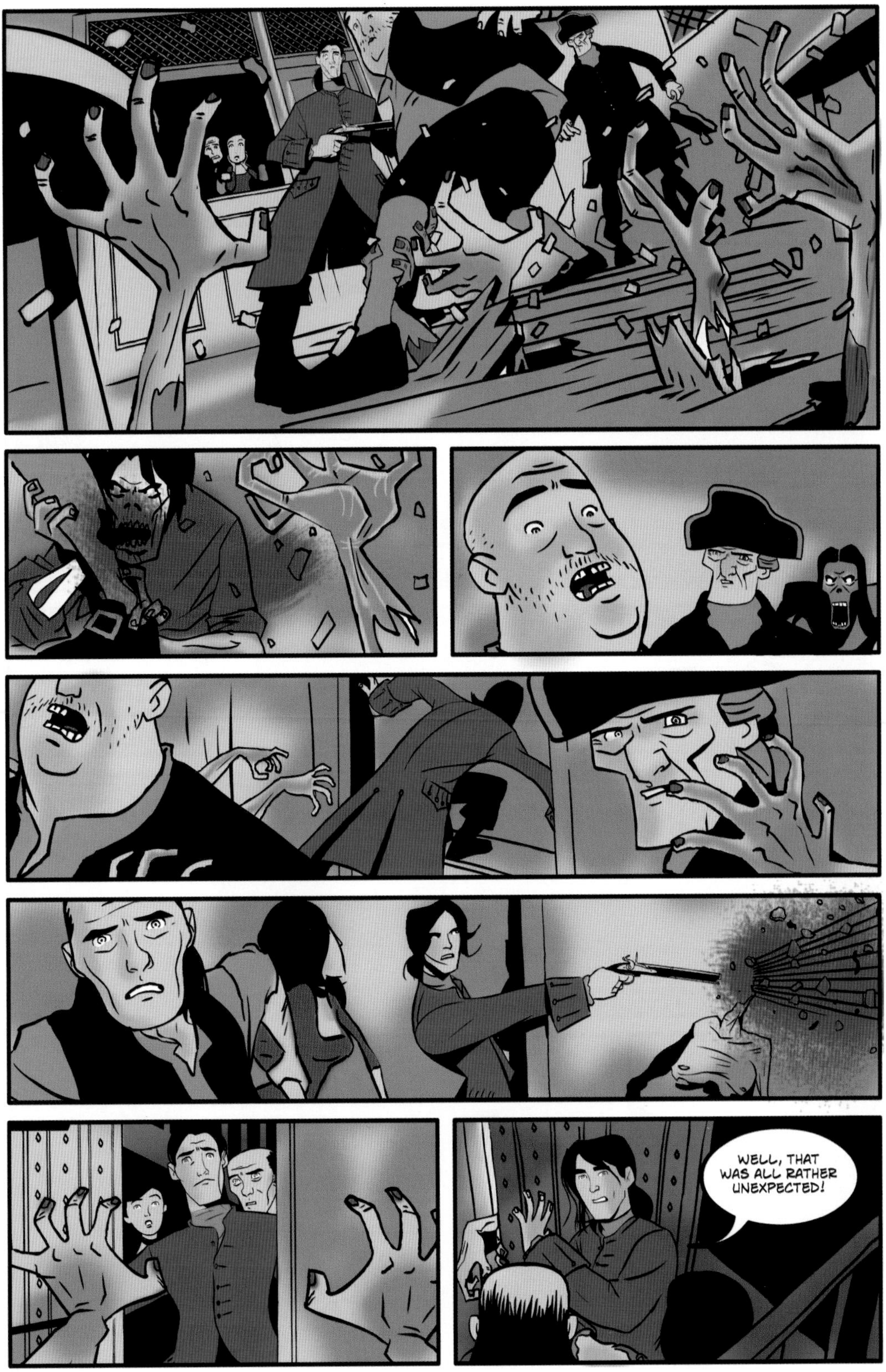
WELL, THAT WAS ALL RATHER UNEXPECTED!

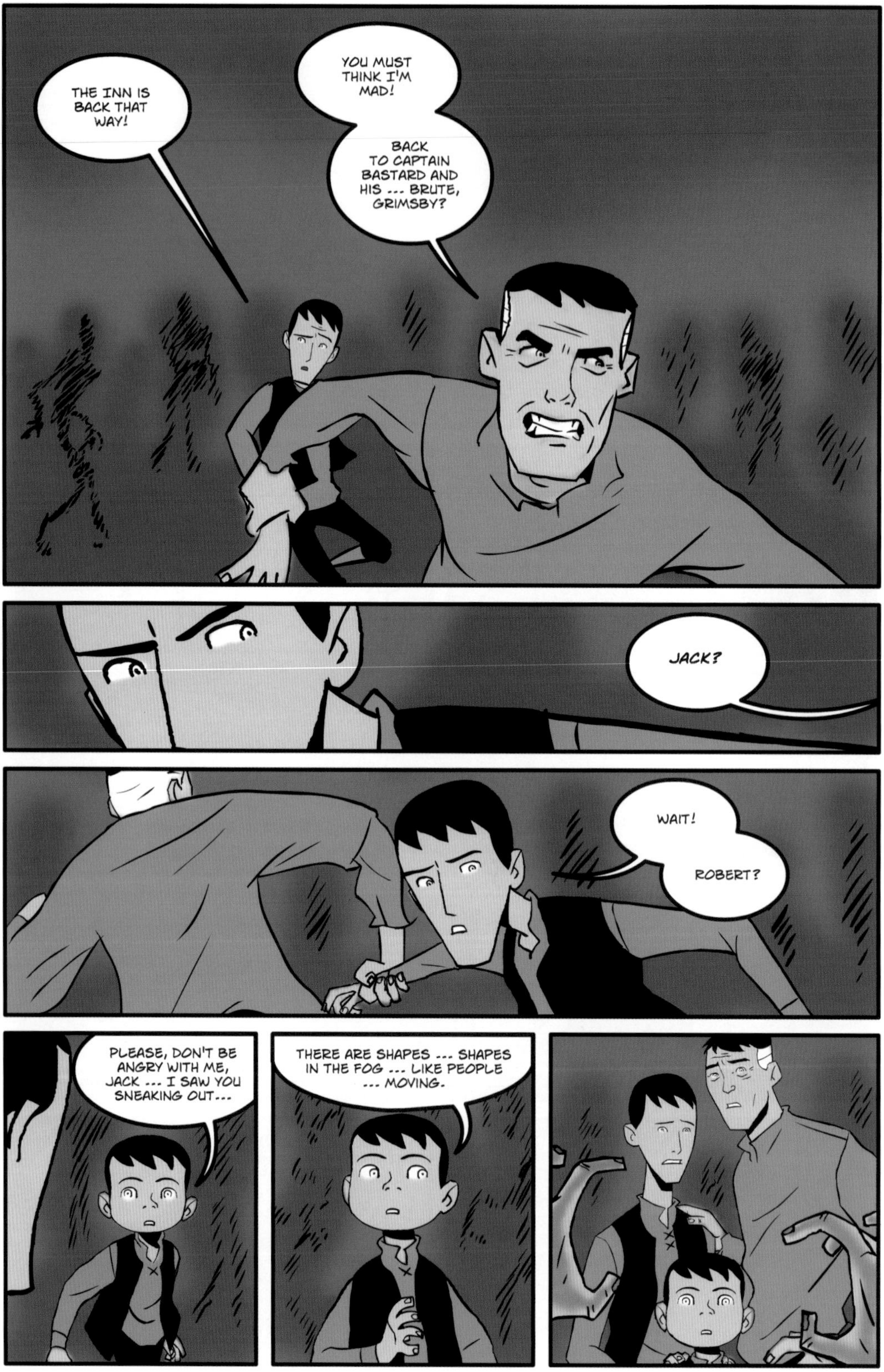
THE INN IS BACK THAT WAY!
YOU MUST THINK I'M MAD!
BACK TO CAPTAIN BASTARD AND HIS ... BRUTE, GRIMSBY?
JACK?
WAIT!
ROBERT?
PLEASE, DON'T BE ANGRY WITH ME, JACK ... I SAW YOU SNEAKING OUT...
THERE ARE SHAPES ... SHAPES IN THE FOG ... LIKE PEOPLE ... MOVING.

THE BOYS! THEY'VE GONE! THEY'RE NOT IN THEIR BEDS!

QUIET WOMAN, I'M TRYING TO THINK!

THUD!

THUD!

OPEN THIS BLOODY DOOR!

NICHOLAS?

IT'S NICHOLAS! QUICKLY, OPEN THE DOOR!

NO.

I'M NOT ASKING YOU, I'M TELLING YOU.

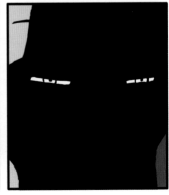

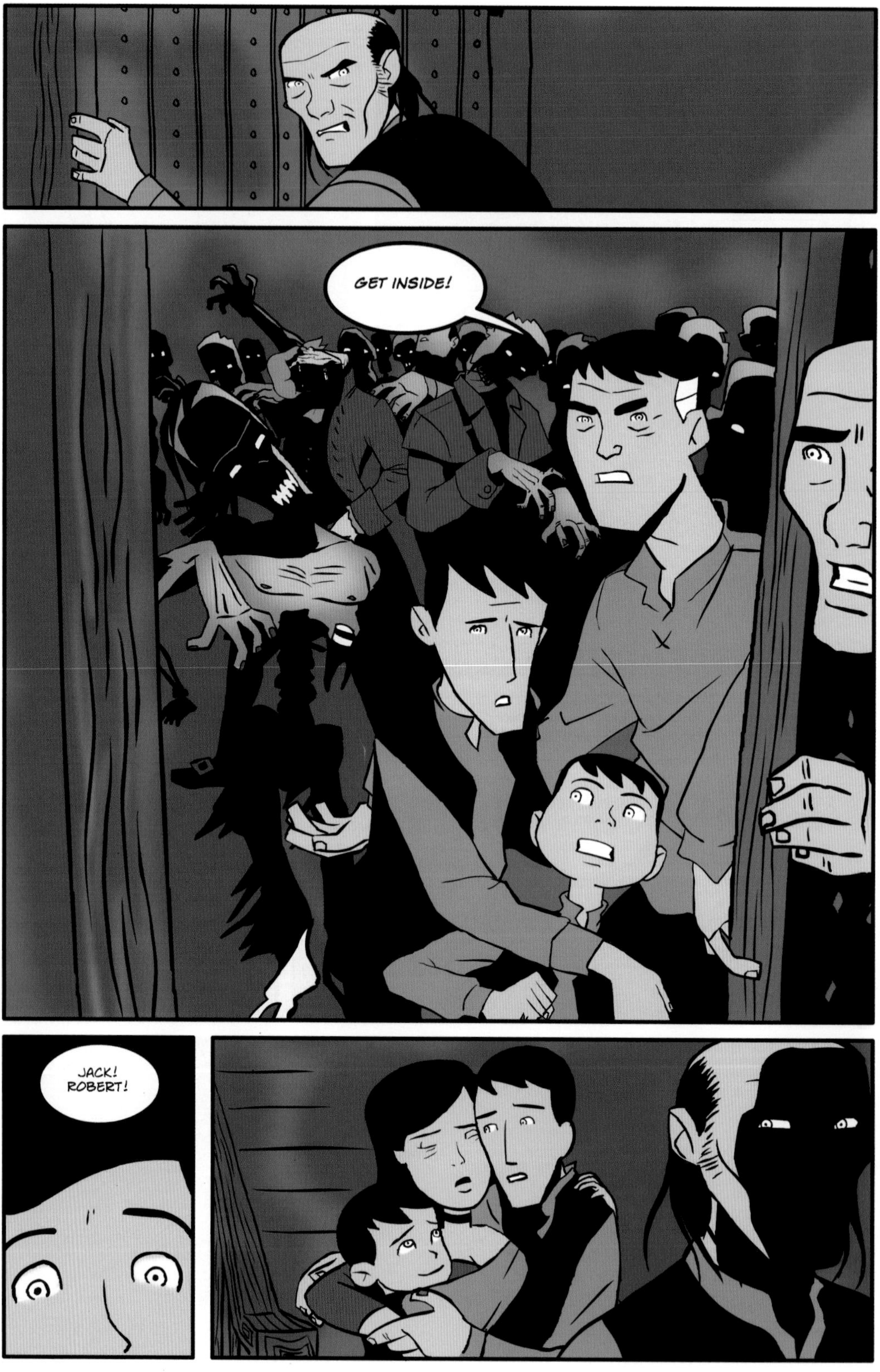
GET INSIDE!
JACK! ROBERT!

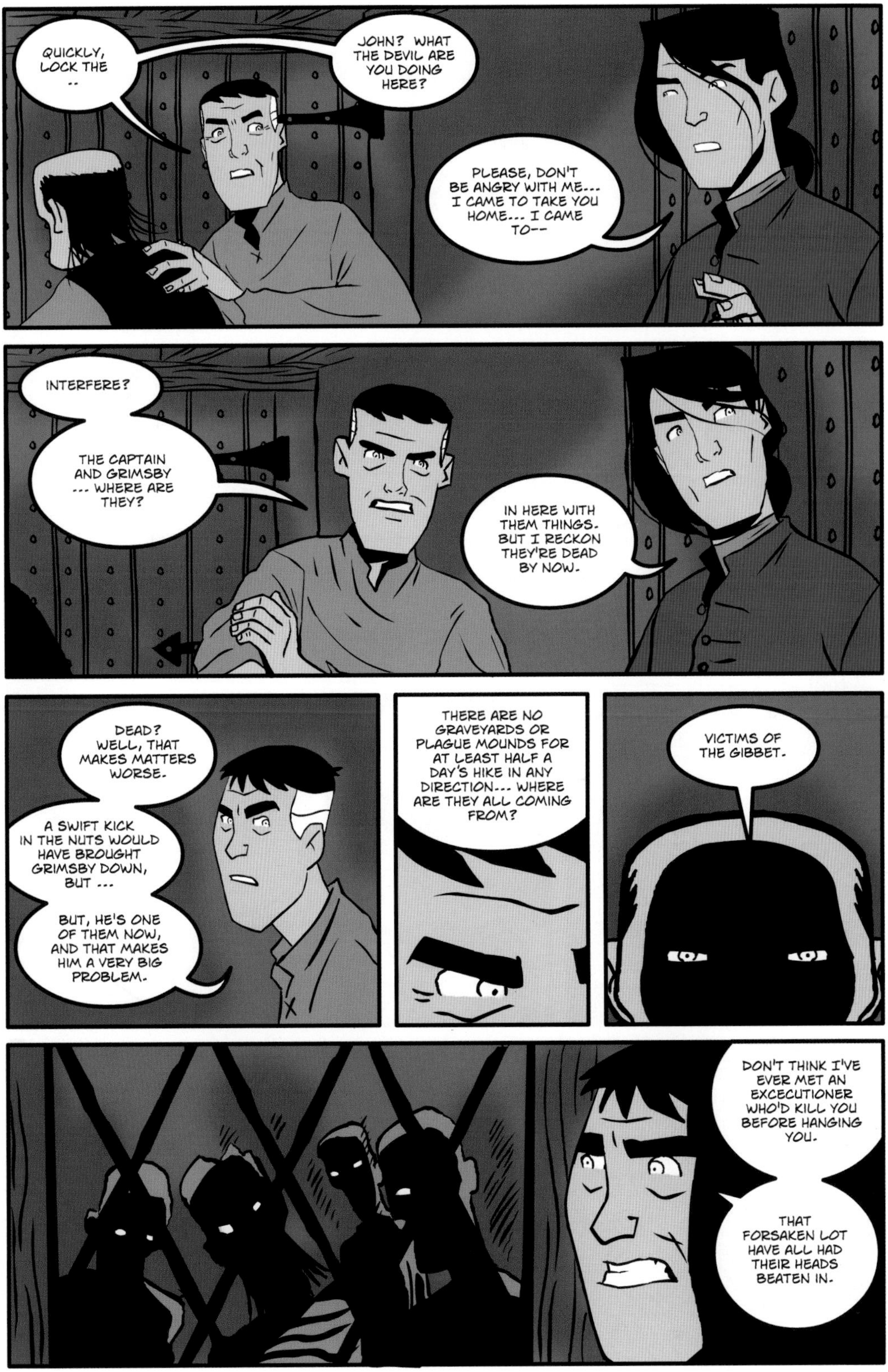
QUICKLY, LOCK THE --
JOHN? WHAT THE DEVIL ARE YOU DOING HERE?
PLEASE, DON'T BE ANGRY WITH ME... I CAME TO TAKE YOU HOME... I CAME TO--
INTERFERE?
THE CAPTAIN AND GRIMSBY ... WHERE ARE THEY?
IN HERE WITH THEM THINGS. BUT I RECKON THEY'RE DEAD BY NOW.
DEAD? WELL, THAT MAKES MATTERS WORSE.
A SWIFT KICK IN THE NUTS WOULD HAVE BROUGHT GRIMSBY DOWN, BUT ...
BUT, HE'S ONE OF THEM NOW, AND THAT MAKES HIM A VERY BIG PROBLEM.
THERE ARE NO GRAVEYARDS OR PLAGUE MOUNDS FOR AT LEAST HALF A DAY'S HIKE IN ANY DIRECTION... WHERE ARE THEY ALL COMING FROM?
VICTIMS OF THE GIBBET.
DON'T THINK I'VE EVER MET AN EXCECUTIONER WHO'D KILL YOU BEFORE HANGING YOU.
THAT FORSAKEN LOT HAVE ALL HAD THEIR HEADS BEATEN IN.

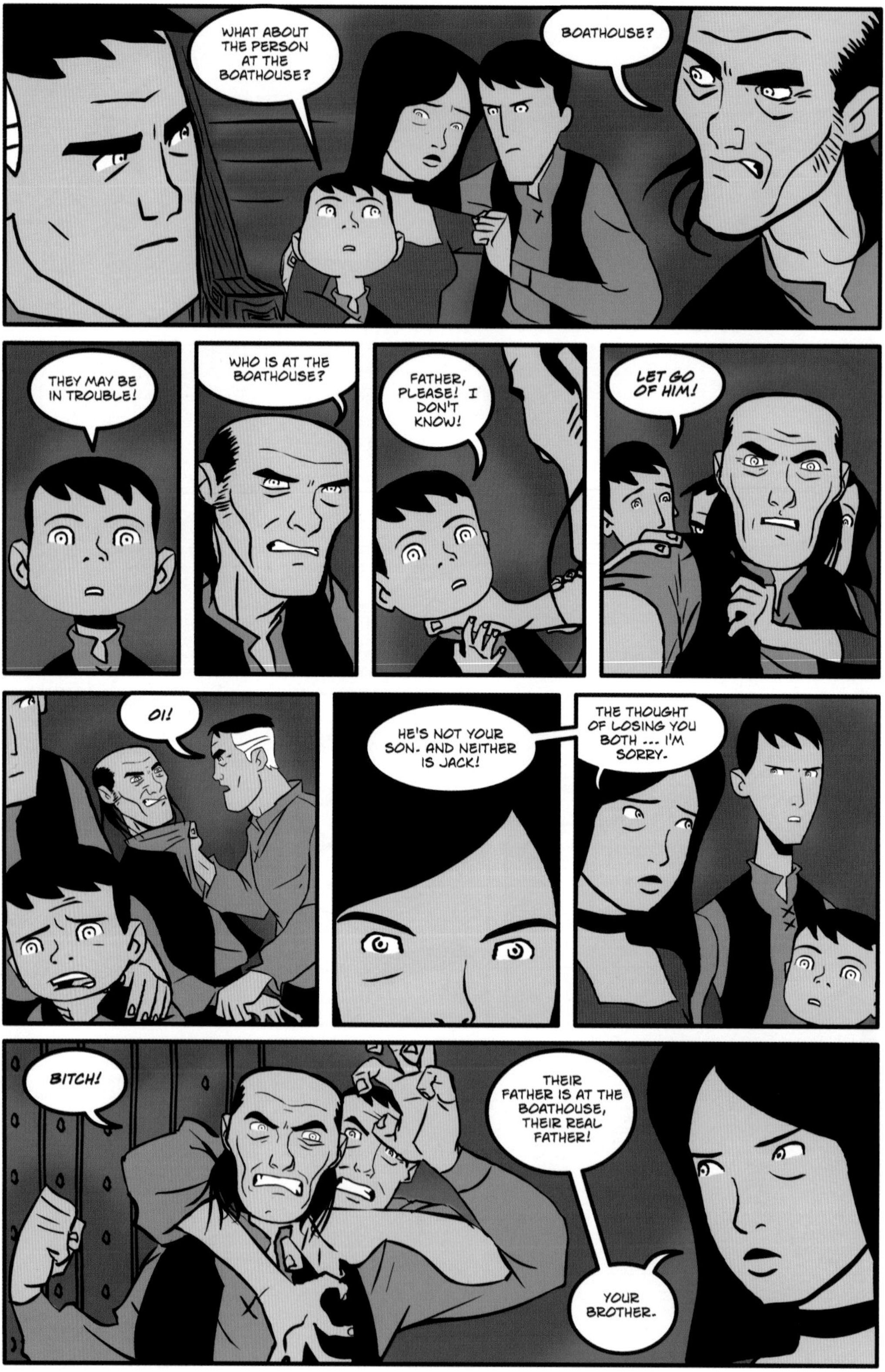
WHAT ABOUT THE PERSON AT THE BOATHOUSE?
BOATHOUSE?
THEY MAY BE IN TROUBLE!
WHO IS AT THE BOATHOUSE?
FATHER, PLEASE! I DON'T KNOW!
LET GO OF HIM!
OI!
HE'S NOT YOUR SON. AND NEITHER IS JACK!
THE THOUGHT OF LOSING YOU BOTH ... I'M SORRY.
BITCH!
THEIR FATHER IS AT THE BOATHOUSE, THEIR REAL FATHER!
YOUR BROTHER.

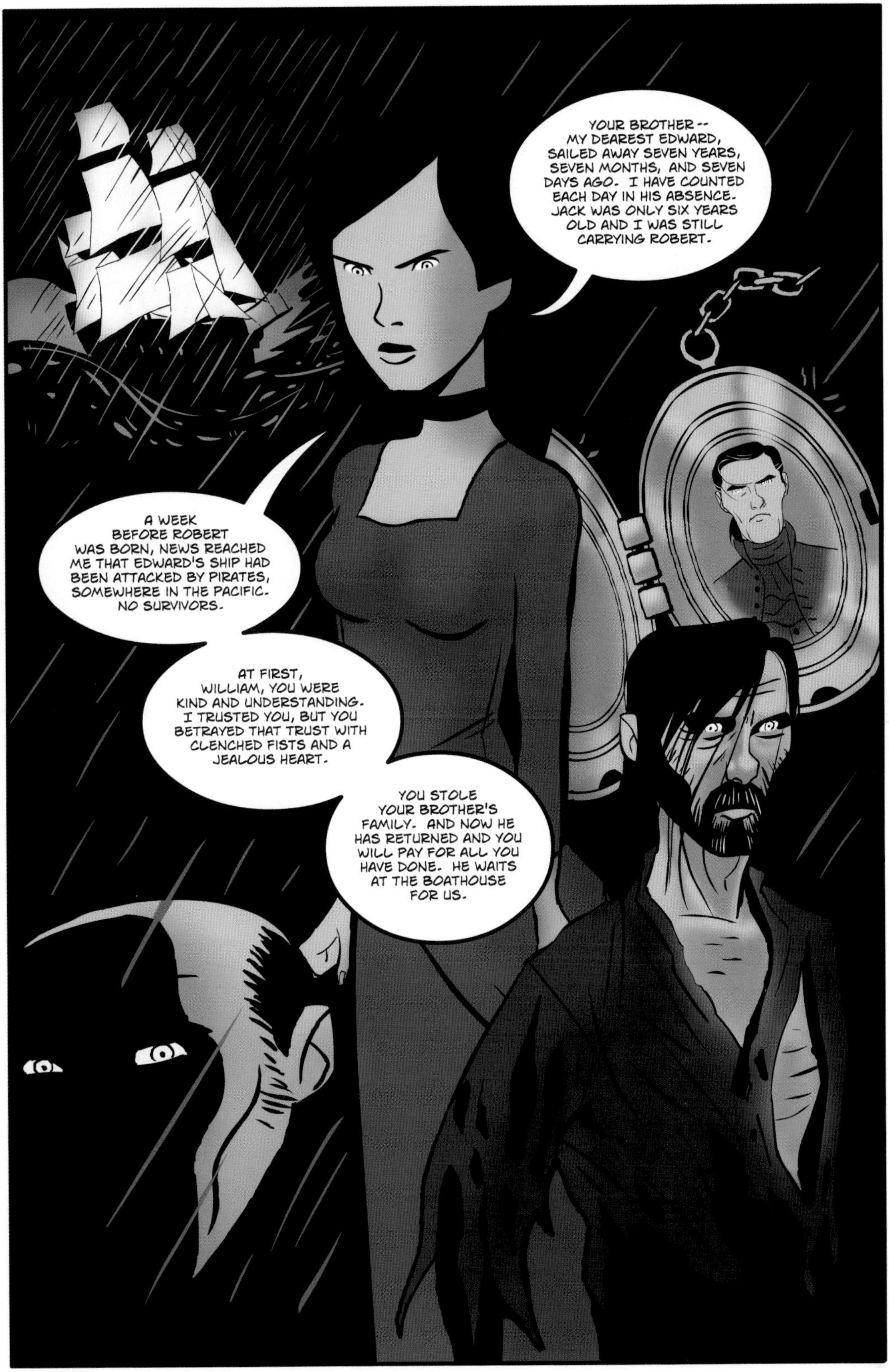
YOUR BROTHER -- MY DEAREST EDWARD, SAILED AWAY SEVEN YEARS, SEVEN MONTHS, AND SEVEN DAYS AGO. I HAVE COUNTED EACH DAY IN HIS ABSENCE. JACK WAS ONLY SIX YEARS OLD AND I WAS STILL CARRYING ROBERT.
A WEEK BEFORE ROBERT WAS BORN, NEWS REACHED ME THAT EDWARD'S SHIP HAD BEEN ATTACKED BY PIRATES, SOMEWHERE IN THE PACIFIC. NO SURVIVORS.
AT FIRST, WILLIAM, YOU WERE KIND AND UNDERSTANDING. I TRUSTED YOU, BUT YOU BETRAYED THAT TRUST WITH CLENCHED FISTS AND A JEALOUS HEART.
YOU STOLE YOUR BROTHER'S FAMILY. AND NOW HE HAS RETURNED AND YOU WILL PAY FOR ALL YOU HAVE DONE. HE WAITS AT THE BOATHOUSE FOR US.

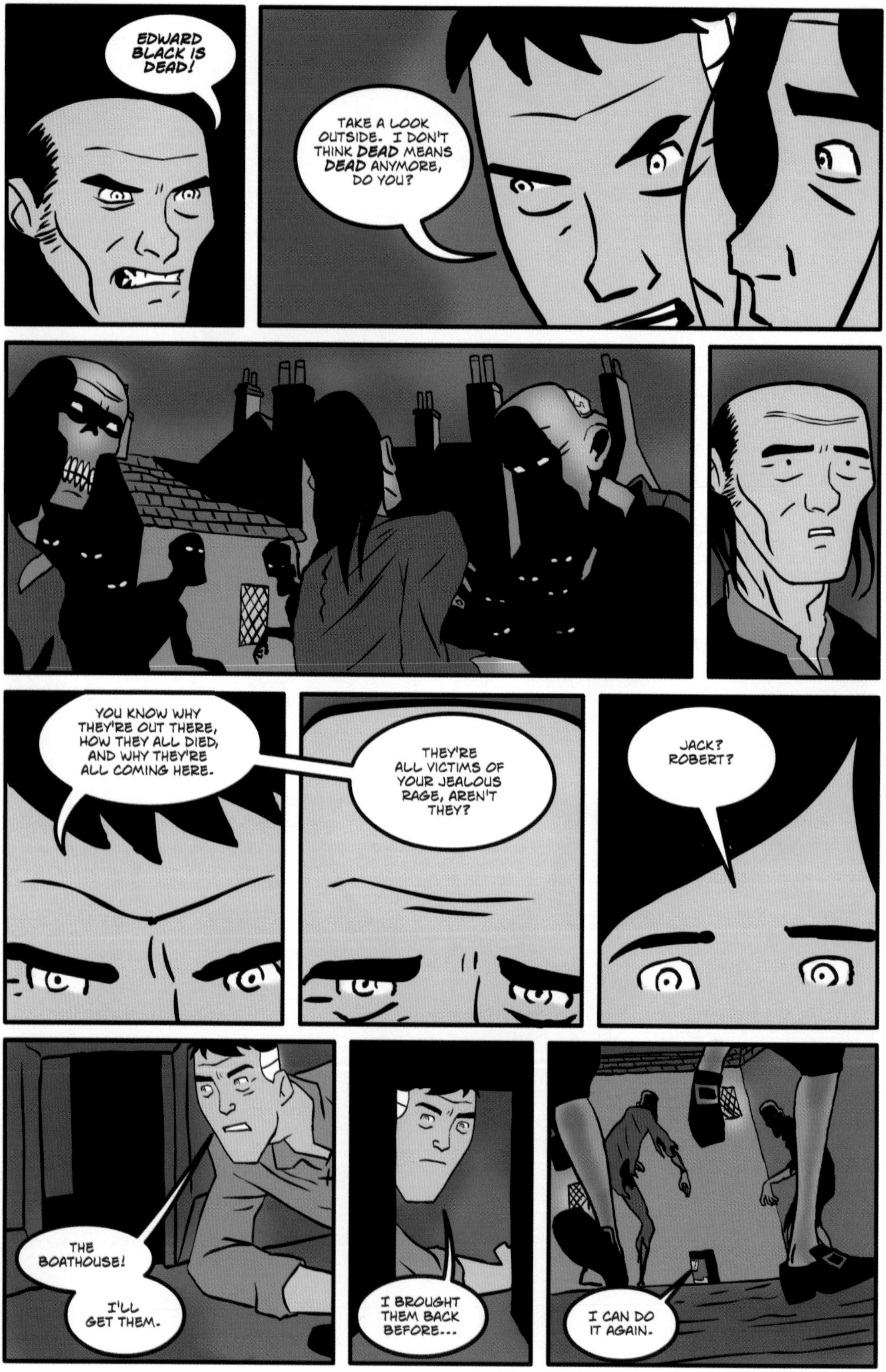
EDWARD BLACK IS DEAD!
TAKE A LOOK OUTSIDE. I DON'T THINK DEAD MEANS DEAD ANYMORE, DO YOU?
YOU KNOW WHY THEY'RE OUT THERE, HOW THEY ALL DIED, AND WHY THEY'RE ALL COMING HERE.
THEY'RE ALL VICTIMS OF YOUR JEALOUS RAGE, AREN'T THEY?
JACK? ROBERT?
THE BOATHOUSE!
I'LL GET THEM.
I BROUGHT THEM BACK BEFORE...
I CAN DO IT AGAIN.

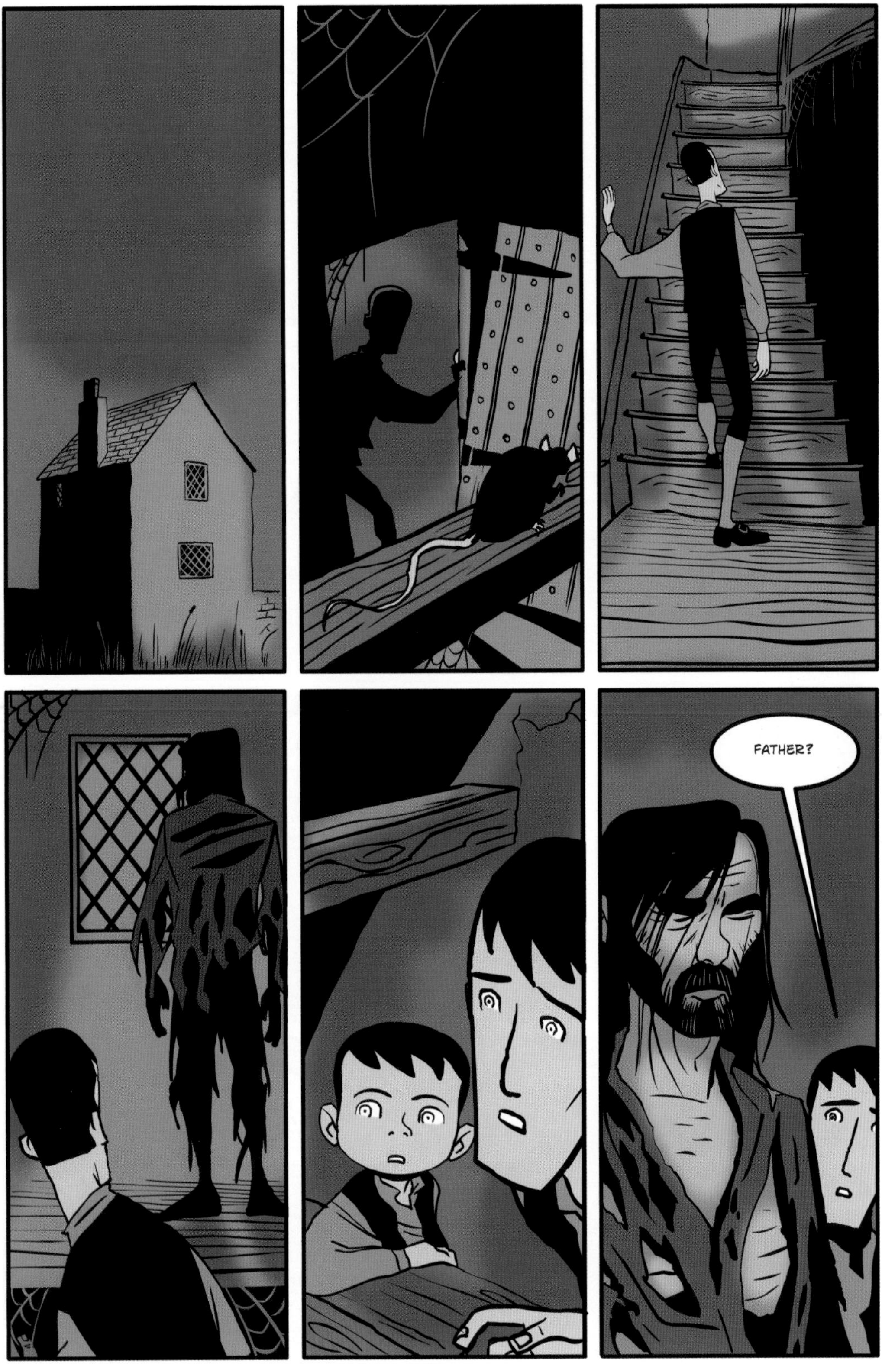
FATHER?

CAN'T HEAR ANYTHING, MAYBE THEY'RE GONE.

OOF!

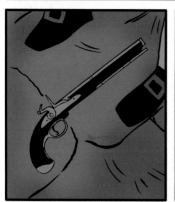

MY GUN, I CAN'T REACH MY GUN. GIVE IT TO ME!

ARE YOU ASKING ME OR ARE YOU TELLING ME?

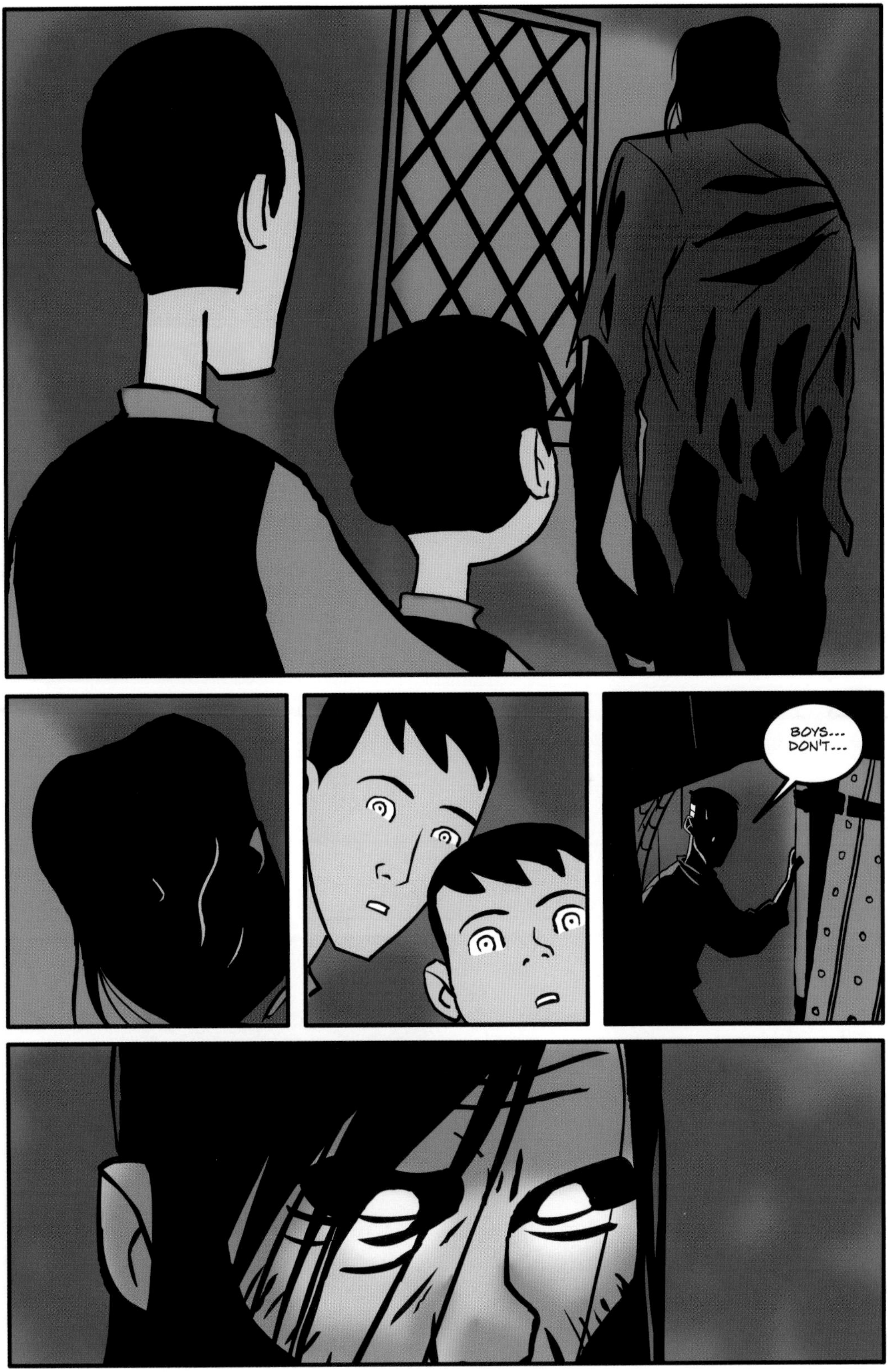
BOYS...
DON'T...

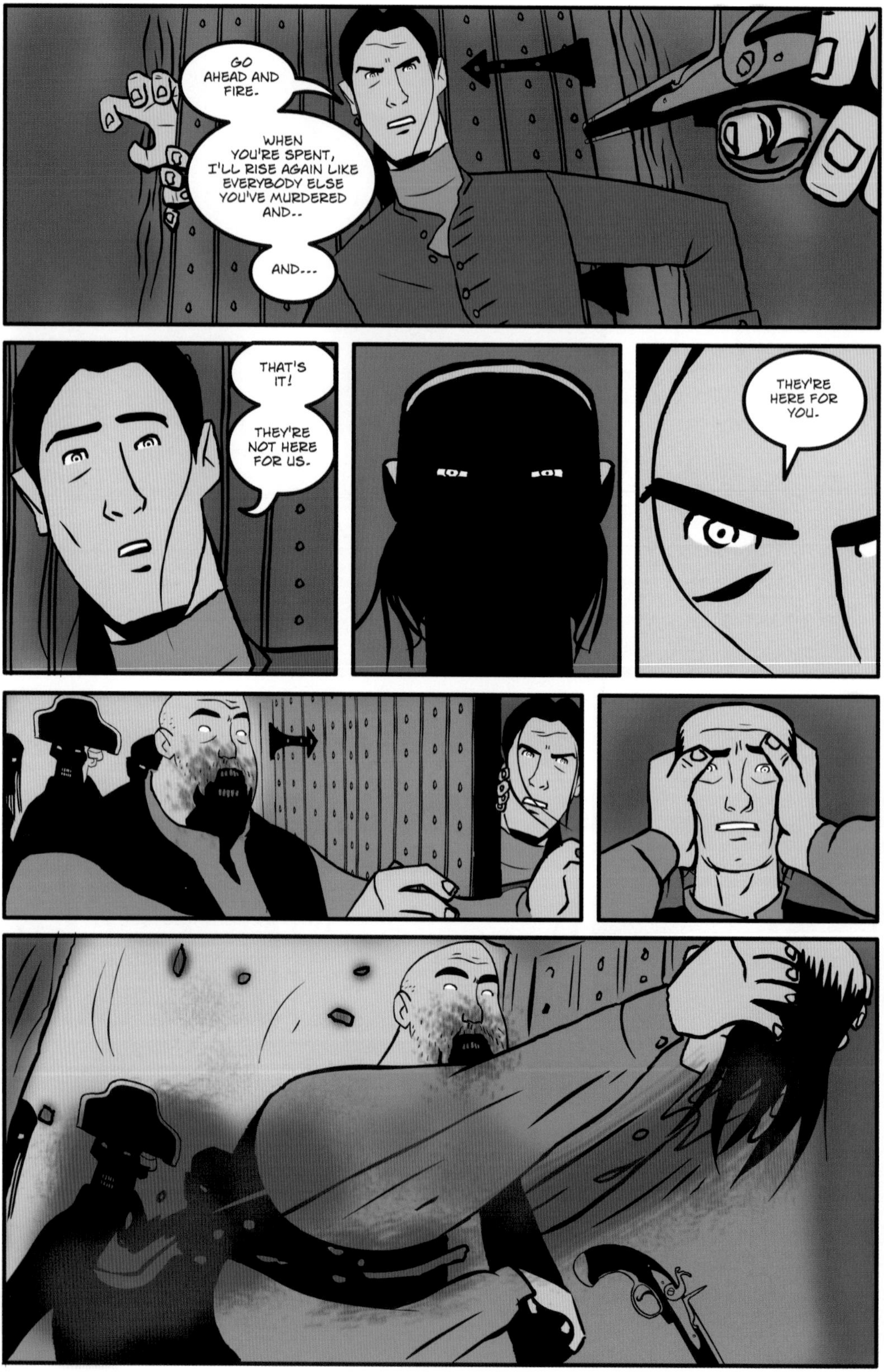
GO AHEAD AND FIRE.
WHEN YOU'RE SPENT, I'LL RISE AGAIN LIKE EVERYBODY ELSE YOU'VE MURDERED AND..
AND...
THAT'S IT!
THEY'RE NOT HERE FOR US.
THEY'RE HERE FOR YOU.

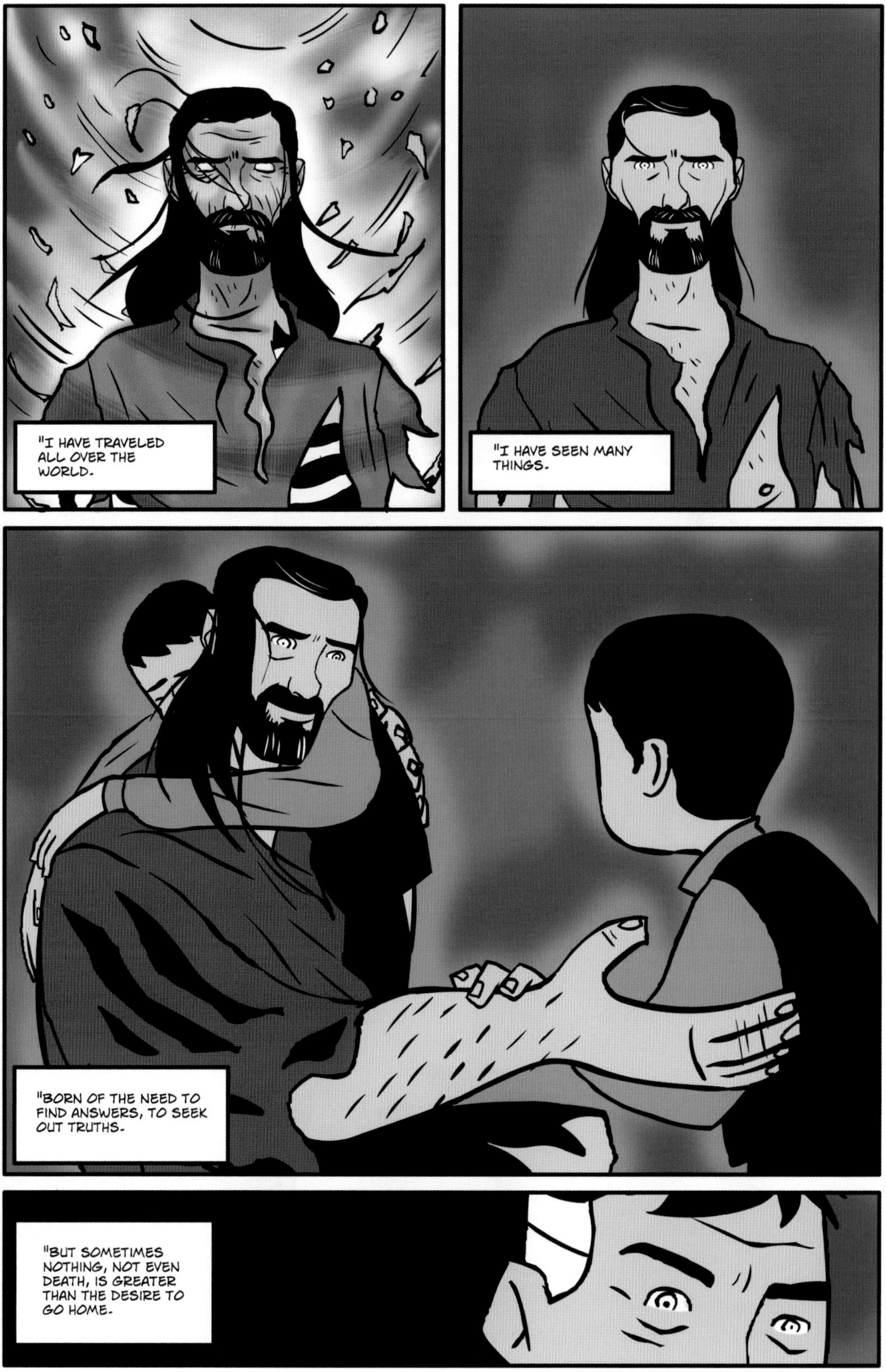
"I HAVE TRAVELED ALL OVER THE WORLD.
"I HAVE SEEN MANY THINGS.
"BORN OF THE NEED TO FIND ANSWERS, TO SEEK OUT TRUTHS.
"BUT SOMETIMES NOTHING, NOT EVEN DEATH, IS GREATER THAN THE DESIRE TO GO HOME.

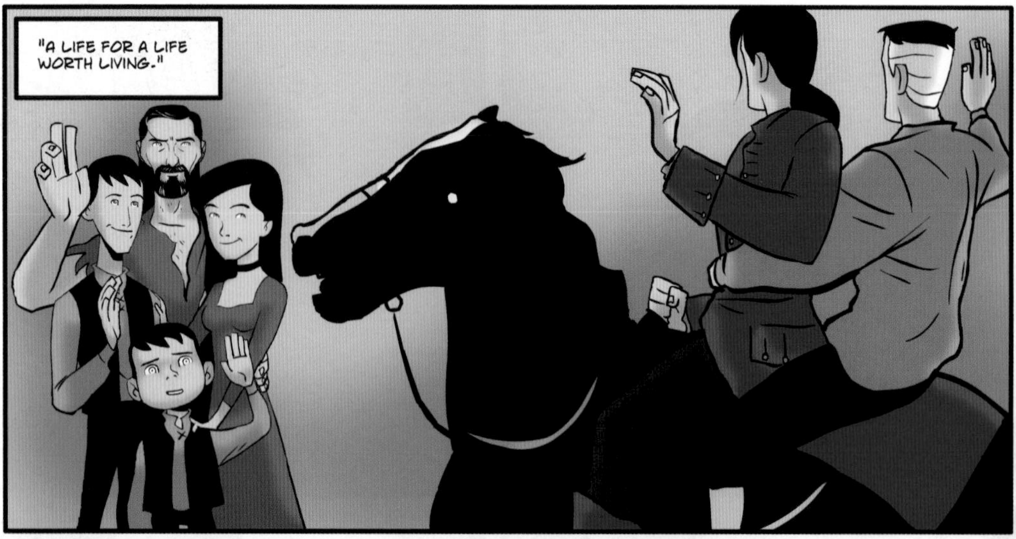
"A LIFE FOR A LIFE WORTH LIVING."

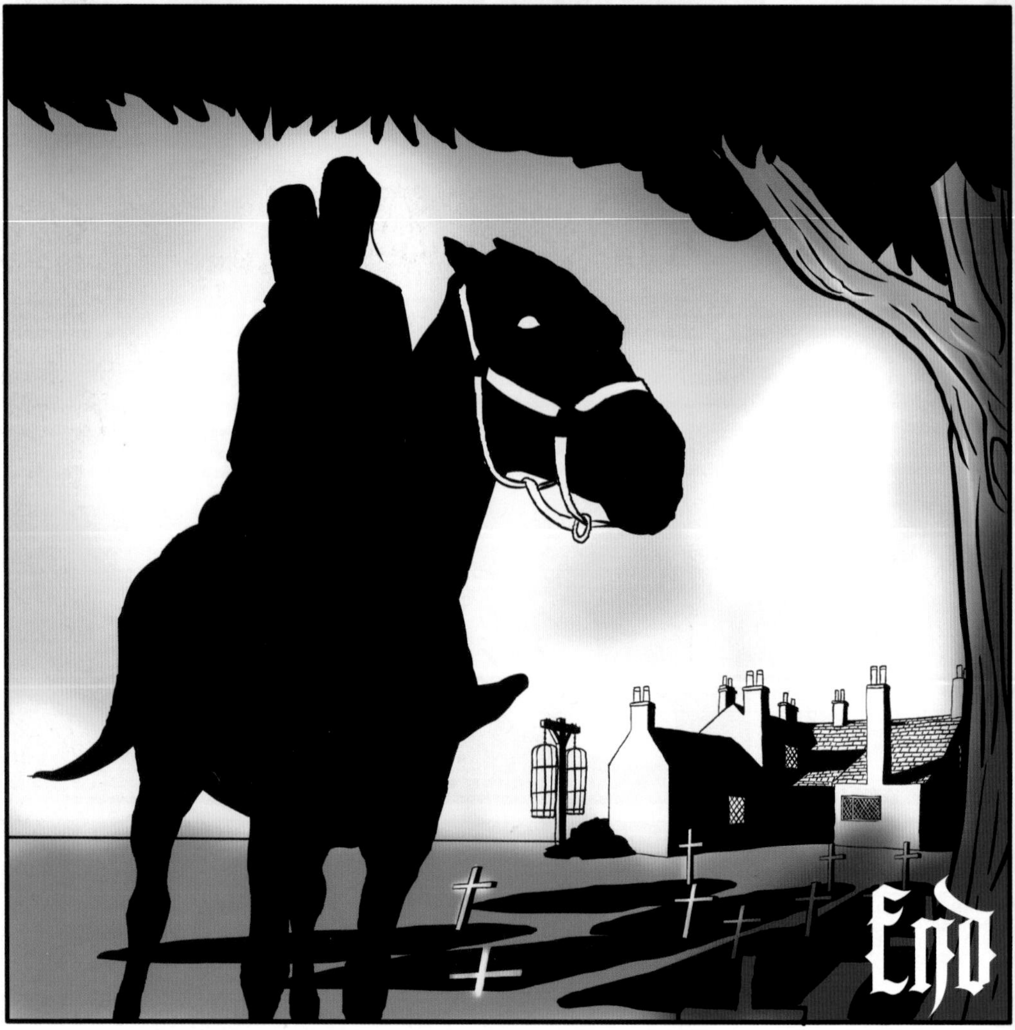
End

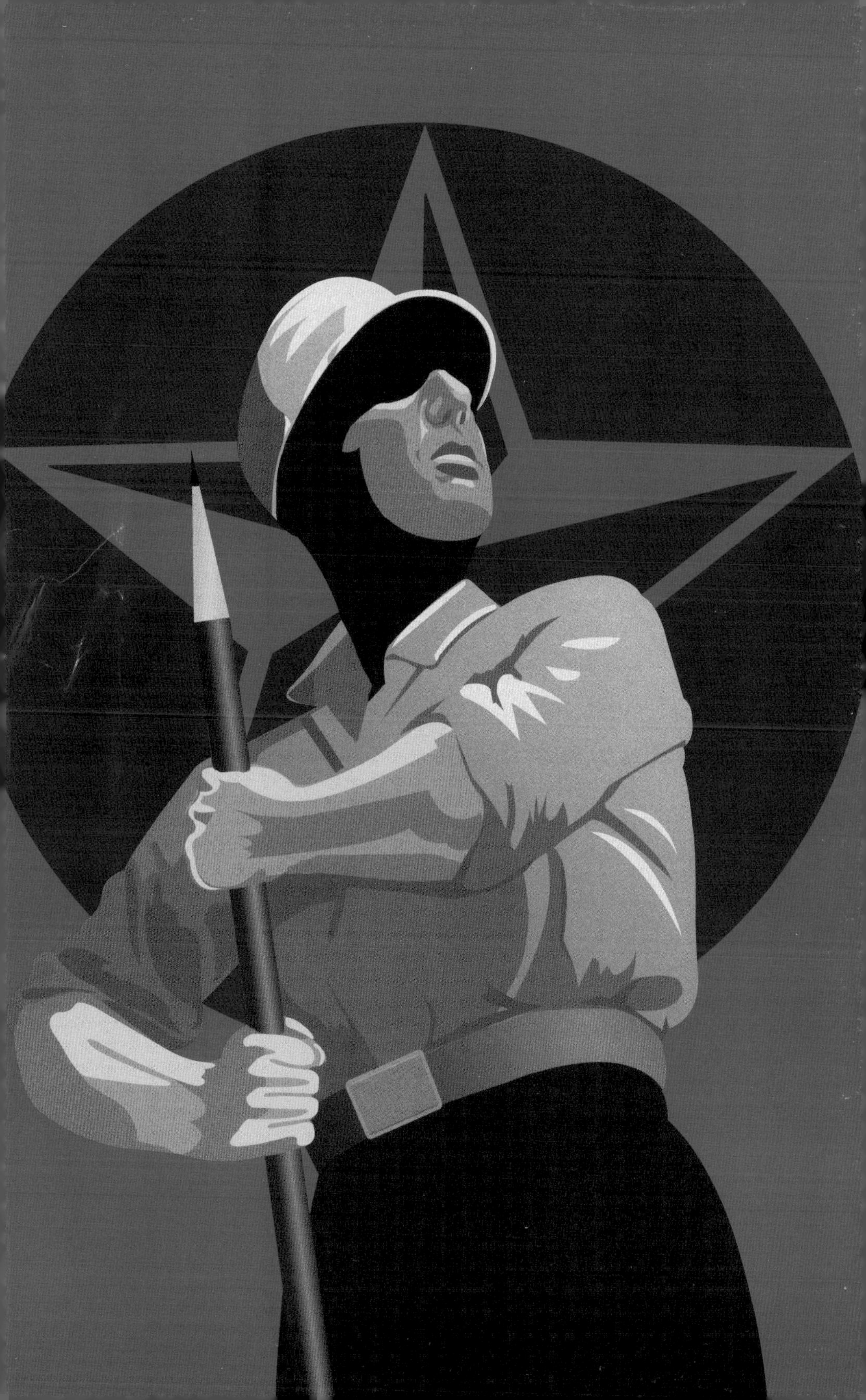